One Step toward Jerusalem

Modern Jewish History
Henry Feingold, *Series Editor*

SELECT TITLES IN MODERN JEWISH HISTORY

Assimilated Jews in the Warsaw Ghetto, 1940–1943
Katarzyna Person

Bundist Counterculture in Interwar Poland
Jack Jacobs

The Children of La Hille: Eluding Nazi Capture during World War II
Walter W. Reed

The Downfall of Abba Hillel Silver and the Foundation of Israel
Ofer Shiff

Einstein's Pacifism and World War I
Virginia Iris Holmes

Leaving Russia: A Jewish Story
Maxim D. Shrayer

"We Are Jews Again": Jewish Activism in the Soviet Union
Yuli Kosharovsky; Ann Komaromi, ed.; Stefani Hoffman, trans.

Will to Freedom: A Perilous Journey through Fascism and Communism
Egon Balas

ONE STEP TOWARD JERUSALEM

Oral Histories of Orthodox Jews in Stalinist Hungary

SÁNDOR BACSKAI

Translated from the Hungarian by Eva Maria Thury

Syracuse University Press

Syracuse, New York 13244-5290

First Edition 2018
18 19 20 21 22 23 6 5 4 3 2 1

"Unification" originally published in Hungarian as "Unifikáció" in Múlt és Jövő, nos.3–4 (2000): 262–67.

One Step toward Jerusalem originally published in Hungarian as *Egy Lépés Jeruzsálem Felé* (Budapest: Múlt és Jövő Könyvek, 1997).

∞ The paper used in this publication meets the minimum requirements of the American National Standard for Information Sciences—Permanence of Paper for Printed Library Materials, ANSI Z39.48-1992.

For a listing of books published and distributed by Syracuse University Press, visit www.SyracuseUniversityPress.syr.edu.

ISBN: 978-0-8156-3543-7 (hardcover) 978-0-8156-3531-4 (paperback)
978-0-8156-5409-4 (e-book)

Library of Congress Cataloging-in-Publication Data
Names: Bacskai, Sándor, author. | Thury, Eva M., translator.
Title: One step toward Jerusalem : oral histories of Orthodox Jews in Stalinist Hungary / Sándor Bacskai ; translated from the Hungarian by Eva Maria Thury.
Other titles: Egy lépés Jeruzsálem felé. English
Description: First edition. | Syracuse, New York : Syracuse University Press, [2017] | Series: Modern Jewish history | Includes bibliographical references and index.
Identifiers: LCCN 2017046575 (print) | LCCN 2017046843 (ebook) | ISBN 9780815654094 (e-book) | ISBN 9780815635437 (hardcover : alk. paper) | ISBN 9780815635314 (pbk. : alk. paper)
Subjects: LCSH: Jews—Hungary—Biography. | Jews—Europe, Eastern—Biography. | Orthodox Judaism—Hungary. | Orthodox Judaism—Europe, Eastern.
Classification: LCC DS135.H93 (ebook) | LCC DS135.H93 A12713 2017 (print) | DDC 943.9/0042900922—dc23
LC record available at https://lccn.loc.gov/2017046575

Manufactured in the United States of America

I would like to dedicate this work to the people who fostered my development as a translator:

my husband, M. Carl Drott, who persuaded me that my dream of translating Bacskai's work could be realized

my son, Milton Thury Drott, who attended Általános Iskola (Public School) during our sabbatical year and provided me with a deeper understanding of the Hungarian language and culture I had formerly experienced only as an expatriate

my father, ifj. Zoltán Thury, who insisted that I endure Hungarian lessons throughout my childhood in America

my mother, Piroska Thury, who wiped my tears and urged me on

Contents

List of Illustrations *ix*
Introduction, EVA MARIA THURY *xiii*
Translator's Note *xxv*
Unification *1*

One Step toward Jerusalem

Guardians of the Faith
Benjamin Abelesz *15*
Ervin Groszberg *46*
Frigyes Rosenberg *66*
Once There Was a Yeshivah in Pest *90*
The Minyan at Kassa *156*
Downward *166*
One Step toward Jerusalem *173*
The Jews of Pápa Go to a Strange Place *188*
Glossary *205*
Bibliography *219*
Index of Places *221*
Index of Subjects *229*

Illustrations

1. Hungary around the time of World War I and later *x*
2. Budapest: the Inner City around World War II and later *xii*
3. Máramarossziget still life: an *alef-beys* table, a map of Romania, and a knot of spring onions *xix*
4. The mortuary at a Jewish cemetery in Galánta *48*
5. Ignác Weisz, the ritual slaughterer, in the cellar of the Orthodox congregation in Budapest *113*
6. Friday morning prayer in the former Orthodox synagogue in Makó *177*
7. Man visiting a gravestone in the cemetery in Makó *181*
8. Jews reading Psalms (Thilim) in the Jewish cemetery in Pápa at the *yortsayt* of Rabbi Grünwald *196*

1. Hungary around the time of World War I and later. Courtesy of Joseph Stoll, Syracuse University Cartographic Lab.

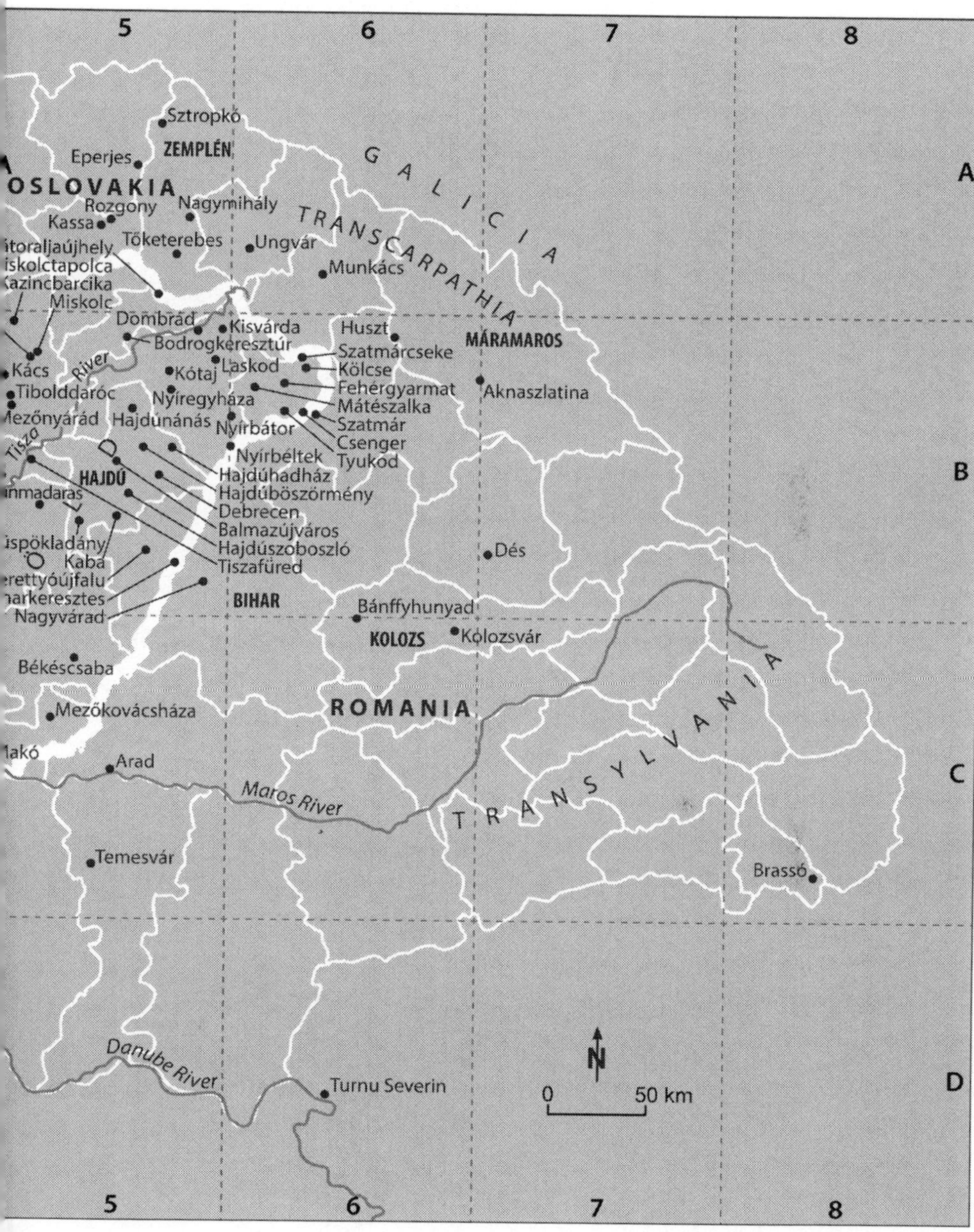
5
6
7
8
A
B
C
D
Sztropkó
ZEMPLÉN
Eperjes
OSLOVAKIA
Rozgony
Nagymihály
Kassa
Tőketerebes
Ungvár
GALICIA
TRANSCARPATHIA
Munkács
Miskolc
Dombrád
Kisvárda
Bodrogkeresztúr
Huszt
MÁRAMAROS
Szatmárcseke
Kölcse
Fehérgyarmat
Mátészalka
Szatmár
Csenger
Tyukod
Aknaszlatina
Kács
Kótaj
Laskod
Tibolddaróc
Nyíregyháza
Hajdúnánás
Nyírbátor
Nyírbéltek
Tisza
HAJDÚ
Hajdúhadház
Hajdúböszörmény
Debrecen
Balmazújváros
Hajdúszoboszló
Tiszafüred
Kaba
Nagyvárad
BIHAR
Dés
Bánffyhunyad
KOLOZS
Kolozsvár
Békéscsaba
Mezőkovácsháza
ROMANIA
TRANSYLVANIA
Arad
Maros River
Temesvár
Brassó
Danube River
Turnu Severin
N
0
50 km

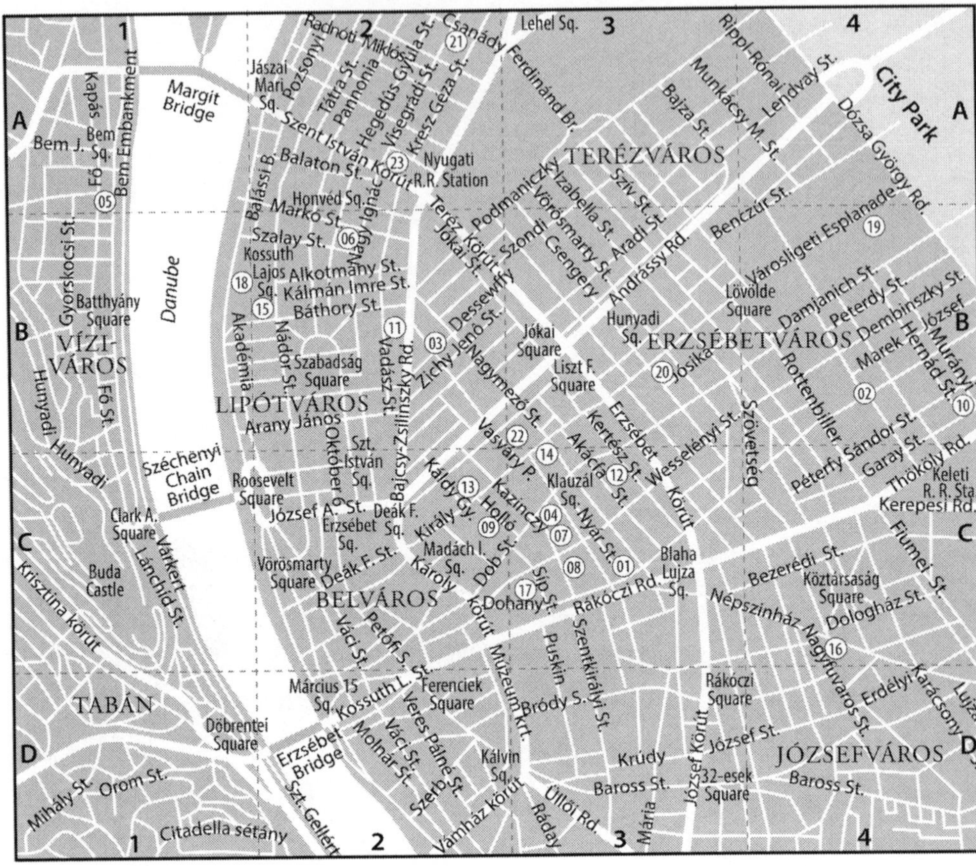

2. Budapest: the Inner City around World War II and later. Courtesy of Joseph Stoll, Syracuse University Cartographic Lab.

Key

01 The Continental Hotel [C3]
02 Shul (Bethlen Gábor Square) [B4]
03 Shul (23 Dessewffy Street) [B2]
04 Shul (35 Dob Street) [C3]
05 Prison (70–78 Fő Street) [A1]
06 The Markó prison [B2]
07 Shul (27–29 Kazinczy Street) [C3]
08 16 Kazinczy Street [C3]
09 1 Holló Street [C2]
10 Shul (48 Garay Street) [B4]
11 Glass House (29 Vadász Street) [B2]
12 32 Kertész Street [C3]
13 26 Király Street [C2]
14 41 Király Street [C3]
15 Kossuth Square [B2]
16 Shul (4 Nagyfuvaros Street) [C4]
17 Neolog Congregation (12 Síp Street) [C3]
18 Parliament [B1]
19 Israeli embassy (37 Vilma Királynő Road, today Városligeti esplanade, q.v.) [B4]
20 Erzsébet Kattler Prayer House (4 Jósika Street) [B3]
21 Small Vehicle Cooperative [A2]
22 Shul (5 Vasvári Pál Street) [B3]
23 Shul (Visegrádi Street) [A2]

Introduction

Eva Maria Thury

Sándor Bacskai is a Hungarian writer and photographer who also researches family history for Jews of Hungarian heritage in documents and cemeteries across Eastern Europe. Since the early nineties, he has written regularly for the Hungarian press, publishing in the weekly *Élet és Irodalom* (*Life and Literature*). He is also a regular contributor to and an editor of the monthly *Fotóművészet* (*Photographic Art*). Besides his journalistic efforts, Bacskai is known for his literary work, primarily creative renderings of oral histories he has collected. Additionally, he has read his short story "Lefele" ("Downward," p. 166) on Hungarian Radio. Bacskai's work collecting oral histories of Hungarian Orthodox Jews has been supported by the Soros Foundation as making an important contribution to the understanding of Hungarian Jewry in particular and of Jewish culture and tradition in general.

Bacskai's *Egy Lépés Jeruzsálem Felé* (*One Step toward Jerusalem*) contains stories told by ethnic Hungarian Orthodox Jews living in Hungary and neighboring countries as well as in Israel that were collected from 1990–1994; the book was published in 1997 in Budapest. In the present volume, I have translated these stories into English and supplemented them by my translation of "Unification," a somewhat tongue-in-cheek historical piece also by Bacskai which has been added to provide background on the material in the ethnographic works. The aim of this introduction is to provide English-language readers with the historical and literary background needed to appreciate Bacskai's work both as material supporting the understanding of the history of Hungary in the twentieth century and as narratives which in themselves are compelling stories that evoke the lives of real people. As a writer, Bacskai blends two genres which are not necessarily connected in scholarly work in ethnography: he functions both as an anthropologist and as the narrator of moving tales whose own personality also emerges in a charming way in the stories he tells.

Bacskai has woven his devotion to Judaism into the fabric of his work, but he is not a Jew and does not represent himself as anything he is not. One of the delightful moments of this volume describes his discussion of Hungarian soccer with the old men at the Kazinczy Street[1] Orthodox synagogue in Kassa,[2] which used to be part of Hungary (pp. 156–57). They ask him if supports the MTK,[3] a national soccer team which was viewed in the 1930s and 1940s as a Jewish club because it had a number of Jewish members. Here is the dialogue that follows:

"No, I'm a Fradi fan."

"Well, I heard what those guys were up to last time, as usual, throwing stones at the clubhouse and shouting, 'Dirty Jews.' They're a bunch of fascists. Decent Jews don't root for the Fradi."

"But after the war they were the first to give jerseys and balls to get the MTK started again. Anyway, I'm not a Jew." Then I had to explain what I was doing there, that I was going to what used to be a world famous yeshivah at Hunfalu where there would soon be the *yortsayt* of Chief Rabbi Sámuel Rosenberg.

"What! You say you're not a Jew, but you know what a *yortsayt* is. If you know what a *yortsayt* is, and you know about the Hunfalva[4] yeshivah, then you must be a Jew. I don't care what you say, as far as I'm concerned, you are," he said, looking at the other men. Several nodded silently.

1. Kazinczy Street: Now called Puškinova Street. (Repeated terms not clarified by an explanation in the text are footnoted once per chapter. If there is no footnote, see the glossary.)

2. Kassa: Once in Hungary, but reassigned to Czechoslovakia by the treaty of Trianon. It is now called Košice and is the second largest city in Slovakia (map 1 A5).

3. MTK: MTK stands for the Magyar Tornaklub, Hungarian Physical Education Club. Fradi is a nickname for the Ferencvárosi Tornaklub, another football team. Ferencváros is the IX district of Budapest.

4. Hunfalva: Hunfalu was known as Hunfalva before 1902: today it is Huncovce (Hunsdorf) Slovakia (map 1 A4).

Beyond briefly explaining Bacskai's stance with respect to Judaism, this sociographic study of the community at Kassa also shows something about his relationship to his work. If Bacskai saw himself only as an anthropologist, his work would have been done, as he has achieved acceptance by the community he is studying. However, he views himself as a writer and that involves a certain style of literary storytelling, as the rest of the narrative shows clearly. While describing the experiences of the faith community and its worshippers at Kassa, it also gives the retort of the hospital porter when he is asked if he speaks Hungarian—"Why, I do everything in Hungarian! I can't even run in any other language!"—and it ends with Bacskai and an elderly Holocaust survivor sharing oranges and tomatoes at the latter's hospital bedside while discussing the days before the Holocaust, when, the old man says, "Life was good."

Through such an account, Bacskai formulates his task as a literary one: conveying the experiences of human beings living the tradition of Orthodox Hungarian Judaism after the Holocaust, in the Stalinist years. Thus, while the portraits of the subjects in this volume are accurate renditions in the ethnographic genre, they also represent literary works of merit that can be read as narratives in the best sense of the word. His Orthodox Jews are not just heroes, they are human beings who have lost much but find the strength to go on because of their tradition, their religion, their community.

English-language readers are more likely to understand that community and to appreciate the struggles of the personages in Bacskai's stories if they grasp the main issues of the historical movements that underlie the Orthodox tradition in Hungary. The first one to be considered is that of assimilation and foreign influence: throughout its history in Hungary, Judaism in general and Orthodoxy in particular have struggled with whether they are perceived as "foreign" or "Hungarian." This affects the Orthodox especially because their mentality was forged from a synthesis of the religious practices of the Ashkenazi Jews who immigrated from Germany and Moravia, and of the Hasidic Jews who came from Poland and Galícia. There is no single answer to this question, and in what follows, we will see that the external accusation of foreignness emerges over and over again in the history of the Hungarian Orthodox, as does the internal question of the right degree of assimilation to Hungarian language and values of those following such an internationally based movement.

A second issue that arises in the history of Hungarian Orthodoxy is resistance to being lumped together with other forms of Judaism, and especially the concern to avoid being governed by any body outside of the Orthodox perspective. In the nineteenth century, the Hungarian Orthodox had reason to separate themselves from Neolog Judaism, which Károly Vörös[5] describes as "a mild variation of the German Reform movement" (188). These two forms of Judaism were very different. The Orthodox were less likely to adopt Hungarian as the language of their sermons, while in the early twentieth century this became the norm in Neolog synagogues (Karady 170). In leadership as well, the Orthodox and the Neolog could not have been more different: Neolog communities relied on lay leadership for all but ritual purposes, while the Orthodox emphasized the role of rabbis to guide their populace (Katzburg 28). Katzburg notes that the Orthodox and Neolog were more deeply divided in Hungary than anywhere else in Europe (19).

As a result of these differences, Hungarian Orthodox Jews placed a high priority on being separate from other kinds of Judaism in Hungary and thus became organizationally unique in the world. They fought to obtain their own independent organization at the 1868–69 National Jewish Congress and viewed this separation as essential to their way of life.[6]

5. Károly Vörös: This introduction incorporates material from modern historians, including Vörös and these others: Victor Karady, Nathaniel Katzburg, András Kovács, Aletta Forrás-Biró, Anna Manchin, László Katus, and Peter Hanák. The full titles of their works are given in the bibliography at the end of the volume.

6. viewed this separation as essential to their way of life: In 1867, as a result of its losses in the Franco-Austrian War and the Austro-Prussian War, Austria was forced to adopt an agreement that restored Hungarian constitutional rights and allowed Hungarians, both Jewish and Christian, to vote. Following this, the Hungarian government called for the establishment of a national organization for Jewish congregations. Until this point, there had been no central organization that facilitated communication between these entities. The government's request resulted in the Congress, at which the Orthodox "waged a surprisingly skillful and eventually successful campaign against the establishment of a single

The planners of this Congress intended to create a unified Hungarian Jewish structure, but the result of the efforts of the Orthodox was the splitting of Hungarian Jewry into separate organizations for the Orthodox, the Neolog, and the Status Quo[7] (Vörös 191). Of this split, Bacskai says, "many are inclined to consider the formation of an independent Orthodox organization as a wrong-headed step, disastrous, and harmful to all Jewry, one that preserved ghetto life rather than enlightenment, civil rights or emancipation. . . . The Orthodox, on the other hand, felt that Progressive Jews had strayed from the path prescribed by their ancestors, that their reforms of Jewish life corresponded to a denial of their religious laws and ultimately represented a denial of Judaism" (*Az Első Nap* 5).

The battle the Orthodox fought at the 1868–69 Congress is the background that explains the importance of the events in the historical piece called "Unification," in which Bacskai describes the National Israelite Assembly of 1950. At this more recent gathering, the Orthodox were required to give up the independent status they had held for more than eighty years; this organizational change was part of a more comprehensive governmental movement to erase the unique position of Orthodoxy in Hungary and to alter the lives of Bacskai's subjects.

Katzburg attributes the "polarization" that attended the split of 1869 to the refusal of the Orthodox to assimilate to Hungarian values (19). However, linguistic Magyarization[8] in everyday life, a key component in assimilation, gradually took root in many sectors of Orthodox Jewry too, especially in the cities and in ethnic Magyar milieus (Karady 170). This raises the third historical issue worth considering by readers of this translation, that of language. All of Bacskai's subjects spoke to him in Hungarian, and, as we shall see, their identity as Orthodox Jews was bound up

---

representative Jewish body" (Kovács, "Hungarian Jewish Politics," 125), in effect declaring themselves independent of other forms of Judaism in Hungary. See also p. 161.

7. Status Quo: Also called Status Quo Ante. Karady describes this as "a milder form of Orthodoxy" (164). See also the glossary.

8. Magyarization: Hungarians call themselves, and the language they speak, Magyar. So this term refers to the process of replacing one's previous language with Hungarian.

with their use of the language; this may seem invisible to those reading their stories in English, but the use of Hungarian actually represents the resolution of a complex issue on the part of Orthodox communities. In the late nineteenth century, the Hungarian people, Jews and Christians alike, were reasserting their independence from Austria, which had encouraged and even forced them to speak German. Thus at this time, speaking their own language and promoting a culture independent of Austria, or Magyarization, was an important movement, and those who spoke the language were considered progressive and forward-thinking. Jews, on the other hand, were accustomed to speaking languages associated with their tradition, including Yiddish and German, and these languages were woven into their customs and their religious rituals.

This language change within Orthodox Jewry took place

> in a Magyar [Hungarian] environment [in] the eastern part of the Central Plain, [where] a rapid and thorough process of Magyarization had been completed by the early twentieth century. The switch to the vernacular went hand in hand with a far-reaching political identification with Hungarian nationalism, with loyalty to the State and government, and with social symbiosis with the Gentile rural environment. In non-Magyar environments, such as [Transcarpathia], linguistic Magyarization amid other aspects of assimilation (except perhaps political allegiance) remained quite limited. (Karady 177)

Thus, as Karady makes clear, the matter of Jewish assimilation can "by no means be reduced to a unilateral process of Jews coming closer to Gentiles in terms of their manners, culture, daily language, etc. Instead, it must be seen as a creative process that engendered a new cultural system (in the anthropological sense of the term), one in close contact with Gentiles—especially those of Magyar and German stock" (169).

Bacskai's interviews poignantly reflect the tensions involved with assimilation for the Orthodox who were often charged with being "foreign" or "not Hungarian enough." For example, Ervin Groszberg says, "Hungarian Jewry wasn't less patriotic than Hungarian Christianity; I am in a position to say so, since, after thirty-five years of life in Israel this patriotism is still within me. I root for the Hungarians in the Olympics,

3. "I traveled to Máramarossziget [a Transcarpathian city now in Romania] to interview one of the Orthodox congregation's clerks about the years after the war. This was once a world-famous Jewish congregation with a large number of members; it endures but is now much diminished. While I was waiting for the clerk, I noticed this nice, and I think typically Eastern European, still life: the *alef-beys* table, the map of Romania, and the knot of spring onions." Text and photograph by Sándor Bacskai.

at home we have a 'Hungarian shelf' with Hungarian books and—please don't laugh—a red, white, and green rosette" (p. 54).[9] Frigyes Rosenberg, on the other hand, tells the story of his friend from Vác who pinned on a red, white, and green rosette but was caught and beaten up by a couple of goyim: "What's this, are you a Hungarian now too?" (p. 86).

The fourth issue that readers of this volume will want to bear in mind is the geography underlying these stories. Over time, national boundaries

9. a red, white, and green rosette: This patriotic and national symbol originated in Hungary's 1848 revolution against Austrian rule.

were redrawn, and this altered the lives of the Orthodox whose communities came to be located in different countries. This greatly complicated the issue of assimilation, which has already been raised above. Karady has studied Jewish assimilation in Hungary in the early twentieth century. He concludes that the positions taken in 1868–69 already reflected the geographic and cultural divisions between Orthodox and Neolog Jews that persisted into the time period of Bacskai's narratives.

Thus, reading the narratives in this volume may be enhanced by an awareness of the geographic locations being discussed in them. Map 1 (pp. x–xi) can serve as the starting point for an examination of these localities. It shows all the cities and towns mentioned in the narratives, giving the present-day boundaries of Hungary as well as representing the country as it appeared from 1886 to 1914. This makes it clear that the mental map of the Orthodox tradition is broader than the present-day boundaries of Hungary.

In fact, the map shows that the two main varieties of Hungarian Jewry were clustered[10] in separate locations in the period we are interested in.[11]

10. clustered: The Neolog predominated in Transdanubia (see map 1 C2-B4) with the exception of parts of Győr, Moson, and Sopron counties. The area between the Tisza and the Danube and also that between the Maros and the Tisza (map 1 C4-B8) were mainly Neolog, except for Bihar county. Budapest was a Neolog center, though it had the largest concentration of Orthodox Jewry in the country. Most of the provincial towns were primarily Neolog, including Kassa (map 1 A5), Pécs (map 1 C3), Szeged (map 1 C4), Nagyvárad (map 1 B5), Arad (map 1 C5), and Temesvár (map 1 C5). The other parts of the country and the large urban centers of Miskolc (map 1 B5), Pozsony (map 1 B3), and Debrecen (map 1 B5) were predominantly Orthodox or Status Quo Ante. Orthodox congregations were in the majority in Hungary's northwest and northeast, the Slovakian and Transcarpathian areas, as well as in the eastern Great Plain and the Upper Tisza region. Transylvania was mostly Orthodox, though it had several smaller Neolog cities (Karady 164).

11. the period we are interested in: Bacskai's stories start near the end of World War II in 1944 and go up beyond the Hungarian revolution of 1956. However, because of the way that the Orthodox hold fast to old-time traditions, by entering the world of these narratives, we find ourselves in a world established at the 1868–69 Jewish Congress. Karady has studied the census records of early twentieth-century Hungarian Jews and has been able to relate these modern records to the votes cast in the Congress. These segments display

We can see this distribution by drawing "a diagonal line across the map of the country from northwest to southeast, that is, say, from Pozsony [map 1 B3] to Brassó [map 1 C8]. Most of the regions south of this line were dominated by Neolog Jewry; those to the north by the Orthodox" (Karady 164). Their concentration initially gave Orthodox communities strength, but their status changed markedly after 1918, with the end of World War I, when Hungary lost two-thirds of its territory and population and the number of the country's Jews decreased by half as a result of the treaty of Trianon (Katus 104). Most of the Jewry whose homes were no longer within Hungary came from the northern, Orthodox section of the country which had been reassigned by the peace treaty to Czechoslovakia and Romania, raising new issues[12] of language and assimilation. However, within Hungary, Orthodox congregations (61.5 percent) still outnumbered those of the Neolog (30.7 percent) and Status Quo groups. "Principally, this was because the strength of the Orthodox congregations was most pronounced in the provincial cities and small towns, where they were dispersed in small units" (Katzburg 27).

Kovács and Forrás-Biró explain that in 1941, the last census before the Holocaust reported there were 400,000 Jews in what is today's Hungary, as well as 50,000 to 90,000 others of Jewish descent who had converted to Christianity, doubtless in large part to escape persecution. Of these nearly half a million people, only between 190,000 and 260,000 survived. However, this was not the end of Jewish life in Hungary. After the war, 258 Jewish communities were reestablished, though as a result of repression by the postwar Communist dictatorship, 60,000 to 75,000 Jews left Hungary in the early 1950s (Kovács and Forrás-Biró 7). This time period is the main focus of Bacskai's sociographic studies in this book. The independent functioning of the Orthodox in Hungary which began with the

---

distinct demographic and behavioral characteristics related to their geographic location (Karady 165).

12. raising new issues: However, after World War I, there was less tension within Hungary between these two Jewish groups, Katzburg believes, because Hasidic influence now fell outside the country (30).

1868–69 National Jewish Congress persisted until 1950, the time of their forced merger by the National Israelite Assembly on which Bacskai reports in the first chapter, "Unification."

There were additional problems for the Orthodox, as we can see from Bacskai's ethnographies. When their numbers were diminished, first by the Holocaust and then by Stalinism, the Orthodox way of life became difficult to sustain in the rural areas in which it had once been concentrated. This is why we see, in the piece called "Once There Was a Yeshivah in Pest," that family after family is leaving the countryside, or at least sending their children to be educated in Budapest (map 1 B4). It is as György Budai says: "We lived in Szatmárcseke, we were the last Jewish family, and in '57 we moved in to Mátészalka [both towns map 1 B6]. In those parts, one or two families still remained, scattered here and there, but there wasn't any serious religious life anymore" (p. 107). Orthodox Judaism calls for a community, and its practice becomes impossible where the concentration of worshippers is too low.

In another piece, Frigyes Rosenberg describes the difficulty of filling positions essential to the community as the numbers of worshippers dwindled. Speaking of 1946 or 1947, he says, "Later we hired a *shokhet* named Roth who happened to be a *talmid hokhem*. I don't remember where we found him, all I remember is that when we called him I negotiated with him until midnight—I said that I could only hire him if was willing to be involved with the children, teach them their *alef-beys*,[13] but he didn't want to undertake this for all the world. I told him that there were ten of us all together and not everyone could afford to kill a chicken once a week, so it wasn't such a burning issue for us to have a *shakter*. You need a *shakter* so there will be someone to be involved with the children" (p. 73). If essential positions couldn't be filled, the Orthodox struggled in their ability to practice their faith.

13. *shokhet . . . talmid hokhem . . . alef-beys*: For italicized Yiddish expressions, see the glossary. A *shokhet* or *shakter* is trained in killing animals for food following the strict requirements of Jewish law. The phrase *talmid hokhem* means "an expert in Jewish learning," and *alef-beys* is "alphabet."

Bacskai likes to point out that most historic accounts of twentieth-century Judaism in Europe end with 1944, but this is where his work begins, with the forgotten stories of those who survived the Holocaust. Some of these Orthodox Jews did return to Hungary and Hungarian-speaking towns in neighboring countries. After the war, the Jews who returned to their homes reestablished the strength of community life. At the end of 1947, 137 Orthodox congregations existed in Hungary; however, the size of the community was soon greatly diminished. In 1950, after the fall of Hungarian democracy, 87 of those congregations ceased to exist. After the Hungarian revolution of 1956, the Jewish Orthodox community shrank further in population. Some Jews emigrated while others, through choice or necessity, remained in Europe. The bearers of the faith who remained had to combat anti-Semitism, anti-Zionism, and the anticlericalism of the Soviet-related socialist system which deployed these forces against the traditions practiced by those who returned. Despite these impediments, as the narratives collected by Bacskai testify, Orthodox Jews maintained their way of life in ways great and small, owing to the strength of their tradition and the force of their will as individuals. The stories collected in this volume testify to the power of their beliefs and represent a narrative that is important for anyone who wants to understand the historical forces that make Hungary what it is today.

Hungarian historian Peter Hanák cautions his countrymen not to allow their character as a nation to be deformed by the inability to know themselves and to question their motives and actions (62). In his work, Bacskai has given his nation, and us, his English-language readers, a series of stories which reveal a defining factor that will characterize the nature of Hungary in history, even though it is not clear what the fate of Hungarian Orthodoxy will be in the long run. Since the collapse of Communism, there have been increases in the number of Jewish communities functioning in Hungary, though they are still tiny, and the Orthodox tradition is the smallest of them. At the time of a 2011 report, there were forty-two Neolog synagogues in Hungary (fourteen in Budapest and twenty-eight in the provinces) and four synagogues and prayer houses owned by the Orthodox, all in Budapest (Kovács and Forrás-Biró 15), as against the fifty that still remained in 1950.

However, Kovacs and Forrás-Biró report that "Jewish life was very much reinvigorated with the fall of communism [in 1989], and more and more Jews have begun to show an interest in Jewish religion, tradition and culture" (8). This rise in interest is occurring in the face of a Communist-fostered culture which demanded that Jewishness should be "invisible": the Holocaust was not an attack on Jews but on "antifascists," and any discussion of Jews as a minority culture was discouraged (Manchin 4). Unfortunately, at the same time, there has also been a rise of open anti-Semitism, which had been officially banned by the Communist government (Kovács, "Antisemitic Prejudices," 22).

In the literary ethnographies of *One Step toward Jerusalem*, Bacskai has portrayed the political, religious, and individual forces which have come to bear on the Orthodox Jewish tradition as it has struggled for survival in the aftermath of fascism and communism during the period from 1945 to 1989. Of his work, Bacskai has said, "During my interviews, I found that crucial facts can be revealed for history in thorough, detailed conversations; moreover these interviews abound in motifs which humanize the abstractions of history" (Bacskai, "The History of Hungarian Orthodox Jewry After 1945," 3).

In addition, Bacskai's work represents an important contribution to the study of Hungarian and Central European cultural history. The living testimony from one of the strongest cultural forces that has ever operated in Hungary can clearly help scholars to shed light on these trends, particularly given contemporary uncertainty over the persistence of Orthodox Judaism in modern-day Hungary. The work done by Bacskai suggests that the transformation of Hungarian culture during socialist occupation was more complex than may be realized. This oral history showing the social and individual factors involved in the creation of today's culture can contribute to a better understanding of the political, social, and cultural forces operating in Hungary at and after the end of World War II.

Translator's Note

My interest in the work of Sándor Bacskai can be traced to my love of mythology, whose devotees understand that the term refers not to "false stories" but to "sacred stories." A people, and a culture, can be understood through the tradition it constructs for others, and itself, describing its values and experiences. Equally influential were the stories I grew up with myself, as my parents described the atrocities of World War II in Hungary and my father's activities in protecting persecuted Jews and resisting the German occupation, for which he, like many other Hungarians, won a medal when the change of regime finally took place.

With this background, I came across the important work of Bacskai in Hungarian and immediately saw that it deserved to be made available to a wider, English-speaking audience because of its moving content as well as its powerful literary style. The Holocaust is much more studied than the subsequent Stalinist persecution of Jews, and Bacskai's stories represent a fine contribution to bridging that gap. I believe that because of their vivid characters and compelling narrative line, these stories will speak, of course, to Jews but also to all humanity, regardless of religion or lack thereof.

This translation represented multiple challenges, as it involved expanding the understanding of Orthodoxy to those who might be unfamiliar with its tradition and practices as well as explaining the unique historical experiences of Hungarian Jewry to a broader English-speaking audience around the world. In addition, there was the need to provide the relevant details of World War II and Hungarian culture to those who were less familiar with these events and experiences.

To meet these challenges, I have supplemented the text of Bacskai's book *Egy Lépés Jeruzsálem Felé* with his article "Unifikáció" (Unification), which sketches for the reader the National Israelite Assembly of 1950, one of the defining historical events for the experience of Orthodox Jews in Stalinist times. In addition, I have provided the reader with footnotes explaining terms, events, and situations that might be unfamiliar in a particular story as well as with an extensive glossary which focuses more broadly on the religious and historical background necessary to appreciate Bacskai's stories to the fullest extent. Terms foreign to the Hungarian text are presented in their original language in the text of the translation and their meaning given either in a footnote or in the glossary. To minimize interference from too much textual clutter, the text does not mark such foreign terms beyond italicizing them. Some ideas or events are explained briefly in the footnotes but have an expanded discussion in the glossary.

The volume as Bacskai originally formulated it has a wonderful narrative flow, so readers with a less historical bent may wish to start with the "Guardians of the Faith" section and return to "Unification" later in their experience of his work. In addition, as readers may choose to read these stories in an order of their own making, any relevant footnotes are repeated in each chapter.

There are also maps that may give the non-Hungarian reader familiarity with the locations referred to in Hungary (map 1) or Budapest (map 2); readers can assume that any places mentioned in the stories can be found by consulting them. The introduction and footnotes contain references to the coordinates of any places mentioned there, but such references have been omitted from the translation of Bacskai's text; the index of places (pp. 221–27) can guide the reader to the correct map and coordinates. In the case of map 2, that index also indicates the direction of some places not included on the map in relation to the parts of Budapest which *are* represented there.

A note about punctuation: this literary work is based on interviews and is thus meant to sound like oral speech. In addition, Hungarians rarely use semicolons; they tend to connect independent clauses with commas. The Hungarian sentence is, as a result of this use of commas, longer and more flexible than the English one; the sentence can convey nuances of connection and meaning that are harder to get across in English. In particular, Bacskai uses this feature of the language to represent speech, and in the translation, I have tried to convey the flow of his thought and the rhythms of his prose through a combination of commas, semicolons and dashes, sometimes without regard to the rules of proper, formal speech in English.

I would like to end by acknowledging with great appreciation the help of some of the many people whose thoughtful reading and broad expertise made possible my translation of this important work. These include Sándor Bacskai, who made available to me the background information I needed in endless consultations; Szonja Komoróczy of Eötvös Loránd University, who first read through my earliest version and supplemented and corrected my translation efforts at regular meetings during my year in Budapest for this project; Rakhmiel Peltz at Drexel University, whose vast store of knowledge has been indispensible to me at every stage of the translation; Ilana Rosen of Ben Gurion University of the Negev, who later read the entire manuscript and made extensive suggestions from her redoubtable expertise; and Peter Czipott, the author and co-author of amazing translations from the Hungarian, who read the entirety of the nearly final version and made shrewd and elegant suggestions for improving it. Special thanks are due to my dear friend Will Mason, who edited the manuscript at multiple stages and provided invaluable suggestions for the translation as well as making multiple passes to research and develop the maps and the indexes. I would also like to thank my husband M. Carl Drott and my son Milton Thury Drott for their readings and suggestions on sections of the manuscript, and my helpful and supportive editor at Syracuse University Press, Deborah Manion, as well as series editor Henry Feingold. *Sine quibus non.*[1] These knowledgeable and kind individuals are of course not responsible for any errors or infelicities that remain. In addition, I would like to thank Drexel University, where I labor happily, for the sabbatical year in which I began this project, as well as Abioseh Porter, my longtime department head, and Donna Murasko, my dean, who supported my subsequent efforts.

1. *Sine quibus non*: Latin, meaning "without them this work would not have been possible."

One Step toward Jerusalem

Unification

On February 20, 1950, Gyula Ortutay, the folklorist, Smallholders party politician and minister of Religion and Education, rose from his sickbed in Budapest, shaved, and, fulfilling his obligations, appeared at the National Israelite Assembly. The meeting was being held for voting on the reunification of the Jewish religion,[1] which had been torn into three parts eighty years earlier, and the provision of a new regulatory administration for the newly unified body.

The National Bureau of Hungarian Israelites, which served both the Neolog[2] and Status Quo[3] congregations, as well as the Orthodox Central Bureau, had informed the minister in December that Hungarian Jewry would like to be incorporated into a single organization. Minister Ortutay approved of the incorporation, and thus he had brought the request of these agencies before the cabinet meeting of January 6. As there was no opposition there either, the ministry was able to issue a proclamation for the convocation of a National Assembly.

Thus Minister Ortutay entered the flag-decorated building of the Neolog Congregation on Síp Street. He took his seat on the podium of the

1. reunification of the Jewish religion: Bacskai is well aware that this was, as Katzburg notes, a forced reunification (29) of the Orthodox community with the rest of Hungarian Jewry. This piece is replete with irony.

2. Neolog: Those Jews who followed the decisions of the 1868–69 National Jewish Congress. Those Jews who left the Congress were called Orthodox or autonomous Orthodox. Katzburg notes that the Neolog aspired to reunification while the Orthodox "zealously guarded their independence" (30).

3. Status Quo: Also called Status Quo Ante. Karady describes this as "a milder form of Orthodoxy" (164). See also the glossary.

Council Chamber. After the introductory remarks of Lajos Stöckler, the president of the congregation, and the greetings of Samu Kahán-Frankl, the Orthodox leader, Ortutay gave his sweeping speech which was rewarded by ringing applause and cheering. He made note of the sufferings of Jewry and he denounced the machinations of reactionary and nationalist Jewish interests, while declaring that, despite delusions to the contrary, freedom of religion was no empty expression for the new government. Finally, he stated his hope that "this National Assembly would certainly represent one of the greatest and most significant dates in the history of Hungarian Jewry, and that it would belong to the greatest dates associated with understanding, peace, and love."*

According to the account in *Új Élet*,[4] the inaugural assembly flowed on in a similar vein. The minister's prediction seemed to have been fulfilled on the spot, as those who took the floor in turn expressed faith in an already unified organization. They suggested that after an eighty-year separation, Hungarian Jews could once again greet each other as family. Only Sándor Jungreisz, the rabbi from Gyöngyös, said some peculiar things[5] that diverged a bit from the others. He alluded to the commanding necessity of the circumstances and spoke of his sharp heartache at the closing of the Orthodox Central Bureau. Later, President Lajos Stöckler declared a little patronizingly that Jungreisz's manner was somewhat overblown, presumably because of his youth.

The next day the assembly continued, moving on to its real work, the debate over organizational structure. The president of the congregation in Miskolc, Alfréd Züszmann, who was no longer young but nonetheless also inclined toward the overblown, declared that, after the inaugural ceremony of the previous day, the time had come for sincere views. As

* This work is based on the documents in section 33 of the National Archives of Hungary, issues of *Új Élet* from 1949 to 1950, and interviews conducted by the writer. Quoted material is drawn from the official record book of the National Israelite Assembly. The starred footnotes are carried over from the Hungarian version.

4. *Új Élet*: The official paper of the Organized Hungarian Jewish Community.

5. peculiar things: This is another good place to point out Bacskai's ironic stance throughout this piece. See also p. 1.

leader of the nation's second largest congregation, he cared less about protocol and could perhaps articulate what Kahán-Frankl, given his delicate position, could not. He declared that the affiliation had come about out of necessity, and that the Orthodox had agreed to relinquish their eighty-year independence only because of external pressure. "Every union which comes into being in the name of God will endure forever, but if it does not arise in the name of God, it will not endure permanently," he added, quoting the saying of the Fathers.

According to the records of the meeting, shouting increasingly interrupted the speaker, but when he objected to the disproportionately small number of representatives proposed for the formerly Orthodox, there were a few cheers. And then President Züszmann turned to the greatest problem for the strictly religious: what will happen given the impossibility of keeping the Sabbath? At this point, Lajos Stöckler decided that the speaker's time was up. He wouldn't like to have the occasion's festive nature disturbed by such an insignificant event. There followed several minutes of speakers distancing the assembly from the president of Miskolc. The most striking utterances came from the journalist Endre Sós, the incoming president of MIOK,[6] who prefaced his remarks by defining himself as "one of the members of the meeting with perhaps the most progressive political views." After this, Sós characterized Züszmann's speech as "unfortunately recall[ing] the sad events of congresses leading to the breach." He advised that they instead return to the path of love, peace, and understanding.

One of the results of the Jewish Congress of 1868–69, the formation of an autonomous Orthodox administration is often considered a flawed final outcome harmful to a unified Jewry, a step which preserved the existence of the ghetto in the place of enlightenment, emancipation, and the rise of the bourgeoisie. Politics and public life are in any case the province of the versatile, cultured Neolog, and the "overly zealous

6. MIOK (Hungarian: Magyarország Izraeliták Országos Képviselete, or National Representation of Hungarian Israelites): The organization established in 1950 as the sole overseer of all Hungarian Jewry.

religious" would be better off if they limited their narrow-minded activities to their prayer life.

However, according to the Orthodox, it was the progressive Jews who had strayed from the path laid down by their ancestors. Their reforms repudiated religious law, and in time their religious innovations would lead to the elimination of Jewry itself. The movement to preserve the faith, the reaction of a people trying to survive without a national state, was the only possible response to assimilation. Therefore, the conservatives also had to come out of their temples and proclaim at every forum the view that their leading rabbis had pronounced years before the Jewish Congress, that Hungarian Orthodoxy considered itself a separate denomination.

Single congregations may have included atheists, reform Jews and Orthodox, and this is how it was in most settlements. However, those religious who insisted on the letter of the law in following the *Sulchan Aruch* Code of Law[7] considered it absolutely necessary to maintain their own prayer houses, in the same way that believing Christians don't all attend Mass in Roman Catholic churches. And if Adventists, Baptists, and Pentecostal Protestants could freely choose their congregations, why would Jews whose religious life is just as diverse be expected to simulate unity and fellowship? Should they continue to represent Jewry as homogeneous to the "outside world" of the state and religious authorities, or should they try to take advantage of the possibilities provided by a liberal political climate and create separate congregations even within the same settlement?

The Neolog, who represented an absolute majority in numbers, usually predominated in the leadership of mixed congregations. It was not to their advantage to allow the divisions in the religious life of Jewry to be reflected also in its administrative life. The Orthodox, however, had voted for a split. Their action made it clear that, despite its own smaller and larger internal disputes, Orthodoxy represented a viable entity, though it was amalgamated from a hundred different colors, cultural backgrounds, and rituals. The Orthodox followed the teachings of Mózes Szófer, the

7. *Sulchan Aruch* Code of Law: The most authoritative legal code of Judaism.

Ashkenazi rabbi from Pozsony,[8] but also did not distance themselves from Hasidism. Their communities effectively resisted the spread of modernism, the Jewish enlightenment, and Zionism; among them, large numbers of children continued to be born; the danger of assimilation was less threatening, and by 1944, their numbers had outstripped those of the WJC[9] and Status Quo factions.

In fact, the leaders of the Neolog protested several times in the years from 1870 to 1944 to the Ministers of Religious Worship that they should rescind the autonomy of the Orthodox, and from time to time they proposed the convocation of a new congress for unification. In 1908, at the request of the Neolog, one such minister, Albert Apponyi, asked the leaders of the Orthodox if they would be amenable to deliberations about unification. At the response that a long-standing resolution precluded them from even tentative discussions, Apponyi himself terminated any further consideration of the issue. The rabbinate of the Orthodox prohibited negotiations with reform elements and imposed religious bans on WJC congregations. Orthodox Jews could not accept positions in these congregations, and they did not recognize the credentials of those who had trained in Neolog rabbinical schools.

The unusual complexity of Hungarian Orthodoxy is manifest in the spirit of its adherents who, despite their parochial way of life, were as proudly patriotic as more assimilated Jews. A majority of them spoke Hungarian as their native language, and as villagers, they coexisted peacefully with their Christian neighbors. Of course, the opposite was true as well: no matter the good relations, or even the genuine friendship which frequently obtained, the Orthodox always and in every instance considered their own laws the only standard. And someone who voluntarily accepts what to the outsider must seem like a stiflingly restrictive framework and undertakes a way of life regulated by 613 commandments but compensated by the joyful love of the Torah is not likely even in hard times to

8. Pozsony: Now Bratislava (Pressburg), Slovakia (map 1 B3). Once part of Hungary, this city was reassigned by the treaty of Trianon.

9. WJC: The World Jewish Congress.

turn against his family, his customs, and his kind. And those who won't abandon their religion at the time of the Jewish Laws,[10] or in the ghetto, or in the camp aren't going to abandon it when the world spins off its axis.

Some Hungarian Jews liberated in 1945 remained in the refugee camps maintained by the American army; others came home and started for the border from there. But there were those who couldn't stand to imagine living elsewhere than Hungary. They considered their most important task the resuscitation of Judaism. From late fall of 1944 to early spring 1945, as the front moved westward, it was followed by the formation of congregations in the Alföld and in the Tiszántúl area. By the time the first groups started home from Auschwitz, Bergen-Belsen, and Theresienstadt, the forced-labor unit workers who returned earlier had cleaned up the temples and organized soup kitchens maintained with the Joint's[11] money. Shellfire still rocked Buda when in Pest a regular morning and evening prayerlife was already being conducted in one of the less battered prayer houses of the Kazinczy-Dob Street building collective. What's more, in Király Street a small yeshivah was already in operation.

In 1945, more than a hundred Orthodox communities were reestablished in Hungary; by the November of '46 there were 136. These numbers could not be compared to those before the war, but tradition and the demand for a religious life endured even in those places to which shockingly few returned. Those who remained saw no reason for organizational changes either. Although the Neolog and Orthodox agencies worked together in a range of things, the idea of unification did not arise.

Despite the revitalization of Jewish life, the number of emigrants grew steadily in 1946–47 as a result of anti-Semitism that developed into pogroms in Miskolc and Kunmadaras (both map 1 B5), and into charges

10. Jewish Laws: These laws placed a ceiling on the percentage of Jews permitted in public life and cultural activities, including higher education, professional life, administrative positions, and commerce and industry in general.

11. the Joint: The American Jewish Joint Distribution Committee or JDC played a large role in the care of those in displaced person camps and provided funds for economic rehabilitation of shattered communities as well as for those who wished to emigrate.

of ritual sacrifice in the Hajdúság;[12] emigrants were motivated by feelings of hopelessness and dejection as well as economic and political insecurity. Even the Jewish soldiers of the Russian army frequently counseled those who returned home to emigrate. The Orthodox, who traditionally preferred small towns or villages, were driven to the relative safety of big cities, especially Budapest, Miskolc, and Debrecen, as a result of the dwindling of tiny congregations, the rise of practical concerns, and an ever-reawakening anti-Semitism. This unintentionally hastened the disappearance of the old value system and culture. In addition, a schizophrenic situation resulted as religious Jews fundamentally repudiated the atheist system which nonetheless could, because of their antifascism, claim them as supporters of socialism.

In many respects, 1948 became the year of the turning point: this was the year that Israel, initially an ally, later a bourgeois-capitalist menace,[13] came into being. The main consequence of this was that, at first, Jewish emigration there was authorized, then suddenly suspended. Next, Jewish schools were nationalized, and in that same year, the government reached agreement with the two Jewish governing agencies concerning the peaceful administration of the relationship between the denomination and the state, assuring the even-freer practice of religion. Beyond generalizations about the freedom of religion, the agreement signed by Minister of Religious Worship Ortutay guaranteed concrete rights, although the struggle against clericalism later made practical qualifications necessary.

In that year, about sixty thousand Neolog and twenty, twenty-five thousand Orthodox Jews lived in Hungary. While the ninety thousand

12. Hajdúság: Originally an autonomous region near Debrecen (map 1 B5). The area includes the towns of Hajdúböszörmény, Hajdúhadház, Hajdúnánás, and Hajdúszoboszló.

13. bourgeois-capitalist menace: Another instance of Bacskai's ironic presentation of historic details: it was not Israel which altered its character but the Hungarian Communist government which changed its stance on Israel. Originally, it was viewed as an ally, in line with Soviet policy, but as early as 1945, it was seen as a force drawing Jews from Hungary and contravening the government's determination to assimilate every minority (Kovács 131–33).

Jews of Poland sustained twenty newspapers and three Yiddish theaters, they employed only twenty-five rabbis. In contrast, Hungary had many fewer cultural institutions but three times as many congregations and rabbis, the majority of them Orthodox. An equally telling statistic is the number of yeshivahs; in Poland, they were only able to maintain two, three in Slovakia, five in Romania, and not even one in Transcarpathia. In contrast, in Hungary there were twenty-five Talmudic schools in operation at one time or another; those at Paks and Soltvadkert, the two most hardy, were blown away only by the winds of the revolution.[14]

Very few Orthodox remained in Slovakia, and the practice of religion was simply "outlawed" in a Transcarpathia long closed off from the outside world. Signs of Hungarian Orthodoxy endured longest in Transylvania, even though the policies of the Romanian government allowed a higher rate of Jewish emigration than those of Hungary. Finally in June of 1949, the great festival of peace, understanding, and love also arrived for Romania's two hundred thousand Jews.

A few months later, in November 1949, there was an article in *Új Élet* about the movement launched by the congregation of Óbuda[15] advocating "one city, one congregation." Among much else, this time was in fact characterized by grassroots initiatives. Naturally, the movement for unification also didn't come from above, it was launched by the community in Óbuda which was small in numbers but possessed of great traditions, and moreover was located in the capital city. Though it was not one of the most influential congregations, the "movement" was launched, and thus required a reaction. Lajos Stöckler wrote an editorial that bowed its head before the common view, and from this a unified Jewish position of national proportions could arise. First a congregation was devised for greater Budapest unifying the Neolog Jews of Pest, Buda, Óbuda, and Kőbánya. Successive editions of *Új Élet* published the names of the

14. the winds of the revolution: During and after the revolution of 1956 against the Soviet-controlled government, many Jews left Hungary.

15. Óbuda: Once an independent town, this community became a part of Budapest (map 2 far north of Víziváros, B1).

congregations which signed on to the noble cause, incidentally all Congressional[16] communities. But, as it wrote, "several Orthodox congregations" had indicated their affiliation as well, and for the sake of readers doubtful of this, it published the view of an anonymous reader who was an Orthodox ritual slaughterer "worried about the eighty-year sickness of Jewry" and who stated that "unification was in the best interest of Jewry."

At the end of November 1949, the Orthodox rabbinate was forced to give up its eighty-year autonomy. At their meeting on the twenty-fourth of November, the twelve head rabbis had primarily to consider what could happen if they held out for independence. They reckoned that Hungarian Jewry could easily end up with the same fate as the Transcarpathians: their prayer houses and temples could be nationalized, and they could lose all their hope along with the physical establishments that remained after 1944. Only one rabbi is still alive from among the rabbinate of those days, Jochanan Szófer, the direct descendent of Mózes Szófer who was then the twenty-year-old head rabbi of Pozsony. In an interview, he recounts that the ministry gave them to understand that they had no other choice; they blackmailed Samu Kahán-Frankl, the president of the Orthodox Central Bureau, threatening him with prison or deportation.

In addition to needing to satisfy the expectations of the government, Kahán-Frankl also had to endure the scorn of several Orthodox who even then proved themselves to be uncompromising. However, he, the president of the Central Bureau since 1934, sat down at the same table as the Neolog against his convictions but with the goal of saving something out of what was left.

The rabbinate did not nullify the eighty-year-old prohibition against the Neolog, and it gave permission for the deliberations only after conferring with the world's greatest rabbinical authorities. When they had obtained the acquiescence of these authorities and had sat down at the same table as the Neolog, they stipulated that the Budapest Orthodox Congregation had to remain a separate division and that a separate rabbinical council had to be established with responsibility for decisions in

16. Congressional: Synonym for Neolog.

every religious matter.* They emphasized several times that it was only because of external constraints that the possibility of the alliance had arisen, that they considered it only temporary, and that as soon as possible, they would again separate.†

Deliberations started on December 11, 1949, agreement was reached by early January, and on February 20, 1950, Gyula Ortutay could give his inaugural speech.

Among other things, the agreement made between the denominations and the state in 1948 guaranteed that the Jewish secondary school in Pest and the rural yeshivahs would be left standing, or rather that the children of parents who kept the Sabbath would not be required to attend school on the Sabbath. The only thing it didn't guarantee was that the parents of Sabbath-keeping children would be able to keep the Sabbath. After the nationalization of craftsmen and shopkeepers, thousands of Orthodox Jews were left unemployed. Although it was possible to get by for a few months through black-market dealings and petty larceny, finally, if they wanted to live, everyone had to accept state employment: there was no alternative. By 1950, the work calendar of the state sector had forgotten Christian Christmas; how would it have remembered Jewish Easter?[17]

The inquiries of Alfréd Züszmann, the president of the Miskolc congregation, about keeping the Sabbath were so unpleasant precisely because they touched on an issue troubling the consciences of many thousand people, and because in addition the one who was then describing his concerns about keeping the Sabbath was in effect also challenging the

* József (Jehosua) Czitrom, the Ros-Bészdin of Budapest, was elected president of the MIOK Orthodox Rabbinical Council; Márton (Mordche) Grünfeld, the head rabbi of Nyíregyháza, was elected vice president. The other members: Jakab Lebovits and Sándor (Amram) Jungreisz, rabbis from Budapest, Nándor (Mose Nátán) Lemberger from Makó, Ede (Jochanan) Schreiber from Eger, Zsigmond (Sraga Slomo) Schnitzler from Békéscsaba, Bernát (Báruch Cví Hakohén) Moskovits, the head rabbi of Paks.

† The Autonomous Orthodox Israelite Community of Budapest became independent again in 1993.

17. Jewish Easter: Jewish Easter Passover or *Pesakh*. Many Hungarian Jews were so "magyarized" (see pp. xvii–xviii) that they refer to their holiday in this way.

fairness of the government's resolutions. Lajos Stöckler shut Züszmann down, but he asked for another minute, and when, after some discussion, he was granted it, he recommended that they immediately request deliberations with the relevant authorities in the interest of obtaining work for Sabbath-keepers. They shouted him down again, they lectured him that he was pounding on open doors; however, it was only years later that the configuration of a few small business cooperatives as Sabbath-keepers was permitted.

After that, nothing else disturbed the work of the National Israelite Assembly, only an elderly doctor named Móric Mayer who professed not to understand why they had to divide up thirty thousand rural Jews into six administrative districts when formerly the five workers of the Orthodox Central Bureau could handle all the affairs of two hundred thousand people. His concern no longer stirred up a storm; they didn't even respond to it; what could they have said anyway; everything was decided long ago; the only thing needed was to vote. They elected the brand-new leadership of the Hungarian Israelite Agency; Lajos Stöckler was chosen president, unanimously, without discussion; and he remained president until the anti-Zionist trials in 1953 swept him away also.

By the fall of 1950, eighty Orthodox congregations were eliminated, along with sixty-six Congressional ones. According to the new Organizational Regulations, there could only be a congregation with independent status where there was a rabbi or assistant rabbi, a temple, and a ritual bath, and the branch congregations which were subordinated to the independent ones had to hold a religious service at least once a week. Requesting the greatest state support and the autonomous status, which meant relative independence, for example, was the Tiszántúl Village District which represented Jews from Hajdú-Bihar and Szabolcs-Szatmár counties and had twelve rabbis, all with temples and baths. The leadership of MIOI[18] rejected one portion of the requests by claiming that the

18. MIOI: Magyarország Izraeliták Országos Irodája, or National Bureau of Hungarian Israelites, the independent body in charge of the Orthodox community in Hungary until the formation of MIOK in the events described here in 1950.

Orthodox Rabbinical Council had not submitted to them the documents attesting to the credentials of the rabbis and assistant rabbis. As if there were an Orthodox community which would engage a rabbi without rabbinical credentials. All together, only four out of the twelve congregations finally achieved autonomous status: Debrecen, Nyíregyháza, Kisvárda, and Püspökladány.*

It's true that, nevertheless, besides the twenty-two Congressional congregations there remained thirty-eight autonomous or branch Orthodox congregations, and where they were forced to unite with the Neolog, the Orthodox still had their own rabbis or rabbi-slaughterers and prayer houses.

Jewry was not homogeneous previously, and it didn't become homogenous subsequently; that was not the goal of the government. It was not because the money matters of the Orthodox Division were handled in Síp Street that so many Jews fled after the revolution. The unification was a demonstration and a humiliation; it may have helped keep anguish alive, but it had no meaning in itself—it was valuable only together with the full score of the age representing all the instruments and voices. A centralized administration, the more transparent handling of congregational resources, the supervision of foreign connections, or the unification conducted for who-knows-what reason did not directly shape the fate of the Jews.

They say that in Pest, they didn't even take away the sign marking the congregation at Dob Street; they only pasted a paper band over it, so the sun would burn it, the rain would soak it, and the rolling wind would blow it away one day.

* Also rejected were the requests of many tradition-rich and relatively populous congregations, which in any case satisfied all the criteria. These included Berettyóújfalu, Hajdúböszörmény, Hajdúnánás, Hajdúszoboszló, Mátészalka, and Nyírbátor, among others.

One Step toward Jerusalem

Guardians of the Faith

Benjamin Abelesz

I don't know if you can tell from the way I speak that I don't live in Hungary. My wife and I converse in Hungarian and one of my sons, who was a fourth grader in '56, writes Hungarian almost without grammatical mistakes. I am seventy-four years old. We are an old Kapuvár family; my father was already born there. We had a grocery store, wholesale and retail, on the main street; many people, not just from the town, but from the region, came to us to shop. More than a hundred Jewish families lived in Kapuvár. The congregation was basically Orthodox, but not everyone kept the faith; a few stores were also open on Saturday, and one of the families even fattened a pig. Later a new rabbi came there who was originally from the Beled region, a "pure" Hungarian, named Ábrahám Ungár, and he began to persuade the congregation little by little, not with hard words but with gentle ones. For example, he told one shopkeeper to keep a ledger and he would see that he wouldn't make less money if he closed on Saturday. And it was true: what he lost on Saturday, he made back on the other days of the week.

In grade school, I studied to good effect. When I was in fourth grade, there was a district contest in the public high schools, and my teacher said I should try it because I was on the same level as the high school's fourth-level students. You had to write a composition, and I beat those who were four grades ahead of me: I came in first. I really loved geography and composition, where I often wrote in verse. I was a good student, but an unruly child, Ds in conduct, all the rest outstanding. Nonetheless, I didn't wind up in the academic track; as first born, I was to have carried on the family business and, in any case, because of the *numerus clausus*,[1] I couldn't have imagined that I would go to university.

At fourteen years of age, after sixth grade, I ended up in Pápa. My father was Ashkenazi Orthodox, but Rabbi Grünwald, who was the rebbe of the Hasidim at Pápa, led a well-known yeshivah—many people learned with him. But they didn't take everybody; anyone who didn't achieve a certain level was dropped. The yeshivah didn't have boarding facilities; we lived in rented rooms and many of us "ate days."[2] All of us lived in poverty and the leaders of the yeshivah wanted us older ones to have some income, so they assigned an older student to each younger one as a *khazerbokher*, to teach him for a few pennies a month. When I first went to Pápa with my late grandfather, I received a letter of recommendation from the rabbi at Kapuvár, stating that I already knew how to learn, even alone. Rabbi Grünwald interviewed me and he said that I really didn't need any help.

In 1939 my father was drafted as a soldier. They created a camp in the district of Petlendpuszta for Polish prisoners of war, he was a guard there. We figured that he would be drafted sooner or later, so I had already earlier familiarized myself with running the business. I came home from Pápa, and at sixteen years of age I filled in for my father. I got used to the work, because we also had a grain business and at harvest time I used to be a bagger there; I would load the horse-drawn wagon at home, and while it went to the station, I would work behind the counter in the store. Then I would bicycle out to the railroad station and load the 170-pound sacks on the freight car.

In '43 I was drafted for forced-labor service. We arranged for me to be declared unfit, so instead of three years I only had to serve for three months. I was supposed to go to Szombathely to be examined by a military

1. *numerus clausus*: "closed number," one of the Jewish Laws. A 1920 law specified that the proportion of Jews in any profession in any given town couldn't exceed the proportion of Jews in the general population. This law also limited the number of Jews who could attend institutions of higher learning to 5 percent.

2. ate days: The poor students were fed in turn by the rich Orthodox families in the town. Each student ate with a different family each day.

doctor named Kuna who was decidedly anti-Semitic; he declared even the dead fit to serve. I received certification from a doctor in Kapuvár that I am sick and can't travel there, and when they called me up again, he gave me a fever injection. At the next call-up, they threatened me with the military police, so we went to Keviczky, the head doctor at the neurology ward. He recommended that we go up to Pest to his professor, Dr. Lehoczky, the world-famous neurologist, and that I should act insane. He asked what I could simulate most easily, and I thought it was apathy. The professor probably knew what was going on, but he didn't show it, and I got into St. István Hospital's mental ward. I lay there all day and didn't pay attention to anything; I only got up to go to the bathroom. They told jokes to make me laugh, but I was able to resist. I only betrayed myself once, during rounds, when the doctor was trying to take my pulse. I was just waking up, and half asleep, I helped her roll up my pajama sleeve. The shout went up that this was my first normal movement, and that I should be given some treatment, I didn't understand what. A doctor who was an acquaintance of mine said this meant I needed brain surgery and he gave me a fever injection—that was how I managed to get out of it.

In the spring of '44, I attended a soccer game for the first time in my life; Vasas and Újvidék played on the Elektromos field. I had gotten out of the hospital back in February, and my brother-in-law and I went to work at a construction company. He had been discharged from the army not long before; we used to rag him that he had, as a machine-gunner, liberated Slovakia, Transylvania, Croatia, and Slovenia. The change to forced-labor service didn't happen all at once in Hungary; one of my uncles, who was a mechanic in an elite division, was still walking around in an army uniform when people were freezing to death in droves in the Ukraine.

We went home sadly from the match: Vasas had lost. Then at home we were greeted by an atmosphere like the fasting on Tisha b'Av. The Germans had arrived. My brother-in-law and I tried to establish contact with the partisans; there was some kind of connection in Király Street, but nothing came of it. In April came the yellow star, then in June there was the summons. We considered which was better, to report for duty or go into the ghetto. The Jewish refugees from Poland said anything was better than the ghetto. We reported to Jászberény. As I had been declared unfit,

I could have gone back to Pest, but I said that I had recovered. The unfit were shipped from Hatvan and directed to Auschwitz; they went straight into the gas without even coming before Mengele.

At Jászberény they deployed us all over the place. They assigned me to the 201st Home Defense Chemical Warfare Company. It was an "elite" company, full of converted Jews with white armbands, but they were short a half-company, that's how I got there as a yellow. They sent me to Piliscsaba for training. You lay down the gas by squeezing it out of the barrel with compressed air and you can fog a tremendously large area with it. It's dreadful stuff, it burned whatever it leaked on; the grass didn't grow again, it ate away the flesh from your hand, right down to the bone. We got rubber gloves, rubber cloaks, rubber boots. That's the only way we could touch it. We suffered a great deal, they thrashed us regularly, so the training was the best part. They had us set out for Várpalota so that we would fog the coal mine, the factory at Pétfürdő and the entire valley around Várpalota. We were stuck for three days at Rákosrendező because they were bombing the Danube bridges; meanwhile Pétfürdő was blanketed by air fire. By the time we got there, the factory had been bombed to pieces; I never saw anything like it; a locomotive had flown to the top of the platform—the blast immediately swept away the deployed air defense battalions, together with all their cannons and men. The German commander, a sixty-year-old Wehrmacht sergeant, said, we're staying here: once they've blown the place up, we won't have any trouble here. He had been a soldier for six years and was tired of it; his only wish, he said, was to see his wife and daughter again.

They divided up the companies into the neighboring villages. I stayed in Várpalota; they placed eight men in one house, six Jews and two Christians—they were untrustworthy elements too, half Communists. A second lieutenant named Farkas became our commander. He stepped to the front of the company: "Boys! Who knows how to play basketball, soccer, or the harmonica?" Everyone knew that you shouldn't volunteer. You know these soldier things, like, "Who has nice handwriting?" "Then go clean the toilet!"—we were already past that. I volunteered anyway, saying I knew soccer, so he said, "Good. Come on." From then on, the company went down every day to the soccer field; the German sergeant liked to play forward, so we played soccer with the ensign. He was a member of the national basketball team, he traveled the world with showgirls, you often saw him with women. "Well, what do you think of my fiancée?" "Which one?" It was unthinkable that forced-labor workers should be in these circumstances in '44.

We didn't know much about what was happening to Jews elsewhere. One night, we heard the airplanes—they always mustered over the Balaton—and the next day, we found a leaflet; on it was a hand, with blood dripping from it into a basin, "Are you washing your hands as well? The government claims that there isn't a single drop of Jewish blood on its hands, even though they have executed 600,000 Jews!" We couldn't believe that this could be true. We had heard stories previously from the Polish refugees, but we just waved them away: these are horror stories, this is Hungary, where my grandfather was already paying taxes in 1850.

Planes arrived every day, twenty-seven bombers to a squadron, we counted the squadrons; it's unbelievable, but one day, three thousand planes flew over us. The earth trembled under them. They consoled us with what a good place we were in; they won't drop a bomb smaller than 500 kilos here, we won't suffer long.

On October 15, our company commander, a lieutenant from Pest, sent home those who were in Berhida. The next day they were captured and sent back. On the eighteenth, the company was gathered on the Várpalota soccer field, and a machine gun mounted on each of the field's four corners. Two MPs, two pilots, and two sailors stepped forward: "Hold your ground! Long live Szálasi!" "Just let him live, then!" said our ensign. They explained that martial law had been declared, they inspected our packages, plundered what they could, and left. The company commanders had to read us our general orders: "Rat-a-tat-boom! Honorable gentlemen! Anyone who murders, steals, or robs will be hung; if he does it at night, he'll be hung twice." He was a real sharpie, and a very decent guy. He allowed things like whoever had money could officially go up to Pest to buy pots and pans,[3] because the company didn't have a kitchen. This was

3. buy pots and pans: The purchase would enable them to cook for themselves.

the "money party." Others went up on the sly; this was the "penny party." Once he called the roll and half the company was missing. As a punishment, he locked us in the barn for days. In the meantime, it was Rosh Hashanah, and I found out that one of the companies had a Torah and a shofar. I asked permission to pray there. He looked at me: "Are you the one who eats kosher? You're crazy enough. But you know what, it may be that you're the one who's right. You I'll let go."

Once after practice, we somehow were left alone in the changing room of the soccer field—in September '44, a Hungarian officer bathes with a Jew!—and he asked me who would win the war. I hesitated. "Don't worry—just tell me, no one can hear." "The Americans." "No: you're wrong: the Russians. You'll see, they'll outwit even the Americans."

When the Russian attack was stopped at the Balaton, our line stayed in the German area. On December 9, we heard the thunder of guns: the Russians are coming. We had a new captain, bearded and wearing laced top-boots; in all probability, he must have been an Arrow Cross. At night we had to march down into the mine; in the morning we would start for Germany through the Bakony. Guards were stationed around the mine so that no one could escape. We heard the officers talking, and one of them said, "Do you want to accept responsibility for their being killed in Germany?" "You're right. Guards, dismissed!" I talked it over with one of my friends—his brother became the president of the People's Tribune after the war—that we would desert. He had been to Russia before, there was something wrong with his heart; I always did the heavy work for him, and he gave me the kosher things he got from home, jam, honey, things like that. He fled first, they noticed him and fired. He hid in a sewer and escaped. Because of the gunfire, I didn't dare to go after him; the next day, we set out for Germany. In the front, on horseback, was our ensign, after him came the skeleton staff,[4] and at the back the forced laborers. As we entered the woods, the company began to stretch out. The ensign came to

4. skeleton staff: Forced-labor units consisted of workers who were considered unreliable: Jews (by definition) and Gentiles (Communists and other unacceptable factions), as well as a "skeleton" or "frame" of regular soldiers who kept the laborers in line.

the back. "What's up?" "Mr. Ensign, sir, I'm going to fall out." "You know that the penalty for desertion from the army is death?" I knew. He got off the horse, we shook hands. "The best of luck!" László Farkas . . . I tried to find out what happened to him, but without success. The company got out to Germany and out of three hundred men maybe twenty came back.

Eight of us escaped, five Jews and three skeleton staff. We kept the shiny black rubber cloak which had gold writing on it, and German military insignia on the shoulders. When we went out on the streets, the Hungarian soldiers saluted us as if there was nothing to say. I said that if we start to beg them for some shelter or a little food, then we are lost. Instead, we go into a village, we commandeer the tavern for the company, and we stay there as long as we can; the Russians would get here at some point. That's how it was; when we saw that they were becoming suspicious in one place, we went on to another village. One day they declared amnesty for military deserters; the skeleton staff turned themselves in immediately, and one Jewish boy went with them too, he wouldn't listen when we told him that it doesn't apply to him. He was probably executed on the spot.

Four of us were left, two from Budapest—the son of one, László Zsigmond, is today the director of Yad Vashem's Hungarian Department—a boy from Mosonmagyaróvár, and I. In one village, I helped a woman carry a few sacks of wheat up to the attic; she came after me and said that from me she dared to ask if there weren't any Jews among my friends. How could you think such a thing, I said, would I be together with stinking Jews?! She broke off a piece of sausage—later I gave it to the others, I didn't eat *treyf*. At Christmas we were in another house. I said I had a stomach ache, I only wanted milk and bread. I went out to the toilet; in the meantime the woman spoke up inside: "What a decent friend you have, he still eats only kosher." It turned out that she was a servant for a Jewish family, and she figured out why I wasn't eating normally. My companions said that's enough, things are not going to work out this way, I was going to bring trouble on them too. So on Christmas Eve I ate *treyf* for the first time, some cake, it had an unpleasant taste, but I had to swallow it, there was no way around it, life came first. I had already thrown my sacred objects into a well earlier; I didn't want anybody to find them on me; that was very hard too—until then I laid tefillin every morning.

In this house, they said that in the mountains, in the woods there was a farm, called Dűltfáspuszta, where the military police didn't go because it was so remote. The owner of the farm was a very decent man, army deserters could always stay with him; we shouldn't tell him we were Jews. We went to this man—his name was Károly Stoltz. He gave us food and he let us hide in his stable. One day, while chopping wood, I cut my foot. His wife bandaged it and meanwhile asked me when I had last had a letter from my parents. I said, it's been a long enough time. And what do I know about them? I saw she was suspicious, and so I confessed that we are Jews. She said she had thought so right away, and she felt extremely sorry for us. From now on, she would try even harder to help us, and she hoped that God in his goodness would repay her by bringing her son, who was a soldier, back safely. The ice was broken; of course we continued to keep our distance in front of the farmhands, but when we found ourselves alone, they would turn on the English radio. We stayed there for weeks, until one day the military police surrounded the farm, and while Stoltz went out to them, his wife quickly explained where we could hide. We jumped out the window, up the mountain, sinking knee-deep into the snow with each step; luckily, the wind immediately erased our tracks.

A few days later, we dared to come down; they said there was no more danger, but it's better that we stay up there, so no one should report us. We dug ourselves a bunker: it was like an inverted letter T; its stem was a four-meter-deep ditch, while there was only enough room in the two ends for us to crawl in on our bellies. We put a ladder at the entrance and inside we huddled together two by two in the cavities. We slept during the day, came out at night to take care of our needs, and every second night we went down to the Stoltzes' for food and to listen to the radio: we became very good friends. Later we put a wooden panel over the entrance and covered it with earth and snow, so you couldn't recognize it. Out of cornstalks we built a kind of ranger's hut over it from which you could look out and one of us always sat up on the ladder and kept guard.

On March 15, the weather was already spring-like and people were already starting to come up into the mountains; László Zsigmond said that on this date something important always happened in his life: his child was born on this day and this is when he came home from Russia.

He hoped something would happen today too. He was a serious man, he spoke seven or eight languages, he had even lived in Palestine, but he had to flee back when the English learned he was a Communist. We always argued because he was very opposed to religion. "Now something good will happen!" The guy who was sitting up on the ladder suddenly ran down into the pit and shouted that we had been discovered. We were used to the fact that he was always imagining things, but this time we really heard footsteps from above, and shots, and then a hand-grenade blew up in the hut. I think it's likely that the Germans, before they bailed out, combed the area, and if they saw something suspicious, they threw a hand grenade in that direction. The hut exploded, they saw the hole, and they threw one in there as well. Nothing happened to us because we were lying in our dens. A new grenade, then another, and there was so much smoke that we couldn't stand it anymore; we shouted out that we surrender. But the grenades kept on coming. Then we shouted in German, they answered in German: we had to come out one at a time, at five-minute intervals, with our hands up. At the entrance to the bunker stood two German MPs from the camp, and further away, on a hillside, was a third.

They took us through the village. "Jewish partisans," they told the people; the women cried. We didn't see anybody who was happy. One of us had a Swiss safe-conduct letter, so we said we were Swiss. They handed us over to the Hungarian authorities, but the Hungarians didn't know what to do with us either—they threw us from place to place like a ball. In the end, we stayed with the Germans. A Hungarian platoon leader came over to me—he's sorry for me, he says, because it will soon be *Pesakh*, and we are here, but he can't help us. We can choose whether they take us out to Germany or we go to Győr, where we can join a forced-labor unit. Naturally, we chose Győr. When we got there, a German asked us, did we know which way Andrássy Street was; I knew the city, so I showed him. We stopped in front of a big building with a sign, "West-Hungarian Gestapo." They had just been tricking us about having a choice; no matter what we had said, they would have brought us here. They took down our personal data. The charge was that from December until now we moved about the front, carrying information to the Russians—this has to be investigated. All of a sudden, my interrogator jumped up with a razor in his hand.

I thought, he's going to cut off my head right here, but he just cut open the collar of my jacket, to see whether there's something hidden there. He questioned us further, and one of the guys who was fluent in German always answered him right away—we learned what we were going to have to say next. The commander came in and asked, what were they discussing with the Jews, just shoot us to death and be done.

They took us over to the prison in Győr, we figured, because they wanted to wait until nighttime, then they'd come for us. When somebody went past our cell—no one should ever have to have that feeling!—we thought, now they're going to take us and execute us. We didn't eat, we didn't drink, we didn't feel like doing anything, why should we? Sometimes the guards would peek in at us. One day passed, then two. There was an air-raid warning, we went down into the cellar where we came into contact with other prisoners, and you could talk. Among others, there were four miners from Szőgyén there who had already put on red flags, but it was their bad luck that the Russians stopped outside of the village; there was a parish priest who spread English news, an officer who wanted to desert to the Russians and two Romanian forced-labor service workers. We found out what the deal was: it took two weeks until they had investigated a person, then they shot him. László Zsigmond asked, what was my opinion, can we escape? I said that in my opinion we could. But, all the same, what were our chances? I told him 50 percent. And this calm man whom I had never before seen stirred up began to shout; he was really bellowing, "You crazy Orthodox, only an Orthodox can be so crazy, didn't you hear, they've condemned us to death! How can we escape from here, then?" I don't know how, but God can help us.

One day we heard the sound of cannons, the news came that the Russians had captured Komárom. They released the criminal prisoners, first those on trial, then those whose convictions were final, and in the end all the robbers, murderers and housebreakers; all that was left were the miners, the priest, the officer, the two Romanians, and us four. We didn't get any food, we couldn't hear the guards; it seemed that they had fled. One of the guards knocked on the door. They had all gone, he was left alone, he was a Communist, so he wasn't afraid of the Russians. Well, then open the door! He couldn't do that: a duty was a duty. At night, the Germans had looked for their prisoners, and then they had gone away. Early in the morning, a young Arrow Cross band came running in.

They had come for us; there was already shooting at Győr, and we were the last ones across the Danube bridge, before it was blown up. There were soldiers lying on the roadside, there was no one fighting there anymore and an officer called out to the Arrow Cross, where were they taking these unfortunates? One of the teenagers answered, "Captain, sir, shut your mouth!" To us he said that we should stay calm, his commander is a decent man, he doesn't torture prisoners long. We went from village to village, the captain wasn't in any of them, at last at Hédervár night set in on us. They began on a farm to divide up the prisoners. "The Hungarians stand here!" We stood there too. "You're Hungarian? You're a stinking Jew!" and he slapped the person at the front of the line, "Stand there!" They let everybody go, even the two Romanians, we alone remained. The SS began to beat us up; I was the youngest of them, I tried to stay on my feet and die bravely; at last I too sank down to the ground, blood poured from my head, they had knocked out my teeth. I lay on the ground and said the *Vidduy*, the confession before death, and then it ran through my mind that if I told this story at home, no one would believe it. I had no idea that this torture, and these murders, were happening elsewhere as well, that they had already murdered my brothers and my parents.

They gave the order to beat us to death; and if we didn't drop dead, a bullet in us. They took Zsigmond and the other guy from Pest, then we heard shotgun fire, well, then we're next. But that's not what happened: the SS men said that they weren't going to execute anyone without the permission of the local commander. This commander got up at night, got dressed, came out to us at the farm and ordered that we be turned over to the Hungarian authorities. This was the night of Seder, the eve of *Pesakh* 1945, according to my calculations.

In the morning it was dead quiet everywhere. I went into a house and asked permission to hide in the attic. They agreed, and I hid. The next day I heard foreign words in front of the house; I spread the thatch a little and saw that the soldiers had red stars on their hats. I wanted to go down, but as soon as I stepped over to the attic stairs, they trained their automatic weapons on me. I was already covered with blood. "Gestapo! Gestapo!" I tried to explain. One Ukrainian spoke Hungarian, so I explained to him that they had wanted to execute me. All right, I can come down. It was a distillery belonging to Count Héderváry; the Russians were making off with the pure liquor by the bucketful. One of them offered me a full water glass, that I should drink it down. I'm not drinking. No? And he raised his weapon. I drank some, but I started to cough and choke, so he had a good laugh and left me there. I washed up at a sweep-pole well; suddenly a jeep braked to a halt beside me, a soldier jumped over to me. He took my watch—I had gotten it for my bar mitzvah, it hung from a silver chain—climbed back on the jeep, and drove away. We had been liberated.

We four split up: one guy thought the situation was still very fouled up, he doesn't dare set out; today he lives in Canada. Another guy went home to Mosonmagyaróvár, while Zsigmond and I set out for Győr. We saw that the Russians on the road were gathering Hungarian soldiers. We sat in the grass and waited to see what would come of this. The soldiers noticed that we were sitting there, so they came and sat next to us, so that in the end there were more people there than there were standing in the formation. The Russians came over and made us stand up too; I told Zsigmond to try to talk to them. He told the commander who we were. "*Jevrej, nye jevrej, Szálasi-szoldát*,"[5] and they slapped us in with the prisoners. They took tens of thousands to Győr, to the Frigyes barracks, English and American fliers, Czechs and Romanians, "You stand here, you over there." We still had time. Zsigmond knew the Russian Jewish types, and one of the translators attracted his attention. I went over to him and told him in Yiddish that the two of us were Jews. He embraced me and asked what he could do to help. I said, get us out of here, the sooner the better. He put us with a group, and in a little while, they let us go. I knew a candy manufacturer in Győr we often bought merchandise from, so I asked if we could sleep at his place. The next morning Zsigmond and I said goodbye; he went to Pest and I to Kapuvár. As an old Communist, Zsigmond became a great man, he taught in the Party school and got an

5. *Jevrej, nye jevrej, Szálasi-szoldát*: Russian, meaning, "Jew or no Jew, Szálasi-soldier." Szálasi was the Nazi-collaborationist leader of the Hungarian government.

apartment. We kept in contact for a while, up until I told him I would like to emigrate, and I asked him to sign my petition. He said this conflicted with his principles. I was no great loss, they couldn't change me, but he couldn't consent to my children not being Communists.

I started homeward. I heard that there was a JDC[6] office in Csorna where they would give you papers so the Russians wouldn't take you away. I went, they gave me papers, but also told me they weren't worth anything, it was better to avoid the Russians. I went the whole way on my own two feet—the old number 11 bus;[7] I set out in the morning, and by evening I was in Kapuvár. In front of our house stood a guard wearing a national armband: the Hungarian authorities had secured our warehouses, so they wouldn't be looted. Later they took away everything—who they were, I don't know—and we got back in to our house. I was the first Jew in Kapuvár, later people began to drift back; those who came from Kópháza or Fertőrákos couldn't even walk, they just lay there and I brought them food and helped them haul back their stolen furniture. We made a kind of soup kitchen and set it up in the house of Rosenberg the ironmonger; he had a very big house and he had been left alone. About a hundred of us came back to Kapuvár, out of four hundred people, 25 percent, a better proportion than most places in Hungary: Sopron county residents were taken by the last transport. Two of my brothers were liberated in Auschwitz—one came home right away, the other was taken to Russian prison. It was a good year after the liberation, in September or October someone wearing a Russian uniform comes toward me and throws his arms around my neck: I didn't recognize until then that he was my brother. He was still a child, sixteen years old.

Rabbi Ungar was killed in Auschwitz; his son came back but he hardly stayed for a few months. A man named Weinberger studied to become *shokhet*, he did the slaughtering. There was a mikveh right away as well, you couldn't feel any decline in religious life; those who once were

6. JDC: Acronym for the Joint Distribution Committee; it played a large role in the care of those in displaced person camps and provided funds for those who wished to emigrate.

7. the old number 11 bus: Ironic: go on foot, using one foot, then one foot.

not religious became religious, everyone persevered and tried to return to the old routine. Christians came to me and gave back everything that my parents left with them, money, bed linens, that kind of thing; they were very decent people. But it also happened that one of our customers from a neighboring village warned me to be careful: I would have trouble, because I go out into the street without a star. I told him to tell his Arrow Cross friends that it was a different world now. There were those who didn't want to give furniture back to Jews. Major Rikov, the city commander, advised us not to argue with them, and in a year we would have more things than they did. There was a Jewish distillery; they started it up, you could get everything from the Russians for rum.

During the war, Rabbi Ungar, who helped many of us avoid being called up, made us promise that, when the war was over, we would get married in a year. And we tried to marry, but there was no public transportation, so we didn't know how to make acquaintances. There were matchmakers, but I was not attracted to the one they intended for me. One day my little brother was bored, so he was reading the commercial offers made by the factories—since the business hadn't started up yet, we hadn't even been opening the envelopes; we thought they would at least be good for heating. So my brother's looking at the letters, and in one of them he finds that Neumann, with whom I studied at Pápa, the son of the rabbi at Óbuda, had a match for me, the cousin of his uncle at Sárvár. There was no other form of transportation, so I covered the more than 50-kilometer trip on a bicycle. We were attracted to each other, and after a few months' acquaintanceship we held the wedding. Slowly we too got our business up and running; with the money I got back from the Christians, I made the necessary purchases in Pest. I traveled on train steps or on top of the cars, and the Russians, of course, swindled me, that goes without saying. Somehow, the local railroad company managed to keep two electric-powered railcars, they called them the dream train—there were windows, and heat—it didn't go in to the Déli Railway Station, so the Russians wouldn't see it. Until the new Hungarian money came, we bartered for eggs, since they could be sold to the Russians for hard currency.

In 1947 the majority of Orthodox Jews voted for the Social Democrats. There were those who sympathized with the Communists, but others like the Social Democrats couldn't come into consideration. For example, Peter Veres, the National Peasant Party's candidate, gave a policy-making speech at Kapuvár and in it he said that the National Peasant Party was "national" because there weren't any Swabians or Jews in it.

My business developed nicely, but we were increasingly feeling mental terror. You felt that you were watched in your every step. We saw that if you were religious, you couldn't remain a Communist. It was also getting harder and harder to get merchandise. After Auschwitz we didn't think that we were going to stay in Hungary. Why should we live here any longer? My wife and I decided that as soon as it was possible, we would get out. We asked for a passport, but they turned us down. With this, the system just contributed to our haste; otherwise we would have waited until we had made a little money.

On May 1, 1949, my brother and my brother-in-law sneaked across the border. I took part in the procession, I took my red flag and my picture of Stalin, all the while waiting for the smuggler to report that they had crossed successfully. We wanted to go to Vienna and from there on to Israel. On June 29, the feast of Peter and Paul, the smuggler took us into the swamp too. A stream was the boundary; I had already reached the other side with the older child, but the border guards heard us breaking through the reeds and they started shooting at us. I had to come back for my wife and child. My friend who came with us got across, and in two weeks he was already in Israel. We remained there, captured. The smuggler squealed that my brother-in-law and another friend also wanted to cross the border; later we learned that they too had been arrested.

The big children were sent home to my sister, the littler one was four and a half months old and still nursing, so he stayed with my wife. We were taken to the Military Police Department to interrogate us. They kept asking, since I had been a wholesaler, where had I put the money? Then suddenly the questioning stopped. In Kapuvár, a man who worked in the bank at Sopron had visited me frequently and urged me to invest my money in dollars—he'd get them on the black market—but I never bought any from him. My wife had received permission to wash diapers, and when she went out to the laundry, she ran into this man. It turned out that he was a provocateur. He must have told my interrogator that he had already tried his scam on us and it hadn't worked: we had no money. In other respects he was decent, he somehow obtained milk for my wife. We were transferred to the ÁVÓ at Szombathely, we went by train, the people watched us, maybe they felt sorry for us, but they didn't dare speak to us. The escort allowed us to buy bread. When we got to the ÁVÓ courtyard, you could hear screaming from all sides, don't hurt me, don't hurt me, I'll confess everything. We were stood against the wall, "Pierce the wall with your eyes!" and when they walked behind us, they pushed our heads against it. There were some who fainted. Everybody was called in turn to the "swag" lieutenant; he was probably a Jew because when he heard why they had brought us in, he began to scream, "To *Erets*! To *Erets*!"—a Christian would have said Palestine. He asked why I had bread with me, I said I only eat kosher. "Here you'll eat even the wall," he said. He sent me on with this, that I should tell them, "No drinking glass." I told them, they recorded my data, somebody typed them, it was good if he typed a letter a minute. The ones who hadn't given the message "No drinking glass" were laid down in a wash trough and scraped all over with a wire brush. Probably the saboteurs, or those who denied their charges, were classified as worse than a simple fence-jumper. For example, one detainee was an ÁVÓ member who had tried to escape to Austria—him they beat all the time. My wife cried a lot because she heard all the screaming, she was afraid that they would hurt me too; they saw she was nursing a little child and they took pity on her and brought her over to me to calm her down.

We were only at the ÁVÓ for two days, we weren't charged with any extraordinary crimes, so one Friday they transferred us to the prison. I had already heard at the ÁVÓ that there is an "Orthodox" cell there, number 52, so I asked in the prison, if it was possible, they should put me there. "Why? Are you Orthodox?" "Yes" "What's your name?" "Abelesz." "You're the one. The whole congregation is looking for you. Don't be afraid. It's already a different world here." A few people knew that we wanted to leave, but we didn't arrive in Vienna, so they suspected what had happened and they kept an eye on the prison, to see when we'd turn up. On Friday night we got challah bread, fish, and wine—by then we had hardly eaten for three weeks—at the ÁVÓ they gave you food like in Auschwitz, or even less.

The next day we got up to the interlocutory cell, a few days after that came the trial, I got a half a year, my wife two months. We asked for a lawyer, and we appealed the decision; they reduced my sentence to four and a half months, my wife's to one and a half. There were only defectors in cell number 52; there was a group who tried to escape to Austria with false passports. The border guards became suspicious of one, so he declared, why pester him in particular, when there were eight of them, so he betrayed the others. We received worse treatment than the "bums," who had been convicted of criminal acts; they got the breaks, they were the elite, they were only robbers. But we didn't have such a bad time, we got kosher food from outside, from the congregation, we could pray in the morning and at night. Every Saturday the rabbi from Szombathely came in, he gave a speech, saying, among other things, that that the laws had to be respected—if a person was not willing to do this, he could wind up in prison. For example, he had heard of an incident in which someone committed a forbidden border crossing, and it was wrong to do this. At the end of the performance, I went over to him, "What do you think, Rabbi, that we are perhaps in prison for murder or robbery?"

Every week they held a political performance as well; probably even the person who gave the speech didn't understand it. "There is no country more beautiful or richer, every man feels that he is free!"—they made us sing this in the prison. My release fell on a Saturday; the way it worked was that on the day before, everybody was taken back to the ÁVÓ, from which they would not have let me out on Saturday or Sunday. I didn't want to spend the weekend there, I was on good terms with the guards, so I asked them not to transfer me until Monday. My wife had been released long before; my brother-in-law had also been released but he was still under parole. On Monday I was released as well. I arrived in Kapuvár, I got off the train, and an unforgettable thing happened to me: Attila Szigeti, the MP,[8] saw me and came over to me in an ostentatious manner. "Greetings. How are you on this very fine day?" And he began to talk to me in a friendly way; he was showing people that he considered me a

8. MP: Member of Parliament.

human being. In '56 he became the leader of the National Committee from Győr-Sopron county;[9] they hold his memory in respect even today.

Before our flight, we left the store empty, they took what was left. We didn't want to stay in Kapuvár; we decided to go up to Pest. We found a sublet on Bajcsy-Zsilinszky Road, with an Orthodox Jew who was sick and only asked that we try to take care of him. But not long after, he died and the apartment was left to us. We still had a little money, we lived from that. In those days, everybody had to work; luckily when they came to inquire about me, our porter, who didn't know that we had done time, always said that we were decent, trustworthy people. Working as a shopkeeper was out of the question because as an observant Jew, I would not work on the Sabbath. At first I worked in the Orthodox congregation's matzah factory, then I undertook housecleaning in the Neolog Old People's Home in Erzsébet Királyné Road. Three hundred ninety forints was my salary, from that 30 came off for Peace Bonds, so I got 360 in hand when the rent was 440. No one asked what we lived on. I detested hauling trash and touching dirty things.

In '53 one of our friends spoke to one of his relatives, who was assistant director of the Building Glass Company, asking if he couldn't find me a job where I could keep the Sabbath. He said that if I were willing to do hard physical labor he could give me Saturday off. All right, I went in to the Personnel Department, they took down my data, the chief asked me if I was a member of the Party. "No." "And of the Hungarian–Soviet Friendship Company?" "No." "Why, are you by chance a Zionist?" "Yes." "Doesn't matter. You'll do for this work." I said that I wouldn't work on Saturday. "That can't be," he said, "there's no such thing." I asked him to call up Comrade Assistant Director. He called him and he said, yes, Saturday was to be my day off. I had one more request, that I needed to step down on Friday afternoons at three. "That's certainly out of the question!" With great anger, he ran out of the room and slammed the door. Then the secretary jumped to the door, locked it with a key, leaned

9. Győr-Sopron county: In 1950, this county was reorganized and renamed Győr-Moson-Sopron (map 1 B2–B3).

against the door and broke into such anguished sobbing that she couldn't be stopped. When she calmed down, I asked what is it, she said that this is her husband's *Jahrzeit*[10]—he was murdered as a forced laborer, and she's happy that there's a man who has remained so faithful to his Jewishness; as much as possible, she'll come to my assistance in everything.

Our children didn't go to school on Saturday. Twenty percent of Jewish children could keep the Sabbath officially. This is how they tried to exert pressure on the parents, each parent had to request the permission separately; if one reconsidered, then the permission was withdrawn. There was a Jewish woman in the school who didn't give permission for a single child to keep the Sabbath, but our teacher was decent, she liked our children. Afterwards she got a pair of nylon stockings or a ballpoint pen, it doesn't matter, the important thing was that she gave permission.

The company hired me. It really was very hard work, you had to carry glass cases, the smallest was 175 pounds, but there were 1,700-pound ones as well; four men stood on an open truck and held the store-window glass, so the wind wouldn't blow it over. On Monday morning they introduced me to the crew. The other three workers didn't say a word to me the whole time, they ostracized me so completely that I can't even describe it. How painful it was to stand there—pick it up, put it here, but nothing else, they went off by themselves and sat in the cab of the truck to warm up, they didn't invite me. It went like that throughout the whole week. On Friday I informed them that I wasn't coming on Saturday, and I left. On Monday morning, when I arrived, they came up to me, shook my hand and asked me to forgive their behavior the previous week; they thought I was a company fink, but they see that I must be a decent man because I keep the Sabbath. And we became good friends, we talked a lot; if somebody left early, the others completed his work without a word. It turned out that their grocery store had been nationalized too, that's why they were there, so we were the "grocery crew." One of their wives was from Fertőszentmiklós; I knew her parents well, they often shopped at our store. The woman repeatedly asked me to visit them, I went and we had

10. *Jahrzeit*: See the glossary, *yortsayt*.

a very good time talking, from this we became even better friends. That's how it went all winter.

From a political point of view, these were the most dangerous years, this is when we were the most afraid; the newspapers wrote about Zionist conspiracies and the Russian doctor suit.[11] There's a joke: at night the bell rings[12] at somebody's house. "Who is it?" "Death's angel!" "Thank goodness, I was afraid it was the ÁVÓ!" Pest is the city of jokes. The boys at our place were also always pulling a prank or two. For example, the company's porter, who was a great Communist, and a stupid enough man, wrote on his booth, "Produce more today than yesterday!" and showed it proudly to the Party secretary, who chewed him out, because the boys had painted over "yesterday" and written "tomorrow." These things always raised our spirits a bit, and we needed it. People bore Soviet rule with difficulty. Once when we were shipping goods to "Red Csepel,"[13] a worker came over to us right away and warned us, this one and that one were Communists, we shouldn't talk loudly in front of them. Another time we were at the airport in Tököl, the Russian officers went along talking and the Hungarian soldier who was providing guard duty[14] hissed across to us, "Would I like to put a couple of rounds into them!" When we got back to Pest from trips to the countryside, the others always asked us, "So did you run into them?" "Who?" "Well, the Americans!"—that's what the mood was like in Hungary.

One day Mrs. Stoltz came up to us and told us the story of how they arrested her son as a *kulak*.[15] The cooperative took away their threshing

11. the Russian doctor suit: In January 1953, in a case thought to be a manifestation of his increasing paranoia, Stalin ordered the arrest of a group of Jewish Kremlin doctors for plotting the murder by medical means of high-level Soviet officials.

12. the bell rings: See also Groszberg, "the great ringing," p. 59.

13. Csepel: A part of Budapest which is a large island in the Danube with an extensive industrial district (map 2 south of D4). The district of Csepel was, even before the war, an industrial area with an unusually large number of left-wing sympathizers.

14. providing guard duty: This convoluted expression reflects the speaker's absence from the native language community.

15. *kulak*: Russian word for a wealthy peasant. Such an accusation before the ÁVÓ was sufficient to initiate action against an individual.

machine and combine, and it seems that they didn't know anything about it, because something broke, so they said the boy broke it out of spite. The matter came before Jónás, the president of the People's Tribune, with whose brother I wanted to escape from the forced-labor camp in Várpalota. I went up to him, he said he would be happy to get me together with his brother, but that he wanted to tell me in advance not to expect favoritism. He did get me together with him, and I told him if the boy is really guilty, convict him, I know that the family can't be the enemy of the system, because in the war they harbored deserters and escaped forced laborers. I asked him to be objective and to make his judgment accordingly. In the end, the boy was acquitted, so I was able to reciprocate their kindness.

In the spring I was let go; at the Building Glass Company, fall and winter counted as high season, there was no work in the spring and summer. I went back again to the retirement home. In the fall I got a letter from the Building Glass Company: they would like it if I went back to them. I asked them to guarantee me work for summer as well, and they promised to do so. In the winter I worked as a delivery person, in the summer in the warehouse. Later I was taken off delivery, but the friendly relationship with the boys continued; I always helped them load up. When they merged the glass companies into a trust, they put us together with the Glass House on Vadász Street—in case you haven't heard of it, in '44 it was placed under Swiss protection. The person responsible for delivery was a Party member, but he didn't do his job; his mind was always on women. Wherever a glazier went, the glass was missing; where they sent glass, there was no glazier—in plain Hungarian, he was a *balagán*.[16] They spoke to me, saying that I knew the places, I knew the problems, I should take over his job. I took it over, on paper I was a delivery worker; they didn't want me to become a white-collar worker, and I didn't either, because then they would find out that I had done time. The work went nicely, I was very good friends with everyone; in addition, from Vadász Street I could go home for lunch every day to Bajcsy-Zsilinszky Road.

16. in plain Hungarian: We would say, "In plain English." The word *balagán* is Yiddish Hebrew meaning "disorderly, or chaos."

One Monday morning, the trust dispatcher, who had supposedly been an Orthodox Jew in Miskolc, said that he didn't see me working on Saturday. I say, and you won't: they've given me Saturday off. He went in to the company director, but he said he had had the best possible reports of me, and it doesn't bother him that I don't come in on Saturday. When he was appointed company director, somebody else had also squealed that I don't work on Saturday, but he had taken no notice.

All this came to light one day when he had me called in. "Comrade Abelesz, you're going to be the work safety representative." I didn't want to take it, because if there was an accident, it was always those responsible for workmen's protection who did time. So he told me the story that when he came there, they squealed about me to him, and the dispatcher resents my day off, but he kept me anyway. If I accept my new assignment, I get Shabbat. If not, I don't get Shabbat. I didn't have any choice.

As soon as I was appointed, the second week, they came out of the ministry saying that they wanted to see the Workmen's Protection Journal. I didn't even know what that was. The director defended me, be calm, everything would be all right. They explained that you had to train the people, you had to keep a journal, and to write a plan in two days for avoiding accidents. For the most part I knew what were the sensitive points, and I wrote the book. I realized that it wasn't enough by itself, so I added how it had been in the capitalist world and how it was today, Comrade Stalin the people's father, and this is how we build the Five-Year Plan—the usual talk. I showed it to the director, he congratulated me; I took it in to the ministry and they said it was very excellent. Wouldn't I like to work there? I would have been brought down that minute, I never wrote my prison record into my autobiography.[17] I said, I want to build the country through physical labor. "Fine, we grant your wish, just work on."

I don't know what kind of organization there was elsewhere, but here I saw with my own eyes what waste went on in the country. They hit upon

17. autobiography: The Communists required workers to describe their life experience in a biographical document, as in a resumé or curriculum vitae, but the narrative was intended to reflect their conformity to the goals of the Party.

the idea of mixing cement with something to save the mortar, and they fitted the top of a tractor factory with the mixture. In the winter of course it froze, and the glass roof broke and fell into the expensive power lathes. Or we got a very large order; a new pipe factory was being built and it had to be ready for Comrade Stalin's birthday. I went out to Csepel, the walls weren't up yet, I thought there's no hurry in sending glass. I received a telegram, what am I waiting for; I sent a message back, and then came an order from the Russians, if we don't send the glass, they'll take all the workers to Siberia. I sent it. The laborers, and hundreds of convicts, worked night and day; they used imported coke to fill a large ditch so the trucks could get even closer. One wall was still missing, but they already put up the stage for the dedication ceremony and they began stoking the furnace so they could pull out the first pipe on December 21. And pull it out they did. Then in January came the new orders, because after the bitterly cold weather, the whole factory had to be refitted with glass.

At that time, it happened that the Party secretary stopped me one morning: "What do you say, Comrade Abelesz, one worker doesn't want to take out a Peace Loan. You know what happened in the National Railroad? Somebody didn't want to take out a Peace Loan, the others took him out to the gate, kicked him and drove him away; they didn't want to work with such a man. I wonder if that's not what we should do too?" I wouldn't have wanted to, but because of my prison past and getting Saturday off what else could I have answered him: "Yes, indeed!" "That's terrific, then in a little while we'll hold a protest meeting, please state your opinion there as well." I saw that he stopped the others as well, and naturally everyone answered, yes indeed, that's how to treat people like that. The meeting started right after the start of work, the Party secretary described what it was all about, what the National Railroad workers did and asked what our opinion was about this. He looked around, but nobody said a word. Finally the best worker stood up and said, if he really doesn't want to take out a Peace Loan, then we need to act this way too, but he doesn't believe it of him, because he's a decent worker. Then I spoke up too that I couldn't believe it either, because he's a very decent and fine worker. So the Party secretary's plan didn't succeed and nothing happened to the guy.

When the situation loosened up in the days of Imre Nagy,[18] cooperatives that observed the Sabbath could be established. These had already existed in the countryside, for example at Kapuvár, when they took away the stores, fifteen or twenty people got together and did carpentry work. But in Pest, Jewish cooperatives weren't formed until '54. I explained to the director that I had been invited into a cooperative and I was leaving; he said that it was a punishable offense to entice a worker from a national company, so he would rather not have heard what I said. Later my name came up at a productivity meeting, some kind of transfer had arrived from the trust; I was surprised that up until now, he had been decent, and now he wants to shame me. But it turned out that I had received a commendation for my work, and I was to receive a monetary reward. "You see what a future you have here? It would be a shame to leave it behind." The workers sent a delegation to the director and the head bookkeeper not to let me go, they are willing to take care of everything on Saturdays, I should just stay there with them. But they couldn't do anything, because the dispatcher kept trying to get rid of me; finally he said that either I went or the director. It hurt a lot, when I left. I was on such good terms with everybody. I took it more to heart than when I left Hungary behind.

I entered the Práter Street Metal, Iron, and Toy Mass Production Cooperative, which had a forty-member kosher section. One item's production norm was good, another's bad, one brought in more money, the other less. We agreed that everybody would work as hard as they could and we would get paid according to the number of hours worked. We manufactured toy telephones out of metal, two men worked on a press, no one wanted to do it because it took a tremendous amount of strength for the pressing, no one could do it for more than two hours. Strange things also happened in the cooperative—the president had to resign because the cooperative's two horses ate up millions, on paper; there are such things today, but they are called "travel expenses." After a year there wasn't much work, people had to be let go. The cooperative wanted to keep me on, but a friend of mine invited me elsewhere, as an outworker

18. Imre Nagy: Chairman of the Hungarian Council of Ministers from 1953 to 1955.

for the Handspinners' Cooperative. A nasty event occurred there. I was praying in the shul in Dessewffy Street, that was the closest to us. When Rabbi Singer made Aliyah, another rabbi replaced him, from somewhere in the vicinity of Soltvadkert. His son-in-law established a cooperative and did some black-market things; they caught him and blackmailed him: if he became an informant, they would let him go. He accepted, and sometimes he would go to the police station and describe some trivialities. But once they asked him for some more serious things; he wasn't willing to go that far, so he went to the shul on Nagyfuvaros Street and hung himself.

Besides my work, I had another important occupation. When the JDC was prohibited as a spy organization, the Israeli embassy distributed aid through a few reliable people, and a friend of mine who succeeded at making Aliyah recommended me to replace him. I always went on Sunday because then the weekly pass was good on every line; I got the money, and I distributed it. The embassy was on Vilma Királynő Road; we always watched to see if we were being photographed, and they turned up the radio when we were talking, as they feared listening devices. The *Új Kelet* wrote that in Romania, those who got caught received twenty, twenty-five years; on Sundays, my wife stood in the window waiting until I got home, but it still had to be done, people were living in such terrible conditions . . . there was an old man in Király Street, he couldn't move, he lay in a dark hole. But I also went to a place in Lipótváros where there were Oriental rugs and a sideboard full of silver; I went back to the embassy and told them not a penny for this man from now on.

We did our work until October '56 came along. I went home and saw mounted police on Kerepesi Street. I heard all kinds of news that there was something with the Russians, they had attacked, or something, but the radio didn't say anything. The next day at five I wanted to go to work, but the porter said I shouldn't go; they had set fire to a Russian jeep on the Kiskörút,[19] and the trams weren't running. By then the radio had begun to say that armed bandits had attacked the public buildings. We lived there

19. Kiskörút: This inner, smaller semicircular ring road in Budapest is made up of Károly Körút, Múzeum Körút, and Vámház Körút (map 2 C2–D3).

on the corner of Bajcsy-Zsilinszky Road and Nagymező Street, the windows faced the street, we saw everything: the protesters came from the Kiskörút toward the Nyugati train station, maybe a hundred thousand of them, covering the entire width of the road, carrying the flag, there were already some injured who were marching with bandaged arms. But a tank unit arrived from Nagymező Street, they met the crowd just in front of our building. The air froze, then the soldiers began to wave, you could hear the relieved sighs. We saw Kossuth Square after the massacre;[20] it was covered with blood. There was shooting from the Defense Ministry into the Killián Barracks, and back; the shells were flying over our heads. I was standing there on Margit Bridge when they brought Mindszenty. On the first Saturday we didn't go to pray in the Dessewffy, on the next Saturday we did, and then we also read the section of the Torah that had been left out last week—such a thing had never happened before. When the Russians withdrew, we were relieved; they sent up food from the villages, for free, so we could shake off the Russians. Opposite us there was a bakery; once when we stood on line for bread, one man began to curse us for being Jews, but the crowd immediately quieted him: there won't be any name-calling here.

Since we had decided to emigrate to Israel, we put our requests in every half-year; sometimes they answered us in a long letter, at others they sent a slip of paper, but they always turned us down. At the beginning of November, the Israeli embassy wanted to send two buses to Vienna with the people they had knowledge of.

We decided where the gathering point would be on Monday. On Sunday morning, the Russians came in. We thought that we would somehow leave anyway. We started work again in the factory, and somebody said that he could obtain a truck and a document with a Russian seal, that we were transporting food. If I promise to take them across the border, they would take me with them. I said I couldn't promise this but only that for a few days we would stay with acquaintances near the border. We agreed,

20. massacre: Russian soldiers fired into the crowd, killing unarmed demonstrators.

at night we bathed the children, everybody put on double underwear. At seven in the morning, we went down in front of the house; the porter somehow figured us out and said, don't go to Israel, we are such decent people, the Jews there will cheat us.

We got on the truck, near the cab; the people at the back were those who lived near Pest so that if they stopped us, they could see we weren't heading for the West. We bought food as part of our disguise: cabbages, prepared vegetables, fruit. We decided that if we were questioned, we would say that we had been bombed out and were going home to Kapuvár. They stopped us a few times, but they never got to us. We arrived in Győr, they told us we couldn't go toward Sopron. I said, then we won't go to Kapuvár from the east but from the south, through Pápa and Beled—they won't be checking as closely there. At Kapuvár I looked for my little sister, but she had left too, they gave me the things she had left behind. The border is only ten kilometers from Kapuvár, but we got stuck in the mud, so we left the food in the truck and set out on foot. It was the end of November and very cold; we went into a stable to get warm, the cows were licking the children. The Russians were beginning to close the border, we even heard shooting; I said I would scout around with somebody, but my wife wouldn't let me go; finally the whole family set out late at night.

The Hungarian border guards took us to the border, they took us across one of the canals with a rowboat, there was a beam across the other and you had to cross holding onto a rope; we crossed into Austria. We had been planning the trip for a long time; every Sunday we went on outings to the mountains, to accustom the children to walking. We went about twenty kilometers with the four children—the youngest was six then, and he put his head on my hand and walked along beside me asleep. We found a spot for ourselves in a haystack; in the morning we saw a village and went in, and the people spoke to us in Hungarian. What had we done? In the dark we had returned to Hungary. It can't be, we didn't recross the river. Be calm, said the people, this is Austria. They put the refugees in a schoolhouse, the rector brought us food. I telephoned the Israeli embassy, we're here, send a car for us. This happened on Thursday, they promised us a car for Friday, but it didn't come. We got a ride on a truck transporting milk to Vienna; my wife sat in the cabin with the driver, I was freezing in the back with the others. When we got off in Vienna, an elegant car pulled up next us with an elegant man in it who had seen that we were Hungarian refugees; he stuck bananas and chocolates in the children's pockets and asked us to spend a few days in his villa. I said, thank you, but we are expected elsewhere. We went to the embassy. For Saturday we got a place in the Nord Hotel, the congregation provided us with food. We had nothing—we got money from the JDC and bought what we needed in a department store. We got a temporary passport that was good for a few days, until they issued the real one; in the meantime we looked up a few acquaintances. My little brother came from London and tried to talk us into going with him, but he didn't succeed: I wanted to go to Israel.

We flew in an older style, decrepit airplane, we even had to make a stopover in Athens. We arrived on November 25, in terrible, sweltering heat; do you know what a *hamsin* is? Hot, dry air, desert wind. We didn't know what life would be like in Israel; I listened to Israeli radio and I had been studying Hebrew, but we were not ready for this, we had come in our warm clothes. What will it be like here in the summer? It doesn't matter, whatever will happen, the important thing is that we are here. The Jewish Agency gave every immigrant a cast-iron bed, a mattress, two blankets, and a crummy little petroleum stove with a few pots, I think. Later they gave us money too, quite little, and they enrolled everyone for three months in the Kupat Kholim healthcare agency. A car took us where we asked to go. A cousin of mine lived in Beer Yakov, and a friend of mine named Spitzer was in Avigdor. We went to Beer Yakov, Spitzer took the children to Avigdor. We began to look around in the country for where we would like to settle down. We wanted to go to a religious *moshav*; Spitzer recommended Yesud Hama'ala, saying that very decent Hungarian people live there. We went, we talked to people, we saw that they worked and at night they studied. They asked us how many children we had, we told them four. "That's a little much." "It's not too much for us"—and I left them. They came after us with a car, but I said, thank you very much, but nobody should do me a favor.

They tried to entice people to some places with money; for example, we knew that if we went to Herzliya, we would get 800 lira,[21] and we would only have to pay 300 for a place to live; if we went to Kfar Hasidim, we would get 600 and pay 600; if we went to Bnei Brak, then we would have to pay 1,000 lira for a place to live, and they would give us only 300. The children were in Avigdor, and we were going around looking at places; in the morning we never knew where we would sleep that night; I was already prepared to live in a tent.[22] Spitzer showed us a Jewish Agency apartment in Jerusalem, I liked it, he showed us another that was even more worth consideration; he told us not to rush our decision. Jerusalem was very extreme, Meah Shearim was too religious, the people who lived elsewhere were too secular. We liked Bnei Brak best: Hungarian Orthodox lived there, the younger Rabbi Ungar, who had conducted our wedding ceremony, had settled there as well, everyone spoke Hungarian, you could run into people you knew on the street. There were orange plantations everywhere, the streets had not yet been laid out, so that one night, when we came home, we ended up in Ramat Gan.[23]

The unemployment rate was high; everyone said first you should find a place to work, there'll be a place to live if you are earning money. A friend of mine recommended me at a textile factory in Petah Tikva. I said that I had done this type of work in Pest; the assistant director questioned me in minute detail about how I fixed it if this and this screw-up happened. At first I did every kind of unskilled labor, I cleaned machine parts, I carried bales. They told me that when the new machines arrived from Switzerland, I would be working on those. With the machines came a mechanic—when he had finished the installation, they sent for me. You had to thread the machine, but my hands were very rough from hauling bales, and the slub came apart in my hand. He looked at me very angrily,

21. lira: Israeli currency preceding the shekel.

22. live in a tent: Israel's founding in 1948 was followed by a housing boom such that some refugees were unable to find housing and lived in tents.

23. Ramat Gan: Like neighboring Bnei Brak, a suburb of Tel Aviv.

but in a minute or two my fingers adjusted to the thread, and by the time he had finished his work, I was done: he was completely nonplussed. He began to show me the machine, I told him I was familiar with it, but in Pest we did it much more simply, he snapped that this wasn't Pest, this was Palestine. The manager spoke up and told me to let him have his way in everything he said, he was going away anyway, afterwards I could work the way I wanted. I was asked, could I work on two machines at the same time; I could, so they installed another machine. I was asked to train others; by then we were working in three shifts, if somebody came in early, the other guy could go change his clothes; if somebody had some business to take care of, we traded with each other. Two more machines were planned, but the four machines would have been so far away from each other that one man couldn't look after all the thread. I had a suggestion that instead of putting the machines in two groups next to each other, they should put them at right angles, so that a man should stand between them as if at the tip of a wedge. The plant's advisor, an engineer at Haifa Technical School, saw this and said, that's great. I got a substantial monetary reward, and after that the advisor, whenever he came to the mill, always looked for me to ask if I had any more proposals for innovations. They sent me to a training course and named me one of the five men who make the decision about important matters concerning the mill. I can say without any immodesty that in every place where I worked in my life, I was an industrious and good worker.

It was with a sore heart that I left Hungary, after all, that's where I spent my life. We had everything we needed, we didn't know what we were going to meet up with in a strange land. However, after the murder of our family we couldn't have remained there; we came to be among our brothers and sisters, and we are happy to be here.

Since then I have been home three times. I looked for the Stoltzes who hid us in '45; at first I couldn't find them, then last year I succeeded, and we met. In the winter, the reason I traveled to Budapest was that at our recommendation they received the Yad Vashem "Righteous Gentile" award.

Before the award ceremony we visited the Stoltzes. It was snowing, the train could only move slowly, so we couldn't stay there very long. I stood in front of the window, where in those days we jumped out to escape from the Germans, and I went up a ways in the direction we fled. Supposedly there's some sort of lime kiln up there; I suspect it's the bunker that we built. I wanted to look for it, but there was such a big snow that I couldn't get there. Maybe next time.

Ervin Groszberg

Our family was strictly Ashkenazi Orthodox; my father learned at the yeshivot in Hunfalva and Pozsony[1] and he received his rabbinical training from Akivah Sofer, the chief rabbi of Pozsony, among others. My late grandfather, Lipót Groszberg, founded the Orthodox daily newspaper *Allgemeine Jüdische Zeitung*,[2] which was written in "high German" transcribed with Hebrew letters, in the nineties of the nineteenth century. He wrote articles for the *Zsido Híradó*[3] and also worked for Jewish newspapers in Germany. In 1919, when Hungary was hacked up, the northeastern Jews who spoke Yiddish as their everyday language and those from Transylvania continued to live in the detached territory, so there was no longer justification for the *Allgemeine Jüdische Zeitung*. Thus, for several years, my grandfather did not occupy himself with newspaper writing; he missed it greatly, and he sickened as a result, the poor man. However, there was a need for an Orthodox newspaper even in post-Trianon[4] Hungary, so in 1925, he decided to publish a Hungarian-language weekly which received

1. Hunfalva and Pozsony: today Huncovce (Hunsdorf), Slovakia (map 1 A4), and Bratislava (Pressburg), Slovakia (map 1 B3). These cities were once part of Hungary but reassigned by the treaty of Trianon. See note 4.

2. *Allgemeine Jüdische Zeitung*: (Germ.) *Jewish General Paper*, founded in Budapest in 1888 under the editorship of Lipót Groszberg, M. Erenteil, L. Freund, and Mór Dornbusch. The paper was published for more than two decades (Ujváry).

3. *Zsidó Híradó*: (Hung.) *Jewish News*, a short-lived weekly published by the Orthodox Community, founded in Budapest in 1890 under the editorship of Dániel Weisz (penname Viador). Weisz was the secretary general of the Orthodox Central Bureau (Ujváry).

4. Trianon: The peace treaty after World War I deprived Hungary of over two-thirds of its territory, including many areas where Jews lived. See Introduction, p. xxi.

the name *Zsidó Újság*.[5] He was fifty-six years old then, and so relatively young, but he had already begun to suffer from illness: he was bedridden and later ended up in the hospital, so my father took over the editing of the paper little by little; he published it in cooperation with the Orthodox Central Bureau but always in a separate edition. He succeeded at making an impartial paper extending a picture that embraced both regional and foreign orthodoxy. It was from this paper that we made our living.

Until I was eighteen years of age, I learned at the yeshivot in Vác and Galánta, then in 1943, I graduated from the Budapest Jewish high school by reading for my degree with a private teacher. Concurrently with this, I was occupied with the organization of the Orthodox youth movement: Dr. Adolf Deutsch, the principal of the Orthodox Jewish school, had asked back in '42 that I establish a youth group within the school. He considered himself a follower of the *Agudah* and he envisioned that, after the conclusion of the war, Hungarian Orthodox would have to undertake a relationship with European Jewry and with the *Agudah* operating within it. For that matter, in '42 the situation was awkward, since most Hungarian Orthodox rabbis opposed the activities of the *Agudah* party, while at the same time in the reannexed Slovakia, Transcarpathia, and Transylvania, *Agudah* members and Zionist parties were active in almost every larger congregation.

After Dr. Adolf Deutsch's request, I recruited several of my friends, and every Saturday and additionally on two or three occasions every week, we obtained a place in the school where we could work with children over ten years old. *Pirkhey Tiferes Bahurim* was our official name. It was already after the liberation, in '45–'46, that *Pirkhey Agudat Israel* became the name of the movement.

I learned a trade at a fancy leather goods dealer on Andrássy Road, and several of my writings appeared in the *Zsidó Újság*. My father would without doubt have hired me as a co-worker if the paper had not ceased publication on the date of March 20, 1944.[6] I was lucky; in November '44,

5. *Zsidó Újság*: (Hung.) *The Jewish Paper*.

6. March 20, 1944: The day following the German occupation of Hungary.

4. "This photograph represents the Jewish cemetery during the commemoration of the anniversary of the deportation from Galánta (today in Slovakia) during the second world war; it was taken from the mortuary, where I had gone to photograph the Star of David on the floor and the casket to the right. Outside, in the cemetery, at the memorial service, prayers are being said, speeches are being made. The figure in the doorway is heading into the mortuary for a brief respite from the blazing sun." Text and photograph by Sándor Bacskai.

I ended up in deportation marches three times, but the farthest I got was Almásfüzitő; from there I managed to get back to Pest. In December '44, my parents and I found our way into the Glass House on Vadász Street, which was under the protection of the Swiss embassy. On New Year's Eve, marauding Arrow Cross bands wanted to take the whole house out to the banks of the Danube, but the Germans—and there are several witnesses to this—drove them away. By then I was lying in the Horthy Miklós Hospital in Kőbánya with scarlet fever; the various Red Cross services brought tremendous numbers of Jewish children there. I was liberated there.

We were starving, our clothes were worn to rags, and for this reason my parents, brothers and sisters and I traveled down to Békéscsaba at the end of February '45. Békéscsaba was one of the first liberated cities, the forced-labor service workers were already returning there, the congregation was functioning, there was suitable kosher provisioning, and we could satisfy our needs for *Pesakh.* We stayed there for two and a half months in a rented apartment; in May we came back to our apartment in Aradi Street. I wanted to continue what I started in '42 and what I was still doing until the Arrow Cross took over power in September '44; for this reason I immediately took part in the Hungarian founding of *Agudat Israel.* I was there from its infancy: our first discussion took place in 35 Dob Street, the ruined offices of the Orthodox congregation.[7] I don't know how many of us sat around the table—if there was a table at all, or chairs—there must have been eight or ten of us. Ábrahám Frank, a shoe dealer from Laudon Street, became the chairman, and Simon Sussman—son of the Budapest rabbi Viktor Sussman, grandson of Chief Rabbi Koppel Reich[8]—was the vice chairman. For some time, the Budapest leather dealer Gyula Link, who was originally from Galánta, was the co-chairman—in reality the *Agudah*'s financial mainstay.

Besides them, I remember Fülöp Ernst and Gottesmann from Miskolc. There were two or three of us who were young; we wanted to be involved with the youth. In the organization of the Children's and Youth Groups, Benő Stein was my most immediate colleague; I learned a great deal from him. He was also from Miskolc; as a forced-labor service worker, he fell into Russian captivity, ended up in Arkhangelsk or somewhere—there he was put to work for the Party, together with István Kossa, one of the leaders of the MKP,[9] later the MDP, about whom he told a lot of stories. Of course Stein didn't become a Communist; he had rabbinical training, and

7. the ruined offices of the Orthodox congregation: After the *Agudah* was established, it set up its own offices in 26 Király Street (map 2 [13] C2).

8. Chief Rabbi Koppel Reich: His full name was Jakab Koppel Reich. He was chief rabbi of Budapest from 1889 to 1929.

9. MKP: Magyar Kommunista Párt, the Hungarian Communist Party. It was later called Magyar Dolgozók Pártja (MDP), the Hungarian Workers' Party.

as soon as he got home, he took part in organizing the *Agudah*. I remember that in February '47 we were in Makó for organizational work, and since we didn't find any sort of vehicle, we went on foot to Mezőkovácsháza; we set out on the fourteen-kilometer walk in the deep snow.

Then there was Ervin Friedmann with whom for a short while I took care of regional matters; he had already left the country by '48 or even earlier. I had two other regional colleagues, one was Károly Grosz—no relation—a very intelligent guy from Kisvárda, and the other was Sándor Roth from Munkács—today both of them live in America. We wore dark blue uniform hats; later I had two hundred hat emblems made in a workshop: blue and white background, with a diagonal white stripe.

We also had female colleagues who organized the *Agudah* girls' group, I don't remember anymore whether it was in 32 Kertész Street or in the girls' home in Akácfa Street: Rachel Ehrenfeld from Makó—she emigrated in '58, and Rachel Adler, who later married Benő Stein—she was his second wife; his first family perished in Auschwitz.

At first we were busy with social activities: we set up a soup kitchen, and we provided dinner to the needy. In those days all the money came through the JDC;[10] they were also the ones who supported the *Agudah*. This was well-organized; there was a committee which distributed the money, and Orthodox and Neolog worked together in this committee.

In May 1945, the *Agudah* moved to the first floor of 26 Király Street[11] and set up offices and a prayer house which was frequented by the neighborhood's Orthodox. In 1946 my late uncle, Lipót Fuchs, the chief rabbi of Biharkeresztes, became the rabbi of the congregation; he and his wife were brought up to Pest from the ghetto in Nagyvárad. That's how they stayed alive. Incidentally, the building had earlier been the home of a

10. JDC: Acronym for the Joint Distribution Committee; it provided funds for economic rehabilitation of shattered communities.

11. 26 Király Street: This was the first headquarters of the *Agudah* (map 2 [13] C2). Until these offices were set up, the group met in the Orthodox congregation offices in Dob Street (map 2 [04] C3).

Jewish dance school, and it was here that, according to plans made during the war, the yeshivah for technicians[12] was to operate.

In the summer of '45, I found an empty apartment in number 1 Holló Street. The Mór Weisz Bread Factory, a considerable baking concern, had previously been in that building; now the Fröhlich Pastry Shop operates in part of it. The way I remember it, the Mór Weisz family let us know that the apartment on the second floor was empty. There were no windows or window frames; I had a carpenter make these, an older man named Mr. Herskovits. For a long time after this, Mr. Herskovits was at our disposal, even then, when we moved to Dob Street.[13] We fixed up the apartment in Holló Street and the boys' section of *Pirkhey Agudat Israel* moved in there. Number 1 Holló Street was a corner house, my office was on the Dob Street side, next to it was a little so-called sitting room, while on the Holló Street side was the boys' daytime center with space for learning, games, ping-pong tables. For the smaller children, we had a kindergarten directed by Isidor Schwartz, and he had two, or in case of need, three assistants: Ella Roóz from Kisvárda, a girl named Glaser from Bánffy-hunyad, and Anna Schwartz, an extremely beautiful girl from Munkács. At first we received our salaries in million, then in billion pengős. From August '46,[14] my salary as "department head" was 500 forints; from this I covered my university studies.

Also in the summer of '46, we organized our first summer vacation program for children in Hűvösvölgy. I don't know whether I would find the building, if I were to take a walk there: the camp was located in the villa located under the number 62 on Hűvösvölgyi Road. This also came about with the assistance of the JDC; they gave us the money, they gave us the food. We took a Torah with us and we set up a little prayer house. We

12. yeshivah for technicians: There were plans for such a yeshivah in 1947, but the school, which was to provide religious studies as well as training in a trade, was never opened.

13. when we moved to Dob Street: The *Agudah* moved from 26 Király Street (map 2 [13] C2) to Dob Street (map 2 [04] C3) in the summer of 1949.

14. August '46: This was the date of the introduction of the forint.

lived according to a strict Orthodox lifestyle. A staff of outstanding educators directed the camp; for example, Rabbi Jenő Singer was the director of the Talmud-Torah; Ödön Gáti, Simon Braun, and Jenő Blasz were the teachers. We worked hard to develop program units with enduring meaning. We provided summer vacations for a minimum of two hundred children, mostly from Budapest; there were also five Polish Jewish children who had been enduring the dangers of the war here. Few children from the countryside came back from the deportation: there were larger numbers of Orthodox children in Debrecen, Makó, and the cities in the Hajdúság.[15] In the summer of '46, I was looking for a location near Miskolc for that summer's vacation program, and I found it, too, in Görömbölytapolca, a pleasant bathing resort. The leaders of the congregation at Miskolc assisted me by pointing out the children in school. Before the war, seventeen thousand Jews lived in Miskolc, fifteen hundred children went to the Jewish school. Then, they could muster twenty children in the school yard—of these a few lived through the war in Budapest, others had been hidden by Christians in various bunkers. I cried so bitterly then, I have never forgotten that experience.

We organized the tent camp in Miskolctapolca, it was very beautiful; in fact we were in that area in '47 as well, in Kácsfürdő, a pretty place, do you know where it is? When I first went that way, you had to get off the train in Mezőnyárád, and I walked though Tibolddaróc to get there. For that matter, we traveled by truck, and we set up the camp kitchen right away, where the professional cook we brought with us cooked strictly kosher. From '48 to '50, we spent the summers in Balatonszemes; that was the last time we camped. Of course there were separate camp divisions for the boys and the girls.

In early fall of '45, an initiative was launched at Mezőkovácsháza: a few people came back from forced-labor service but their children had been exterminated; they longed for children's voices, and in addition, they had space that wasn't being used, so they turned to us to establish a children's home for orphans from Budapest and the Hajdúság. I believe that one of

15. Hajdúság: A predominantly Orthodox region near Debrecen (map 1 B5).

my contemporaries, Ignác Brüll, still lives there, sometimes I see his name in the *Új Élet*.[16] He began to organize the boarding school with us; we set about the thing together. From our point of view, Mezőkovácsháza wasn't an ideal place: it was a typical, large lowland village near the Romanian border without a water system, or anything else. But it also had a certain attraction, the children could taste village life; every morning, they helped with the milking, this was a great experience for city children. We also organized a school for them, everything was going along nicely. Then in '46–'47, we moved the children's home to Csorna, a cultured provincial town, where the conditions were much more favorable. There I discovered a superb educator who had returned from forced-labor service and later went up to Pest. The rabbi was R. Mordkhe Arye Moskovits; he had been learning with the older boys already in Mezőkovácsháza.

Where children returned in greater numbers, a local *Pirkhey Agudah* group was immediately established, launched from Budapest. In 1946 we first organized the Agudist Youth Days; in those days, every Zionist organization held such events. In '49 we were in the Nagyrét in Hűvösvölgy, in '50 in Makó; in '48 we decided to hold our demonstration in Debrecen, since there was a local group there then as well as a children's home. At Lag b'Omer, we organized a nice little procession in the Nagyerdő, local groups from Hajdúnánás, and Hajdúböszörmény and Balmazújváros were there, besides large delegations from Budapest and Makó. The groups processed with their flags and their banners, then we set up camp and there were speeches and skits—all this didn't cause much of a sensation: people accepted that those who had survived the Holocaust wanted to live. But in the same way the sight of the occasional religious Jew wasn't of especial interest in those days, whether it was in Budapest or Pápa or Berettyóújfalu.

The *Agudah* had a considerable influence on Orthodox youth, more so than the *Mizrakhi*, the Zionist religious party, especially on boys who were around fourteen, whom we guided to yeshivot. Since the old ones had

16. *Új Élet*: The official paper of the Hungarian Jewish organized community. See also the glossary.

ceased to exist during the war, we established a new one on Hűvösvölgyi Road—in that villa where we organized our first camp. We founded it under the leadership of Simon Posen the former chief rabbi of Sopron—it was the first yeshivah since the liberation. Later others were established; the one at Hajdúhadház and the one in Békéscsaba were also founded by the *Agudah*. In other places, as in Eger or Paks, they were established on initiatives from the local chief rabbis.

The other area where we had an influence on the children—and you're not an ÁVÓ case official, so I can safely tell you about it—was making Aliyah. Until '48, when the Jewish state was founded, there were countless difficulties with this. The groups first went to France, where they took part in *hakhsharah*, or "preparations."

In the beginning, the *Agudah* was not a declaredly Zionist party. The Jewish leaders thought that what had been interrupted in '44 would continue, that, though they had been manhandled, the religious congregation's organizations would be rebuilt. Hungarian Jewry wasn't less patriotic than Hungarian Christianity; I am in a position to say so, since, after thirty-five years of life in Israel this patriotism is still within me. I root for the Hungarians in the Olympics, at home we have a "Hungarian shelf" with Hungarian books and—please don't laugh—a red, white, and green rosette.[17]

But in '47, after the blue-slip elections and the elimination of the Pfeiffer party and the Barankovics-style Christian People's party,[18] even a blind man could see that the Communists were going to take power. Thus making Aliyah was part of the spirit of the times. I wouldn't say that this would have been our main occupation—our main occupation was our everyday work. But subconsciously, it became our main objective that the children who had survived the Holocaust should sooner or later get to *Erets Yisrael*.

17. a red, white, and green rosette: This patriotic and national symbol originated in Hungary's 1848 Revolution against Austrian rule.

18. Barankovics-style Christian People's party: In the Communist-rigged 1947 elections, two Hungarian parties opposing the Communists did well; the Hungarian Independence Party founded by Zoltán Pfeiffer was banned in 1947, and the Christian Democratic People's party founded by István Barankovics was dissolved in 1949.

In 1947, we received an invitation from the *Agudah*'s then-headquarters in London, to participate in the congress at Marienbad. We decided that the participants should be Ábrahám Frank, as well as Benő Stein, Ervin Friedmann, and myself. Incidentally, my late grandfather had represented Hungary with three others at the founding congress of *Agudat Israel* in the year 1912, and my father was a delegate at the congress in '37 at Marienbad.

We didn't receive legal entry permits because of current Hungarian–Czechoslovak relations, or something else, so a dear friend of ours, Pál Levin, the only member of our community in Rajka, invited us, and then helped us get over to Pozsonyligetfalu, the Czechoslovak side. As I remember it, we slept at his house while he first obtained the documents for us at the local administrative offices that proved that we were residents of Rajka, and then, with these in his possession, he obtained the border-crossing permits as well. This is how we crossed the area near Oroszvár, which was annexed to Czechoslovakia not much later. We spent Saturday in Pozsony, took a night train to Prague, and then on Sunday traveled to Marienbad. We arrived a few days after the opening of the conference, and fell to work. One of the main topics was the relationship with the Jewish state which was in the process of being born; another important area was reviving Eastern European Jewish religious life—this last was primarily urged by the English and Swiss delegates. We met many people and had many conversations. Afterwards, they sent us prayerbooks and other things to help the preparations of children here.

At this time, we published the newspaper called *Akhdut*,[19] which I edited. The newspaper reported news and stories about the lives of our organization's Budapest and regional groups; I wrote reports and editorials. Unfortunately, I don't have even a single copy of it, as my wife burned them all after the ÁVÓ arrested me.

I completed my university studies in 1949. I had already applied to the university in May '45—since childhood, geography and education had been hobbies of mine, and I decided I would somehow link these

19. *Akhdut*: (Heb.) Unity.

two areas together. I had to write a dissertation, and my professor and I agreed that I would write about transportation in Switzerland. I would have liked to make on-site observations, gather information, and obtain books, so it came at the most opportune time that a Swiss religious social organization invited twenty-three children for a holiday who had suffered lung injuries as a result of the Holocaust. I selected children from Budapest, eastern Hungary, and Makó—among them was Efraim Frisch from Hajdúnánás, who recently became the director of the endowment school[20] in Wesselényi Street.

I completed the university, I even have a certificate of completion, only I never received the doctorate, although the rector put my name forward to Gyula Ortutay, the minister of culture. They sent me to Rákosi, that I should obtain permission from him, but, needless to say, I didn't go knocking on his door. Each people has its traitors; Rákosi betrayed the Hungarian people and Jewry.

In the beginning of 1949, the *Agudah* ceased to exist. If I remember correctly, the directive about the dissolution of Zionist organizations came out in March. At the end of '47, when the ruling was born about the division of Palestine and the creation of two new states, then Hungarian government policy and the press, especially the *Szabad Nép*, related very positively to this. Understandably, since Andrei Gromyko had a significant part in the creation of Israel, and the Soviet Union was the first to recognize Israel. But shortly after this, they began to realize in Moscow that Israel was leaning toward the West; at first they bought weapons from Czechoslovakia, but after that they shifted to cooperation with the French.

At the end of '48 a certain anti-Zionist drive was already palpable, in around '52 it had been somewhat converted to anti-Semitism. At the end of '48 there were Zionist legal actions in Romania and Poland, so the decree about our dissolution didn't seem entirely surprising. Many people attempted unlawful border crossings at the time, and we thought it was to be expected that those who were caught were thrown in the clink—the law is the law.

20. the endowment school: The full name is the American Endowment School.

The *Agudah*'s prayer house on Király Street continued to operate for a while, the offices had to be closed. The daytime center for boys on Holló Street and the daytime center for girls which existed at 41 Király Street continued running until the summer of '48, after the termination of the *Agudah* as an organization of the Orthodox congregation. Then, following the socialization of the schools, the school building at 35 Dob Street became empty, and the daytime center was unified there with the Talmud-Torah. Then I took over the children from *Bnei Akivah*;[21] some of my colleagues—Benő Stein, Ervin Friedmann—went abroad, and new people came to replace them, among them Jenő Steinberger, who became my successor after '57. Many in my circle of friends said I should leave too, but I was very tied to the place—I loved working with the children.

In 1950, an important event occurred in the life of Orthodoxy, although I don't know much to say about it.[22] Gyula Ortutay, the minister of religion and education, called for the unification of the Orthodox and Neolog religious congregations. The idea was not raised by the Jews, even though the Neologs had several times insisted on it, and there had earlier been noises made in Síp Street to the effect that the time was ripe for the unification. The Orthodox didn't see any other expedient. The unification was, of course, to their disadvantage, since autonomy is of the essence of Orthodoxy—it has to manage its own affairs, it has to lead a religious life independently from the Neologs. Although the right to this was guaranteed, more and more of the leaders left the country, for which they received criticism as well: the captains were leaving the sinking ship. For example, Sándor Jungreisz, the chief rabbi of Budapest, departed in '53 and became rabbi of Jazur,[23] a town near Tel Aviv. This was entirely out of keeping with his position here, and he himself was clear about this. The public officials in charge of the Orthodox at the time, the chairman Samu Kahán-Frankl and his assistant, the legal advisor Dr. Imre Reiner,

21. *Bnei Akivah*: International Zionist youth organization.

22. important event: See the first chapter, "Unification," in which Bacskai describes the National Israelite Assembly of 1950 and its effect on the Orthodox Denomination.

23. Jazur: The medieval name of the area where Azor was founded in 1948, in the Tel Aviv District of Israel.

had already emigrated in 1950. They were involved in the leadership of the JDC, and when the government broke off its connections to the JDC, they were afraid of being held accountable, since it had also financed the Zionist movements. In fact, they did arrest the president of the JDC and Lajos Stöckler, the president of the National Neolog Bureau. In my opinion, there is no doubt that this would have been the fate of Kahán-Frankl and Dr. Reiner as well. I have known both men since I was a small child, morning and night I went to Kahán-Frankl's place in Eötvös Street to pray, I understood their cast of mind: for them, Hungarian Orthodoxy was a concern of the heart, so it was not baldly a matter of saving their skin.

Fifty-two and fifty-three were very oppressive years. We lived in fear.

The law forbade anti-Semitism. But if somebody on the tram said, "You stinking Zionist!" that was no crime, and everyone understood what he was talking about. The press was full of anti-Zionist propaganda, every day, political speeches contained accusations of Zionism.

As a reaction against the anti-Zionist movement established in Eastern Europe, people in Ramat Gan[24] attacked the Soviet embassy, and because of this the connection between the Soviets and Israel was broken and reestablished only in the time of Khrushchev. The Israeli embassy continued to operate in Budapest, but we knew it was not advisable to enter it: they even had the neighborhood under surveillance. When Chaim Weizmann, the first president, died, a few friends of mine and I went in anyway, to express our condolences. I had a rather good, personal relationship with the embassy's people in those days.

If I reconstruct the events today, nearly forty years later, I can say that what happened after this was a logical consequence of my activities and the times then, although de facto I did not propound activities which satisfied the criteria for Zionism. Later at the ÁVÓ, my case official once spent the entire night preaching about this; all night the topic was, "What is the *Agudah*?" "The *Agudah* is not simply a Zionist organization, it is much worse than that. It is in part a nationalist organization, and in part an ecclesiastical one, and to be sure, ecclesiastical nationalism is the

24. Ramat Gan: A suburb of Tel Aviv.

greatest sworn enemy of socialism." This of course is not true—neither can its working be considered nationalism, nor does its religious approach cross those boundaries which the Hungarian constitution then permitted under freedom of religion.

In Prague in '52, the Slánsky case[25] was being tried, and shortly thereafter in Moscow they made public the affair of the doctors.[26] Here at home there wasn't a single Zionist organization operating anymore, neither above ground or under ground. Nonetheless, the press was always talking about the Zionist menace; we felt that something was imminent.

On February 28, '53, on a Saturday, my wife and I were taking a walk. We had been married four months. We stopped in front of a shop window on the Körút,[27] and I was reading an article in the *Szabad Nép* which was displayed there, "The sorry plight of Zionism." I saw what the issue was, but I still didn't feel that it also affected me. That evening—it was Purim—I learned in the shul that two of my former pupils had been arrested. So that, when in the middle of the night—the night which would dawn in Purim, you understand the significance of the holiday—at around eleven o'clock came the great ringing,[28] only then was I taken aback to discover what was happening. They didn't use the word "arrest," or I just don't remember it, because I fainted, they had to throw cold water on me to bring me around. Then I already knew that they were going to lock me up, but I was hoping that it would only be for a short time. I could only

25. the Slánsky case: At a trial in Prague in November 1952, Czech Communist Party leader Rudolf Slánsky, who was Jewish, was found guilty of "Trotskyite-Titoist-Zionist activities in the service of American imperialism" (Kniesmeyer and Brecher 62–64).

26. the affair of the doctors: In January 1953, in a case thought to be a manifestation of his increasing paranoia, Stalin ordered the arrest of a group of Jewish Kremlin doctors for plotting the murder by medical means of high-level Soviet officials.

27. Körút: The streets of central Budapest are laid out like a wheel, with the grand boulevards of this semicircular ring road forming the rim (map 2 A1–D3). The Körút is broken by spoke-like cross-streets into Szent István körút, Teréz körút, Erzsébet körút, József körút, and Ferenc körút.

28. the great ringing: The visit from ÁVÓ in the middle of the night was notorious. See Abelesz, "the bell rings," p. 34.

bring the most minimal things with me, so I was in the same clothes for eleven months.

The car went around and around, the windows were covered with curtains; I didn't know where I was. In any case, my impression was that we can't be traveling far from Budapest. The took me to Fő Street, there they took away my gear—my watch, and the Megillah and tefillin which my father very naïvely gave me—and threw me into a cell. For a while I looked around; I had never seen the inside of a prison.

In come two prison guards, they take me by the arm, we run to the corridor, they throw me in the elevator, we stop somewhere, they take me in to the middle of a room, state security authorities are sitting all around me, and one asks, "Do you know why you have wound up here?" I answer that I don't know. "Well, just think about it!" and they are silent for a few seconds. "I don't know." "Because you are the enemy of the people," they reprimanded me . . .

Afterward they didn't ask me anything, but ordered me to write a sixteen-page biography and no less, or else I'll rot there in my cell for time out of mind. They brought me back to the cell, gave me paper and pencil, I should start writing. I was young—except for the war years I had nothing behind me at all—I wrote down two–three pages.

Monday they brought me in to my case official, he introduced himself, not by name, just that he was my case official. I didn't know the degrees of the ranks, I learned them after I was set free; he was László Székely, state security captain. He looks at the papers, well, this is nothing! Back into the cell, sixteen pages. Meanwhile, from Sunday night to Wednesday morning, they didn't let me sleep; when my eyes began to close, immediately a kick in the door, from this my eyes opened, even involuntarily. Again, just write. Well this doesn't work! I had fallen into a more or less unconscious state from lack of sleep, a little wet rubbing, a little washing helped after a fashion. Then I scribbled down everything, but things like, when I was three and spent my summer vacation in Kecskemét, and the swings there were such and such. I remember that I included this; in this way I pulled together eight–nine pages. My case official looked at the sheets, asked something here and there, then on Wednesday morning, he allowed me to lie down on the bunk to sleep. By then it was May 4: Stalin died the next day, and I didn't know about the whole thing, I didn't notice anything in the world. As far as I was concerned, he died on August 24—that's when they took me over to the Markó Street jail, and I learned about it there from my cellmates. My 178 days in Fő Street were all spent in solitary confinement: I had no interaction with anyone except my guards and my interrogators.

First they asked me about my foreign travels, so I described my trip to Switzerland. "Careful, don't play the fool! Slomo Groszberg goes out to Switzerland and takes a tour of the railroads," said my interrogator cynically, but he never returned to this topic.

On March 11 started the second range of subjects, my connections with the Israeli embassy. I explained that I knew Moshe Dak, the secretary of the legation, and Zwi Chaskel, the immigration attaché. Then he asked me about the nature of the relationship: where did we meet, what were the furnishings in the room, where did I sit, what did the chair look like. What did the two gentlemen want from me? Nothing at all? And what did I want from them? I explained that at one point I had been considering emigration, and so I inquired about placement opportunities. "You're trying to snow me again," he said.

On Friday night, I'm sitting on the bunk when in come two prison guards, and they make me stand between the two bunks. When they go out, I want sit down, they kick the door loudly, "Keep standing!" I asked for how long, "Stand!" I stood like this for an entire week, night and day, they let me lie down for two hours a day. During this time there was no interrogation. The week after this, on Thursday, they interrogated me again, from ten o'clock to four in the morning. "What did Moshe Dak and Zwi Chaskel want from you? "They didn't want anything." "Stand against the wall and don't turn around until you remember what they wanted!" Around dawn he pulled aside the curtain and said, "It's already morning, and you are burying yourself here. You'll never become a human being like this!" Then he sat me down and said that they knew well that Moshe Dak and Zwi Chaskel wanted to enlist me in the overthrow of our government. I was in such pain, my two ankles were swollen, my skin was red and festering; I was going through superhuman torments. "I'll sign whatever he wants," I thought to myself. He put an affidavit in front of me,

"I admit that I led a movement aimed at overthrowing our government, which I wanted to accomplish through the illegal Agudist movement in cooperation with other anticommunist, antidemocratic organizations, and that Moshe Dak and Zwi Chaskel, the officials of the Israeli embassy, entrusted me with the direction of this plan."

They took me back to the cell. It was Friday noon; I could lie down as long as I wanted, I could sleep as long as I wanted.

On Monday morning, a new interrogation started: how much money did I receive for the carrying out of the plan. None. "Well, that's not possible," said my case official, and with this started a new round of wrangling that lasted the entire week. On Friday they put me in chains, I had to stand like that until the next Thursday. The next morning I said that I had gotten 10,000 forints. "Well, what's 10,000 forints to an Israeli embassy?" he asked, and in this way we got to some inflated sum that satisfied him. He wrote the affidavit and I could rest again for a few days.

In April, a calmer period ensued. At *Pesakh,* I cried terribly at the interrogation—you know, don't you that the night of the Seder is a family holiday. My interrogator said that if I were honest, then the time would come when I would celebrate. And this was a human voice after all the threats and curses. Later he asked me about my school activities: how did I let the faculty know that the children were to be raised in a Zionist spirit? For this, I stressed the parts of some of our prayers which dealt with Jerusalem: it was comforting to be able to recite these at *Pesakh.*

After the holiday, however, he returned to Moshe Dak and Zwi Chaskel. By then I had recuperated a bit, there was some resistance in me, so I didn't say anything. On April 20, a Sunday, a man in a white cape came in to see me and asked, did I have any complaints. I said none. He thumped my back, "You look very bad; you need to be getting injections." In a few days, I could feel that something had changed, I began to be in a better mood, to sing softly to myself, "Quickly away ran those years, while they are keeping me inside." A new cycle of interrogation started, by then I had become completely unresisting, I continued to receive the injections. They plagued me with questions about spying and delivering documents. If I hadn't read spy novels when I was a child, I wouldn't have known what to concoct. So I made up a story, that I had gathered information about textile manufacturing from the father of one of my students, who was the engineer of the textile factory at Kelenföld, and from another of my former students, Éva Katz, and I had transmitted this data to the Israeli embassy. This was my arrant nonsense of a spy story, but they were satisfied with it. In mid-May, my interrogator still asked me some questions about the leaders of the Orthodox in those days, but it was clear that he had closed out my case. I last saw him on May 22.

For two weeks, I lay idle in my bunk. They didn't concern themselves with me; three times a day, they handed in the food and were done. I wasn't even allowed to go for a walk. In all my time at the ÁVÓ, I never once got to go for a walk. I had a certain daily schedule: I reconstructed fifty psalms from memory; I recited these. I thought a lot. I prayed: I never neglected that, not even in the "twenty-six hour days," and I took care that, despite everything, I shouldn't lose track of the Hebrew date, so that I would know when it was a holy day. I tore a handful of black lining from my coat, and I held this over my head while praying.

On June 10, I was assigned to a new man; he was a very congenial lieutenant named János Kádár.[29] We talked for three–four hours every day, about all kinds of things, books, movies—let's say I didn't have much expertise there—we even discussed matters of religion. In July he began to delve into my earlier confessions. He ordered face-to-face sessions. Éva Katz was summoned for Tisha b'Av: I was to say to her face that I had asked for data about the textile factory! "But you never asked any such thing!" said Éva; the session was inconclusive. For the next day, they summoned Miss Piri, who even today is a kindergarten teacher at the Orthodox Division.[30] Miss Piri was then a young teacher at the Talmud-Torah, and they asked her what instructions I had given for Zionist pedagogy. This session was inconclusive as well. Then they took me in to some high-ranking official—I don't know but he wasn't a colonel, who asked me in a

29. János Kádár: not the dictator.

30. the Orthodox Division: This was the designation of the Orthodox Community within the unified entity created by force in 1950. For the complete story, see "Unification," p. 1.

fatherly tone to tell him the truth. Bitter tears burst forth from me, I blubbered out the conditions under which I had made my confessions. "And what is the truth?" The truth is that I taught the geography of Palestine to the children. He wrote a one-page record of this, and by it he nullified the approximately four hundred pages which had been recorded earlier.

They transferred me to the public prosecutor's department. On August 24, they put me in the Markó. That was when I learned that Stalin had died and Rákosi had been replaced, and that Imre Nagy[31] had become the prime minister.

They combined my case with that of Géza Kornitzer, who was the treasurer of the *Agudah*, and they were accusing him of maintaining the organization's financial position after its dissolution.

They set the first trial for the middle of December, but nothing came of it; the Markó was full of Titoists and Rajkists[32]—that's when they emptied the internment camps—there were thousands of them.

The real trial was on January 13, '54. Vilmos Olti, the president of the tribunal, read out the charge, the crime of inciting to emigration—he was the one who at that time tried the Mindszenty and Rajk cases as well. In my defense, I explained that I had been a teacher of Palestinian geography as a foundation for the history of the Jewish religion. They acquitted both of us, by noon of that day I was eating lunch at home; my late mother awaited me with my favorite foods, she cooked matzo ball soup and stuffed peppers.

A significant political thaw occurred when Imre Nagy first became head of the government. After I was freed, the Orthodox congregation received permission for the establishment of a children's center which I led, along with continuing the leadership of the Talmud-Torah school and the daytime center. On October 23, 1956, I still had six hundred students, all Orthodox children from Budapest. At the end of October or the

31. Imre Nagy: Chairman of the Hungarian Council of Ministers from 1953 to 1955.

32. Titoists and Rajkists: The Soviet Union perceived the policies of Marshall Tito in Yugoslavia as threatening its hegemony. In 1948, Rákosi, the Stalinist Hungarian ruler, mounted a concerted effort against what he called Titoists and followers of László Rajk (Kontler).

beginning of November, you could expect anti-Semitic atrocities, but it wasn't from these that people fled—the far right would never have triumphed in Hungary. Jews were much more afraid of a future Communist retaliation that would destroy their religious life.

By March '57, after the wave of emigration had subsided, the Talmud-Torah was depopulated; I had maybe two hundred children, most of whom had moved up from the countryside. A king without a country, I gave my keys to my successor, Jenő Steinberger, and we too emigrated to Israel.

"Well, it seems as if," said my father, "it was just Rákosi who held together our Orthodoxy."

Frigyes Rosenberg

It's so interesting, the way Hungarians talk today—they don't talk like we did. Can't you hear the differences in rhythm? The other day some people came here from Pest, and I was talking to a couple I met in the bus. I said to them I don't know how to adjust myself to talk to you people from Pest today because we talk completely different, we stress words different.

Tov,[1] let's talk. I'm not going to reveal any kind of secret to you, not to mention the fact that I don't even know any secrets. We were liberated in Bor[2] and that's the truth, though I don't know the exact date, but it was sometime in October. It must have been near the end of October, because we spent the holidays there. I could tell that the empire was crumbling when the Germans blew up their central garrison, set fire to it with two hundred fifty injured in there. The peasants came and rescued them; these things were already written up back then. I think it must have been the end of October when the Russians came, though we were actually liberated by the partisans and the Russians came right after them. If one gave you something, the other took it away, but anyway, that's not interesting.

Then a couple of friends and I, we started for home on foot, it was still November '44. And we walked from dawn until late at night. I think it was on the second day that I said to my friends, "I'm not walking any further, because in a day I can walk eighteen or twenty-four miles, but if I find a car, in an hour it can take me further than that. So if I sit here from eight o'clock in the morning and I stop a car at five in the afternoon, I'll be six hours further along than if I had walked all day." And it was true: we sat

1. *Tov*: (Heb.) Good.

2. Bor: a city in eastern Serbia (south of map 1 D6).

down at an intersection and along came a Russian car that had been carrying munitions and they were going back empty. We asked for a ride and we really did get further along than we could have gone on foot. There were two drivers—one of them came back to us and said, "Money! Who's got money?" Where would we have gotten money? A Serbian peasant who was with us paid the way for all five of us. We got to I-don't-know-where and slept there. Then we managed to find a car that was going toward the border at dawn, but it wouldn't take us unless we gave them something. One of us had a cigarette lighter, the other a pen, little things that happened to be left in our pockets, and with these the car took us as far as the Danube, where there was a ferry. We got on the ferry and it took us to Turnu Severin, that's already in Romania. We left our baggage on the riverbank with one man to watch it while the rest of us went to find out if it was worth it to go into town or what. We were so hungry that our eyes would pop out for a hatful of food, and they had everything in the world: the stores were open and the pastry shops were full.

When we saw this, one of us ran back and brought a blanket from the baggage. We sold it, sat down in a pastry shop, and ate its value. Only after that did we go to look for the shul—people told us where it was, where Jews lived—and we went to sleep there, in the shul. There were Hungarian Jews there, because they spoke to us in Hungarian, not Yiddish. The congregation was functioning, but they didn't give us anything, not a thing, maybe because they didn't have anything to give, I don't know.

In the morning we got on a train to come home and as I looked in the car, all of a sudden I saw a Jew with a beard. I hadn't seen a bearded Jew for a long time; in Hungary even the rabbis had been forced to shave. He turned out to be a Jew from Temesvár.[3] I sat down next to him and we started to talk. I had gone to yeshivah, first at home in Salgótarján—my late father, who for twenty-five years was the congregation's *gabe*, didn't want us to have to study away from home, so he talked it over with his

3. Temesvár: Now Timişoara in Romania, the major city of the historical region known as the Bánat (map 1 C5). This area was under Hungarian rule from the tenth century until the Turkish invasion in 1552. Today it is divided between Romania, Serbia, and Hungary.

older brother that they would bring in a rabbi to run a yeshivah, and they brought in Rabbi Günzler from Sátoraljaújhely—after that I studied with the rabbi in Verpelét, and finally I was in Csorna.

Since this Jew saw that I was more religious than the others, he invited me to eat with him on Shabbat. He couldn't invite the others, in the first place, because he had so little, and besides, he was getting ready to emigrate, and all his belongings had been sold—he was coming here to *Erets* in two or three days. So the others just slept there, but I don't know where they ate. When we started to talk, he asked me right away what I ate. I told him what, what—I know how to eat what there is. He said to me, as soon as you are in a place where there are other Jews, you can't eat everything anymore.

My original line of work was baking; I was a baker in Salgótarján in '35, but when I married and settled in Vác, I gave my bakery to my little brother. In the camp at Bor there were five bakeries, and in the last few weeks, when the Germans couldn't make enough bread, they assigned me to be the director of one of them. Several times, the Germans brought in young porkers cut in half for me to roast in the oven. I had a cousin there who said, they don't want the fat, they only want the meat, so store it for yourself. I took a jug and filled it with fat. I was so hardened that I didn't even mind, because I knew well that if a man eats a gram or two of fat a day, he can extend his life with it. I got hold of a big box of some kind of margarine, that kind of fat, and I had about two or three cans as well. That Jew says to me that I shouldn't be eating these things anymore and I knew he was right.

But I'll tell you about one more thing: right after we were liberated, when the Germans fled, we right away went into the storeroom, and I grabbed a silk blanket and gave it to one of the boys and said, hurry off to the *shuk* and buy everything you see. He brought eggs and flour and I don't know what else, and I got to work right away making pancakes. But by the time I mixed up the batter, a bunch of partisans came and chased us out, saying they needed the building as a hospital. I saw that they were right, not to mention that they had weapons and we didn't. Not too far away, there was a sort of restaurant; I spoke Serbian and even Russian tolerably well, so I went to the restaurant owner and asked him to let me cook the pancakes. The partisan leaders were meeting in there, and, as I was making the pancakes, they grabbed them right out from under my hands. I said to the owner, "Hey! I'm doing this because I'd finally like to have a dinner to eat once again," and he said, "Just give them everything and we'll eventually get dinner too." I made a great pot of pancakes and I never even got to taste them, they grabbed them all. When the pancakes were done, I said to the restaurant owner, what about dinner. He says they ate everything, but he gave me a can of ham. I can tell you, I had never eaten such good meat, before or since. The best meat in the world, at least the best I ever ate.

For two more days I cooked pancakes for the partisans, and their commander gave me a document that I could go, along with the other six men who worked under me, to eat in any restaurant I wanted, whenever I wanted. So for a few days while we stayed there, I'd go into a restaurant and show that slip of paper and without a word, we'd get what we needed. I don't know what kind of agreement they had, but he gave me that document and I accepted it without a word. To this day, I regret throwing it away on the road, but I was afraid of the Germans and terrified of the Russians.

Well, with that Jew from Temesvár, I of course went to an Orthodox shul. I was very happy. On Sunday morning, we went to Arad, which was one of the gathering places for Jews, and we went to the JDC,[4] where it was mostly my friends sitting in the offices, those who had managed to get there faster from Bor. We sat and talked while the city Jews, mostly women, came and took a man here and there home with them. I happened to be well dressed, because when I joined up I took a decent suit with me, knee pants and a nice jacket I had had made not long before.

When we had left Bor on foot and first stopped to rest, right that minute, I opened my backpack; in it there was a brand-new summer coat I had not worn even once and two pairs of pants. I took off everything, put on the good suit, and kept three or four pairs of socks and two shirts; the rest

4. JDC: Acronym for the Joint Distribution Committee; it played a large role in the care of those in displaced person camps and provided funds for those who wished to emigrate.

I handed out to the guys. I already knew that proverb from Russia that even a toothbrush was heavy for a man to carry—why should I carry it? I handed it all out.

These ladies came: a very well-dressed, elegant woman walked up to me, the wife of a lawyer—they were well-off people. I should come right along to their house, they would provide me with everything. I said to her, I'm sorry, but I need to ask, I want to go only to a place where they keep kosher. She says she can give me everything I need in the world, but she doesn't have kosher housekeeping. I say, then I am infinitely sorry, but I can't go. She asked me to recommend someone else to her. There was a young boy, a real gentleman, and I don't remember, somehow I was friends with him, so I said I know that boy, I recommend you take him. She took him away with her; the boy came back in two hours dressed like a prince, brand-new suit, new shoes, hat, a greatcoat, tip-top from head to toe.

I ended up in a house where the man was already retired; he had been the head bookkeeper of Arad's yeast factory, and his wife and his son also had a shop. I stayed there with them for three months. On the first day, when I got home from the shul, the wife said to me, Mr. Rosenberg, what will you do? I said, at the moment, I have no idea. She says, if you don't have anything better to do, my son has a shop—she explained where—go to him and see what there is. I went to the store and stood at the end of the counter; the son was waiting on customers, mostly Russians, and he couldn't talk to them. He knew English and French so well that he didn't need to translate the English or French newspapers, he could read them straight off in Hungarian. He said he was the only person in Arad who spoke Romanian well, better than the Romanians. But he didn't know Russian: I saw he wasn't getting anywhere and I interrupted, telling him to give this and that to the customer. And then the boss said to me, Mr. Rosenberg, please come and stand here behind the counter; you know how to talk to them better than we do. I stayed there.

Three or four weeks later, I went with him to Temesvár; he took me to a couple of factories where he used to shop for his goods, and he introduced me to everyone. Two weeks later, I was the one who went to do the shopping. The only unpleasant part of it was that if something cost, say, one shekel,[5] there would be ten shekels of tax on it, so what it came down to was that the one-shekel goods cost eleven shekels. If you could, everyone tried to save themselves the tax. I bought lace—it was a dry-goods store—and stockings and that kind of thing, so I would wrap myself around with fifty kinds of lace and save him a fortune. But if they catch you . . . if I saw even a slightly suspicious-looking man get on the streetcar, I would already be jumping off the other end. I stayed there with them for three months. After three months, I heard that it was now possible to go to Hungary as well, so the day after Purim I went back to Hungary.

There was a train that hauled lumber and I don't know what else. I managed to climb up on an open car, there were quite a few of us there. As we sat there, airplanes began to bomb the railroad line, so the journey was no honeymoon. Around me sat several old ladies; all of a sudden it seemed to me that a woman fell off. Later, somebody asked, was his sister there? I was sitting on the edge, so the wind wouldn't be as piercing. It was late at night, I couldn't see a thing, so I began to feel around and at last I said, she's not here. Ai-ai-ai, he started screaming there, and when the train stopped at a station, they got off to look for her, but, of course, the train didn't wait for them—we traveled on. When we reached Pest, it was Friday and there was no train, so we had to wait a couple of hours at Pest and then home to Vác. Of course we traveled well into Shabbat because the train went so slowly—it was winter and it was snowing—that it would have been faster to walk. And then we arrived home.

About eight or ten of us who came home were observant Jews. There were others there as well—they were Jews, yes, but they only held to some customs here and there; they hadn't been observant before either. Later, after that, my wife cooked for the JDC and one or two came there to eat, but the majority were scattered among the goyim.

Let me explain something about Neolog Jews: not long ago I read in a book that the rabbi from Dés was explaining how much it hurt him that a boy who had been his student in yeshivah went off to Pest to the

5. shekels: Rosenberg, who now lives in Israel, transposes Israeli currency to the Romanian town he is describing in his story.

rabbinical seminary. They said to him, now why does this bother you; an Orthodox congregation is not going to hire someone who completes the rabbinical seminary, and why do you care about the Neolog? The rabbi says, I'll tell you a story. In the first world war, after the Germans drove back the Russians, there was a place in Galícia where the dayan went out to check to see if the *eruv* was in place. I don't know if you know what that is: you have to fence around the city for it to be permissible to carry on the Sabbath. The dayan went out Friday afternoon, and he was caught by a German guard patrol *shefteling*[6] with some wires. He must be making a telephone line with which to spy for the Russians. They took him in to headquarters, where an officer questions him and the dayan explains that this is a religious regulation, you have to encircle the city with wire for it to be permissible to carry on the Sabbath. The officer says he's not going to swallow such a lame story, but he'll inquire into it right away, because they have a chief rabbi in the camp, a Neolog rabbi. He telephoned, the rabbi came, and the officer said to him, "Hey buddy, this man has come with some kind of a story that he has to wrap wire around the city." The rabbi says he's never heard anything so stupid. Five minutes later they shot the poor dayan. The rabbi from Dés says that what's so unfortunate about the Neolog, they don't know anything. That's why it bothers him that his student went to become a Neolog rabbi, because he'll tell people that something should be done this way or that, but he won't know anything, he won't have any idea how you are supposed to do things.

We put together a minyan and it lasted until '50, when the nationalization took place. One *shakter*, Áron Duved Glancz, came back, but we could only pay him with great difficulty. The little shul survived and the big one wasn't torn down either, but it was all broken up inside. There weren't windows, there wasn't a door, there wasn't anything. I led prayers, on High Holy Days, on Shabbat, on weekdays, any time; it was

6. *shefteling*: messing. The word means using intelligence to come up with a solution. The *eruv* had to be created in an ad hoc fashion from the structures already in place. The word *shefteling* can have the implication of doing something less than legal; the action here was not underhanded but was perceived as such.

me or someone else. The *shakter* asked us to hire him as a rabbi, because we paid him so little, and if a person was hired somewhere as a rabbi, the state would subsidize his salary. He asked us to hire him, but he had opposition: in the end he changed his mind and left for Szombathely, he was hired there. This was in '46, or maybe '47. Then it was arranged that someone would come from Pest once a week for slaughtering, and later he called himself the rabbi at Vác, but in the meantime no one in the world would hire him. Later we hired a *shokhet* named Roth who happened to be a *talmid hokhem,* he really knew how to learn, he died recently. I don't remember where we found him; all I remember is that when we called him I negotiated with him until midnight—you have to understand that by then there were three- and four-year-old children and we needed someone to concern himself with them. I said that I could only hire him if was willing to be involved with the children, teach them their *alef-beys,* but he didn't want to undertake this for all the world. Not everyone can work with children. I told him that there were ten of us all together and not everyone could afford to kill a chicken once a week, so it wasn't such a burning issue for us to have a *shakter.* You need a *shakter* so there will be someone to be involved with the children. With great difficulty I talked him into it; later the grown-up daughter of one of my pals who had completed *beyt yakov* school agreed to work with the children. We had a little nursery school with I-don't-know-how-many children, five or six, maybe more, because there were little girls there as well. I believe this girl was involved with them in the morning, and in the afternoon the *shakter* taught them their *alef-beys.*

A rabbi from near Miskolc, Elezer Weiser, made it his business to help Jews cross the border. They caught him and sentenced him to three years. In prison, he found himself in the same cell with a Jew who had come back to Hungary from Israel—they were together for three years, so he learned excellent Hebrew from him. He filled out his three years, but he wasn't allowed to go back to where he had been rabbi. He was forced by the state to relocate, either to Vác or to Tét. Well, he chose Vác, because his older brother lived there. On Friday towards evening he was brought to Vác, and he was with one of us for Shabbat; we had three *kheders,* one of which we gave him so he would have an apartment;

afterwards he also brought his family. By then there were more children, and he concerned himself with them as well. Later he left and became a rabbi in Vienna.

Unfortunately no one had such a *brayt parnose*. I had a store, and so did others, Yosi had a fabric dyeing business, and Benő a stationery store. I wasn't the president—we had a big need for a congregation president for ten people—Uncle Chaim was chosen; I led the *Khevrah Kadishah* and I was the treasurer, but we did everything together. Burials were not that frequent, *borukh hashem*, but they did happen: not far from Vác, someone was hit by a train and they brought him in for us to bury. There were weddings as well; we got married there too, in '46 and a few months earlier my brother married my wife's little sister.

This *shakter* Glancz had a pet habit, he was inclined to let people wait for him for an hour or two. If they told him the wedding was at one o'clock, he'd come at two thirty or three. When we got married, I said to him, pay attention, the wedding has been set for one o'clock. If you are here at one, then you give the *khupah-kidushin*. If you come one minute after one, then you don't. This was the only occasion that he was on time.

In '48, I got involved in an ugly story. There was a law in Hungary; I don't know if it is still in effect. If you come visit me and we talk away the time so it is too late for you to go home, you stay here, take the ring off your finger as you lie down, put it on the night stand and go to sleep. In the morning you grab your clothes but forget the ring on the table. The law says that if I don't report it at the police station within twenty-four hours, I have committed a crime. No one in the whole world knew about this law, including the lawyers. My little brother lived in Pest. Once someone climbed in his neighbor's window and stole a lot of money, so the insurance company notified my brother that they wouldn't underwrite his insurance until he put bars on his windows and locks on his doors and I don't know what else they required. It so happened that I went to Pest that day. My brother says he has some gold objects here that he doesn't want to keep here—I should take them to Vác and we'll bring them back later. Also, he had some gold coins that he had bought from a friend who was a jeweler. The jeweler got caught, and as they began his interrogation, of course he probably got smacked around a little, so he quickly related who he sold these gold coins to. I had a pants factory, a shop—well, I bought cloth, cut the pattern, and had the pieces sewn outside. That time too I happened to be in Pest, I went shopping with my brother; we come home and there are two detectives at his house asking who he is; he tells them, they say, yes, come with us. Who am I? I say I'm his brother. I should come with them too. They took us in to the district police station, interrogated us there and my brother says that he gave the gold things to me because he was afraid of a break-in. They put me in a car, took me out to Vác, I had two or three gold bracelets there and a big pile of gold coins that were mine, they returned that to me without a word, I have them to this day. The rest they took, and how much of it they pocketed only they could tell you. They took me back to Pest and the investigating judge arrested me. For a week or two I was there in the Markó and after that, for the most part, out in Buda, I don't know the name of that prison. Our lawyer stopped several other lawyers and asked them if they knew that such a law exists; there wasn't a single one who had heard of it. But it was a law nonetheless. I had kept gold and I had not reported it within twenty-four hours. One guy who was mixed up in it had gotten a letter from America the day they arrested him that contained one dollar. ONE dollar! He got an extra year for that, because he didn't, as soon as he got it, take it straight to the bank and quickly.

They had no case against me, I didn't do anything, I just kept my brother's valuables at my house, but they didn't want to acquit me, 'cause I could of sued 'em for keeping me locked up for no reason. At the trial, they began to read the sentences. I didn't know what order they were going in, but it looked like it was according to when they arrested us. The first one was L., who sold my brother the gold, the second was my brother, the third was me, and after that there were I-don't-know-how-many others. When the judge read that L. had gotten twelve years, everything in front of me went dark for a minute. Twelve years? How much would the sentence go down: to ten, to eight, to five, to three? That would still leave me with a couple of years! Then when he read on, that my brother got eight months, I said to myself, it's easier to come down from that. In the end I got two months. But the trial was two months after my arrest and they counted everything, so I could leave the next day.

In the morning a detective came and took me over to the police station, because it's only from there that they release prisoners; besides, I had a "Return Request": the police request the return of most convicts, and then they get to decide if the convict can be set free or not. But they let me out smoothly, there was no problem, I got into a taxi and had myself taken home, I paid when I got to my house. I stayed there in Pest for another three months and tried to arrange bringing my brother out of jail. I had a few good friends who held considerable positions; one was the executive director of a division at the Ministry of the Interior, so first I went to him. A second lieutenant stood in front of the door, I said that I'd like to speak to my friend—I don't want to mention his name, since he's probably still there—he said, someone's in with him, they're in conference, I should sit down outside. I sat for a while—meanwhile another friend of mine comes by who's a police officer and is even some kind of distant relation of mine and I talk to him for a while. Then the executive director was escorting out the person who was with him and sees that I am there. He comes over and says, hey, buddy, what are you doing here and I say I want to talk to him. Well, come on in. I go in to his office and there's a captain in there, but he says to him, captain, this is more important. He sends out the captain so he can talk to me—you can imagine what good friends we were. I say to him, I'd like some help from you. What's up? I explain to him that I'd like to bring out my brother. "Listen here, you know that I would do anything for you that could be done, but this is a financial matter, and I don't dare to start trouble with the financial police." Such an influential man says he's afraid of them. I say to him, I have another friend who's a high-ranking official, but I don't know where, find him for me. What's his name? I say such and so. He says, that's impossible, someone with a such a Jewish name can't be with the police. I say, that's what he's called and he's not going to change his name. He calls a number and says, comrade colonel, is it possible that we have, in the heart of the police department, someone with such a name? "There are police officers by the thousand, wait a minute, I'll get back to you right away."

We waited there for an extremely short time and he called back; yes, he's the president of the disciplinary tribunal, he's stationed at police headquarters. Thank you very much, I'll go see him. I went to police headquarters and I say, I want to talk to this man. They say this guy doesn't exist, you can't go in and see him. I say to the commanding officer, please, tell him I would like to talk to him. He called my friend, who asked to have me brought to him with a policeman as an escort. A policeman walked me to his room, I went in, well, hi there, how are you, what's new? I say to him, I would like to talk to you. There was a fellow sitting in his office, I don't know who he was, he says to him, "Go look in the next room, see if I'm there!" The fellow went out and I explain what I would like. "I'm reluctant to touch this." I say, a man doesn't always get to do what he would like to. "*Tov*, for your sake, I'll try," and he calls someone, probably the one in charge of this stuff, but he's not in, he's on vacation. I say, given the position you hold, you have more than one friend, more than one acquaintance. Whoever occupies such a position is above everyone, because he handled all the disciplinary matters for the entire police force. Well, for him district judges were like little boys. He tried with this one, he tried with that one, finally he sent me to somebody, but I couldn't get anywhere there either. "So, you see, I can't do anything!"

I tried to take care of things a different way. We hired a lawyer, we offered money, we paid here, we paid there, everyone said that he could take care of everything. At the end, each of them said this is a financial matter, nothing can be done.

I went back to that high-ranking friend of mine; I thought, since I knew that you couldn't just walk in on him, that I would catch up with him in front of police headquarters. I went after him and said I can't settle things any other way, I'm going to have to come back to you. He said, come back in, and then he looked at me—it happened to be *drayvokhn*, the three weeks when we don't shave, from Shavuot to Tisha b'Av. He says, are you going to come like this, do you imagine that they'll let you in? You know what, I'll wait 'til this holiday is over, and after that I'll come in. After Tisha b'Av, I went in to see him, but he was away on vacation. Where does he live? They finally told me. He lived outside of Pest—I went there and told him what the situation was and what I had tried already. He starts to write a letter and then all of a sudden I see he's tearing it up and throwing it away. He says, "Well, do you think I've lost my mind? How can I let such a letter out of my hands?! If somebody else reads this, I'll be sitting in prison right away." All the same, what can I do now? He says, "There's one more thing I can do for you. Go to the Ministry of Justice, go right up to the minister's personal secretary and tell him I sent you. And how will he know? I'll let him know that you are coming to him." The next morning, I went there with my sister-in-law, the office was full of people; well, I couldn't start talking about this business in a crowded office. Finally, we waited until they were mostly gone; most of them had left, except two or three, when I went up to him and said that Tibi had sent me. "Tibi? Who is Tibi?" He called you on the telephone. Oh, he said, yes, I know. What is this about? I explain it to him. Well, this doesn't belong here, I should go to such and such a district judge, and he'll talk to him for me. I went to the district judge; until now the matter was in his hands, but just that day it was moved higher up. Then I went to that guy, he sent me away with some story I don't even remember anymore; in the end, when I had gotten to the third judge, they phoned him while I was there that they were transferring him to another office. I say to him, listen here, until now you sat here, and this matter was in your hands. There's no rule such that if they told you five minutes ago that this is no longer any business of yours, then you have nothing to do with it. He turns it over this way and that, "You know what, I'll take care of it." He calls a number, "Gyuri, is that you? Please, that Rosenberg case that I handed over to you, take care of it." In one minute it was taken care of.

This story is even hard to tell, never mind to live through. But there were many Jews in the police. Jóska Szaberszky, the director of the ÁVÓ, was a good friend of mine. I didn't know Gábor Péter personally, but his assistant Miska Szabolcsi happened to be a lad from Salgótarján. The Jews there were so bad that, for example, a friend of mine was brought in and his friends, whose lives he had saved in the work camp, beat him like a horse. I knew a few of them, but never a religious one. Most of them were Communists and therefore a priori atheists, and they were full of their own crazy ideas.

But if someone got in there, it didn't even matter if he had been a *yeshivah bokher* before. One guy who was a major told the story, and he happened to be a *yeshivah bokher,* that they got hold of a letter; some Jew received a postcard and there were suspicious parts in it. The Jew lived in a village—they went out to him, and when they went in, he sees that there are Shabbat candles on the table. It didn't matter, he didn't come because it was Shabbat or it wasn't Shabbat, so he interrogated them and he saw that the whole thing was insignificant, there was nothing to the letter. When he went out, he wished them a good Shabbat; it was an older couple, and he could tell from looking at them that a great weight was lifted from their shoulders. He went out to the car, well of course the police had come out to a Jew, so all of the few Jews that lived in the village had come running and there was one who knew him and said accusingly, "What are you doing here?" He says, "What could I do, I jumped in the car and drove away." It didn't even occur to guys like him that it was or wasn't Shabbat.

By the time I got home from Pest, my partner had wrecked the business. Before the war, he was a very poor man; here and there I did him some favors, nothing interesting. After the war, when he wanted to be my partner, my friends warned me not to go into business with him. I said, in Auschwitz this man had already been put out in the yard because he was dying. He heard that my brother was there and he sent him a message. My brother had been assigned to work as a servant, and there was this shikse there with them who had been adopted by a Jewish woman. That girl always stole some food and gave it to my brother; when my brother had food, he gave it to this man. You know how it was, sometimes even one mouthful of food will help a person, so in the end he recovered his strength and even came home. I said, a man I did so many favors for is not going to cheat me. I was locked up for two months and for three months I attended to bringing my brother out, and during that time he *wirthshafted*, I don't know how. I called him to *din Torah*,[7] he didn't come, it doesn't matter.

I was left with nothing; a relative of my wife's had a leather store, so I went to work for him. A friend of mine had called me earlier; I went over to him and ran just about the whole business because he worked in Pest four or five days a week. A lot of things came in there to him—how do I know—somewhere, a lot of paper got spoiled, it was torn, and he bought it

7. *din Torah*: (Heb.) A judgment of the rabbinical court, or *bet din*.

and brought it home. I took it to a printer and had it cut into business-size paper and packaged it nicely into stacks of 250 so you could make some money from it. But while he made these deals and tracked them down, he had to spend four or five days in Pest. He was always at home on Friday, otherwise I was alone practically the whole week, unless his wife had time, then she came and helped me in the store. This is how it was until the nationalization. Then we really took a bath.

First the bigger businesses were nationalized. But it was done in such a brutal, mean way! For example, I happened to become acquainted with a Jew, he came out to Vác, he was some kind of unskilled laborer there; I was chatting with him and he told me that he had had two cable factories in Pest. One day he went into the plant to take care of business, and for some reason took his wallet out of his pocket and put it in a drawer of his desk. The next morning when he went in to work, the porter didn't open the door to him, the business had been nationalized, he had no right to go in. He tried to get in his car, sorry, the car belonged to the business. He asked to be allowed in, his wallet had been left on his desk. The porter said whatever had been left in the office had been nationalized. "What could I do, I walked home because I didn't even have enough money for the trolley. When I got home, my wife was sitting on a chair in the hallway, and I say, 'Why are you sitting in the hallway?' We had also been turned out of our apartment, because the apartment was nationalized. I, who had owned two factories, was left without a penny, a piece of bread, a change of underwear, without everything." Somewhere he managed to get some food for a few days from friends, so they survived. And after that, he told me, his brother sent him clothes and some money. When I knew him, he wasn't destitute anymore, but his livelihood had been taken away.

The business was taken away, I don't even know what became of the stores. For seven years after the nationalization, I went in to Pest to work. I had to leave at daybreak, we went to morning prayer in town, and on to work from there. It was a regular Jewish life—maybe the shuls weren't full, but there were large minyans, not like in the country. If I was in Pest, I prayed in the Vasvári. I won't say I never went to the Kazinczy, but I didn't go there often; once or twice, I also went to the József, and the Visegrádi and the Bethlen. Once I was there in the shul and I see an older man—the *gabe* or the shul attendant asked him, "Well, why weren't you here last time, you usually come to shul on the Sabbath." He responded, "You know very well, if I come to shul, I usually *shnoder* a lot of money. Since they nationalized, I can't even *shnoder* a korona.[8] I thought I'd rather not come to shul, so I wouldn't have to *shnoder*." There were guys like that, filthy rich men, and from one day to the next they didn't have a *krajcár* to buy a piece of bread.

If they knocked on someone's door in the middle of the night, those people were finished. My first wife had a cousin who lived in Tátra Street, they were in the fabric dyeing business, well-to-do people; for months she didn't dare to undress at night, she sat in the window and lay in wait for when they would come to move her out.

Well, we were left from one day to the next without any livelihood. My boss lay around at home for a while until they took over his business. Another friend and I went to look for work. The Neolog were just starting a matzah bakery in Vezér Street,[9] and they hired us there. I worked for a few weeks. I happen to be an expert in this too, because in 1913 my late father was persuaded to start a matzah factory, but the business had hardly gotten underway when he enlisted in the army in '14 and he only came home in '19. Kohlmann, my father-in-law, on the other hand, had a big bakery; Vác supplied the whole country with matzah. This wasn't the first time I was in a matzah factory, I could see they were baking complete *khamets*. For this, you need to understand that after eighteen minutes, the dough begins to rise. Every eighteen minutes, you have to shut down every machine for cleaning. Here they shut them down once an hour. I wanted to talk to the head rabbi. The head *mashgiakh* said to leave it to him, he'll take care of it, and then after that he tried to talk me into becoming a *mashgiakh*, he saw that I understood these things. I wouldn't have to work, I just walk around, for double the pay. There isn't enough money in the world to get me to be a *mashgiakh* here! To sell Jews *khamets* for *Pesakh*?!

8. korona, krajcár, pengő: Rosenberg mixes up the type of money spoken of.

9. Vezér Street: Rosenberg's memory seems to be faulty here. The Neolog bakery is on Tüzér Street (map 2 A2).

I wanted to transfer over to the Orthodox matzah bakery on Kazinczy Street, but a cousin of my wife's was the manager here for the Neolog and he wouldn't let me transfer. Wouldn't let me! We were not on good terms.

I don't remember what the cantor's name was, he was once a rabbi, he studied at Pozsony, he was trained by the rabbi from Erló, but after the war he didn't want to be a rabbi, so he joined the Vezér Street shul as a cantor. We were on very good terms, and I told him that I would like to transfer to Kazinczy Street but the manager won't let me. He didn't say anything, only I see that after morning prayer, he goes into the office and looks for the manager. What he said to him, I don't know, but the manager, when he came out of the office, didn't dare to stop and talk to me; he just said as he went by me that the rabbi had arranged for me to transfer to Kazinczy Street. There I was a *mashgiakh*, or rather the head *mashgiakh*'s assistant; there were six *mashgiakhs* and I supervised them. Unfortunately, six *mashgiakhs* were not enough, not because we needed so much matzah, but they had so little expertise. There also I had a lot of *tsores*, because the machine got gummed up. Amram Jungreisz was the *rosh bet din*[10] then, and he said the machines need to be cleaned every sixteen minutes. Sixteen minutes is fine with me, I have the time. There was a big fuss about it, the foreman came over to me, that every machine was gummed up. None of them knew how to clean them, I had to do it, a salary violation; I don't know if you're familiar with these Communist whatchamacallits; they took off my head. The foreman said to me, listen here, don't you need a salary? I said, if I get one shekel, or whatever, one *pengő* less, I notice the lack of that pengő. But to do something against my convictions, that I am not ready for. *Tov*, then he will talk with the chief rabbi. Let him talk! The next day, of course, I proceeded in the same way and the foreman says, didn't the chief rabbi tell you not to be so strict about things? I say, the chief rabbi didn't speak to me, but I can tell you right now that, when the chief rabbi tells me not to take the work seriously, right that minute, I am not even here anymore. There were eternal battles arising from this. The manager would already be shouting down the steps, "Rosenberg, to the

10. *rosh bet din*: Head of the rabbinical court, which must be consulted for ritual matters.

office!" and then he would lecture me . . . They assigned me to the yard, hauling this and that here and there, when they needed some raw material. For two or three days I worked in the yard.

I transferred to the Construction Materials Company as a central-heating repairman. They had already declared that this would be a company where you could keep the Sabbath. There was a machine wholesaler they had nationalized and a mechanical engineer, and these two agreed that they would start a cooperative for those wanting to keep the Sabbath. In the end, they didn't succeed at establishing it, but they arranged for six of us, we had ministerial authorization that we didn't have to work on the Sabbath. I couldn't be there until four o'clock Friday, because if we were out working in Kőbánya, then I had to travel an hour to get to Pest and another hour to Vác and I had to get home by at least three, so I already had to leave work by noon. You explain to a goy that Saturday starts on Friday afternoon. They couldn't understand it and my supervisor said that I was the best worker among all the workers, but it all went for nothing, since I leave my work behind and he has to finish it. I had a lot of *tsores* from this. People tried to lure me a hundred different ways with better conditions, more money, but I didn't dare to leave because of the Sabbath.

I had an acquaintance, a goy, the director of some vegetable warehouse. I should come to his warehouse. He said I wouldn't have to work on Saturday, there would be two directors, the other one would rather be home on Sunday than Saturday; I work Sunday, he works Saturday. I say to him, that's fine, but what do I do if they order an inventory on Thursday? An inventory takes four or five days, and that runs into Saturday. What do I do then? So I didn't dare to make a move. I stayed here until the last day, until I came away: until January '57.

In '56, when the revolution was, then they began to persecute Jews very much. Before that, not so much . . . look, there were always anti-Semites. If I sat down in a bar, because you know how it is, these workers, they are always drinking, they can't be without that; oops, here's a bar, let's go in! Then we had to go in and sometimes I'd drink four or five glasses of beer; I didn't want a sixth one, and I hadn't needed the five, either. But with goyim you have to drink, and you know, right that minute, as soon as a goy starts to drink, it's not possible for him not to start in on Jews.

There's no such guy. And then they'd notice that I was sitting there with them; "you know, good buddy, we don't mean you, after all, you're with us, you're one of us, we mean the rich Jews." Would they had rotted right there, where they were.

Since summer, I had been working at headquarters: when the mechanics went away on vacation, the director of the main warehouse said, they're on vacation for a week, in the meanwhile I should go in the warehouse. I went in the warehouse and saw that they were robbing this man blind. You know, in the construction business, they had everything, pipes, and toilets and all, and the mechanics were making off with all these things. In a week there, I fixed things so that nobody could steal anything, and by the time the week was over and I wanted to go back to my work, the president, who was an ÁVÓ captain at that time, went in to the director of the warehouse and said, "If you take Fritzi out of the warehouse, then I'm leaving too. I won't stay without him. Until now they stole everything of mine, now everything stays put." So I had to stay there in the warehouse.

One day I telephoned one of my relatives that we hadn't seen each other in a long time—I would like to talk with him. He was a friend of Rajk;[11] I don't know what he did, because when I asked him once, he said, "I'm not the one who sweeps the steps." If I called him, someone else always picked up the receiver and if I asked who is speaking, he said he was the office manager. This time too the office manager gave him the telephone. He said, "Listen here, I'd like to talk to you too, you know what, I'm done with work at four, you finish around four too, come here and let's go out to your place in Vác. I'll sleep at your place and at least for once we'll get ourselves all talked out in due course." One o'clock, one thirty, what do I know what time it was, and then I hear the din outside. I ran out. What's going on? Revolution. Well, never mind, we stayed a while longer; I say to the boss, look here, I think we've had enough of this, I'll close up the store, let's go home. I closed the warehouse and I went there, where my relative was waiting for me, not far from Kálmán Imre Street, the third side street, perhaps. I go there, and wow, the house has been demolished down to

11. Rajk: László Rajk, minister of the interior from 1946 to 1948.

the ground. I don't know what kind of office was there. I never succeeded at finding him anymore. I traveled home. When I reached home it was late at night, even the train crawled along. The next morning I went back to work, the train went as far as Rákosrendező or something like that, I am not remembering. It stopped a couple of miles before Pest, and I had the good sense to pad along on foot to Pest. I went to the shul to pray, my tefillin was there, I kept it right in the shul. I said my prayers, found a friend of mine there who lived in Pest, we went to their place and we didn't try too hard to go out, because there were snot-nosed kids running around in the streets, shooting up and down. Later we went out anyway and went to Vilmos Császár Road—what do they call it now? Bajcsy-Zsilinszky Road—and we saw some sort of a gathering, a bakery, bread, that's what we came for, to buy bread. We stood there for a while, and about two dozen army vehicles came out of one of the side streets, each with an automatic weapon with a soldier behind it, and as they go along the street, they are firing. We hid behind a doorway, and when they had passed by in good order, then we went home too. In late afternoon, I nevertheless went out to the Nyugati train station. They said that in not too long there would be a train to Vác. I boarded the train and waited one hour, or two hours, what do I know how long; they were shooting right and left, firing from the roof of the station, and from the streets. Then somebody crawled on his belly forward all the way to the engine and told the engineer to start. He started the train, and as we got underway—we hadn't even gone maybe ten meters yet—they began to shoot at the train from both sides. We hit the ground; he had the good sense not to stop, so we got nicely out of the line of fire and after that I managed to travel home. But what a ride it was: on an express train, Pest-Vác is a half hour, it doesn't stop, except at Újpest and Göd; on other trains it's forty or fifty minutes. It took five or six hours before we got home! But I got home. Then I didn't go in for a day or two. I went around to all the stores: there was nothing available, but all the storekeepers in Vác were my customers while I was in the paper business, and I was on very good terms with them all. There wasn't a store where I wouldn't get something, and there were some where they let me in the back door, bypassing the line. In one day, while I was home, I don't know, I gathered up more than forty pounds of sugar. And also flour, and I don't know what else, that you couldn't get. Then two days passed, and it was already possible to go to Pest.

It's not true that the Russians left,[12] they were there all along. They set up an automatic weapon by the Margit Bridge and the story was that in one day they shot twelve thousand people to death. They were even firing behind the Parliament. I had a friend here in *Erets* who was a veterinarian, I think he was a captain in the Russian army, and he used to say that they didn't care about anything, wherever they went, they started the machine gun, whoever it shot, it shot, it didn't matter. A good friend of ours from Vác was in Pest; he looked out the window from the fourth floor or somewhere, and just that minute, they shot him. I didn't see it, but there was a story that someone threw a plate down when a Russian tank went past a six-story house. They thought that it was a bomb thrown down, so they turned the tank around to face the house and they kept shooting until there wasn't one brick on top of another. For another two or three days, we didn't go in to Pest. When I went in next, here and there on Andrássy Road there was an undamaged house, and out there where that Kárpáti or whatever they called that general who was a resistance fighter in the revolution, the one who led the rebellion in some barracks—not Maléter, there was also another guy—well, anyway, on Üllői Road, in that section where these guys barricaded themselves, there wasn't one undamaged house.

One friend of mine, the poor guy died already in Canada, did a stupid thing in Vác—I was never up for such things—"It's the revolution!" and he pinned on a red, white, and green rosette.[13] As he went out in the street, a couple of goyim caught him; "What's this, are you a Hungarian now too?" and they beat him up pretty thoroughly. There was a lot of anti-Semitism there too; in fact the anti-Semitism was so great that a friend of mine said, let's buy weapons, so we can defend ourselves. I went

12. the Russians left: Official histories reported the Soviets retreating from the city for several days.

13. red, white, and green rosette: This patriotic and national symbol originated in Hungary's 1848 Revolution against Austrian rule.

in to the city hall and got a revolver; I went home, but my wife said that I couldn't come in with it, because she wouldn't stay in the same house with me. So I took it back.

Everyone went away. We were among the last, because we left with passports. I requested one, and I got it. We left the day we got our passports. January 17.

The *Sokhnut* had a law that you couldn't travel towards Vienna, but only through Yugoslavia, because many who went towards Vienna stayed there and went to America from there. But through Yugoslavia you could only come here—by train to Milan and from there by boat. My wife's mother is buried in Vienna and she hadn't been on *kever avot* for twenty years. Let's try to go that way! We went with my sister-in-law to the Austrian embassy; there were a lot of people there, we got in line too. In the doorway stood a gray-haired gentleman, he asks what we want and I tell him, we want to go to *Erets* through Vienna— we'd like a visa. Fine, we should come in. Inside I go to a woman and say, I'd like a visa—they have orders not to give visas. "I don't know, a gentleman is standing in the door outside and he said we should come here." "Who is he?" "I don't know who he is." The woman goes out to look and comes back and says, the ambassador is the gentleman standing out in the doorway. Well, if he says so, then there is no problem. The next day we took our belongings through customs, we arrived in Vienna on Thursday night, I believe; we went to the Continental—everybody went there—and we slept there. The next morning I go to the *Sokhnut* to notify them that we are here, I show them my passport; they won't take us. And what is more, they immediately called the Continental that we can't stay there, they should put us out. For a week, anyone who had arms or legs that worked, who had any influence, who had anything to say about Jewish matters in Vienna, they all ran around in my behalf. No matter what I did it was all in vain; the president of the *Mizrakhi* went to the *Sokhnut* on my behalf, the president of *Agudah* went, all in vain. When I told the story in the shul that I want to come to *Erets* and I can't, at first everyone laughed in my face. "You're coming with such a lame story, that they won't take you out? They're standing in the streets with lassos to catch people and bring them out!" but us they wouldn't take for all the world. I had to go to a hotel, Vienna in those days was full of Hungarian refugees, I had to ask for money from my friends, so I could pay.

I didn't know anymore what we should do. We were with three tiny children. My bad luck was that I didn't know that the leader of the Vienna *Sokhnut* was a friend of my brother's. If I had known this and called my brother that we are here and they don't want to bring us out, he would have sent a private flight for us. But did I know who his friends here were? Thursday or Friday I went in again to the *Sokhnut*, and I find a friend of my brother's there; he worked there in the embassy, but somehow I didn't notice him before. He called Paris, because our highest authorities were in Paris, and he got permission from there to send us out here. I got some money from him and he arranged that we should go by train to Milan and from there we came here.

Just the day we arrived, it snowed in Jerusalem, you couldn't make a move out of the city, then when you could get out, my brother came for us and took us there. We looked around and got an apartment near Naharya, in Trumpeldor. I talked to people there and they all told me it wasn't my kind of place, I wasn't even going to be able to find a minyan. A religious man who came there with us and got an apartment on the same floor was gone in a couple of days, so there weren't religious Jews there, and they didn't even come there. Then my brother said, we live in Jerusalem, you live in Trumpeldor, we work all week, and we're busy, we don't travel on Shabbat, we're never going to see each other. It would be better if you came to Jerusalem. We gave back the apartment, I got some kind of loan and some money from my brother as well, and we bought a crummy old place at the end of Meah Shearim, twenty yards from the Jordan border.

For twenty-seven years I worked in the same plant—we made must, soda water, essences, and syrups. I went there as a laborer, and in a few weeks, I was already the one who repaired the electricity and worked on the machines. I threw the water mechanic out because he didn't understand anything. It was a pile of ruins, that's the truth, and every week each repairman had to come to adjust something so we could work. There was a Romanian manager who wouldn't even change a fuse, if a fuse blew out, he went into the office; a repairman should be called because there was no power. An electrician was called—either one was sent, or he wasn't, we waited an hour or two, during which we sat there. This is not the goal, to sit here for nothing; the next time, I went over and put in a piece of wire and then we worked on. The machine broke down, again we had to wait three or four hours, a repairman came out and adjusted something on it. I say, I know how to give that machine a poke too; you don't have to come here for this. Next time I poked it and it started up. When two months had passed they didn't call anyone anymore; by then I did everything myself. The furnace was ruined, they bought a new one, and I connected up the water, steam, and electricity: anything you want. I worked there for twenty-seven years. As for pay, they didn't pay well there either. It could be it was my fault.

We must have been in the country a few weeks—I was waiting for a bus at the *shuk* when a Jew with a long white beard stands in front of me and asks if I remember him. I don't know where I would remember him from, he doesn't seem familiar, he says he learned at the yeshivah in Salgótarján and, for a year and a half, he ate with us on Shabbat. Then he was a young child, and now he stands in front of me as a gray-haired man—well, how could I recognize him? Later this man was Shaye Kereszturer's[14] *shames* in Bodrogkeresztúr; unfortunately, he died a few years ago; I have a little book here which he published about the rebbe. He stands next to me and says, when I look at you, I can tell you are a new *oleh*. Do you already have work? I say I have. Who do you work for? I say I don't know what they call him, I only know about him that he is a *Szatmár Hasid*, a religious Jew, the man I work for. He says to me that I should leave this man immediately and go somewhere else; it's not worth it to work for a religious Jew. Said a bearded Jew to me. The *shames* of Shaye Keresztурer. If only I had listened to him, if I listened to him, I'd be a millionaire today. Not that I want to complain to you; thank heavens, we don't lack for anything. *Borukh hashem*!

14. Shaye Keresztурer: Yeshaya Steiner, rabbi of Bodrogkeresztúr (Shaye, short for Yeshaya).

Once There Was a Yeshivah in Pest[1]

My forefathers were great personages learned in Judaism. My great-grandfather's cousin, Mordekhai Benedikt, was the chief rabbi of Moravia seven generations ago; his residence was in Nikolsburg. One of my uncles, whose name was Mark Benedikt, was chief rabbi of Szombathely. People had a lot of respect for him too, but he unfortunately developed throat cancer and could hardly talk. He preached only to small groups, at weddings or congregational meetings, but he did perform his other tasks as a rabbi; he was respected because he was very strict in religious matters. He must have been around ninety years old when he was deported to Auschwitz.

—What was your father's occupation?

—He was a businessman, a textile merchant. He was born in Aranyosmarót, in Bars county. He came to Pest when he was three or four years old, and when he married, or even earlier, he opened a textile store at 13 Murányi Street. For a while, we lived in 45 Garay Street, later we moved to Aréna Road. When the Germans came in, they took away the apartment, and my parents never got it back, not even after the war. After four years in public school, I went to rabbinical school, not so that I would later function as a rabbi, but to become familiar with the Jewish faith. That was the custom with us in our circle. My grandparents on my mother's side lived in Eperjes, and since my parents didn't want me to be alone in a strange place, I went there to live. The next year I went over to Galánta,

1. Once There Was a Yeshivah in Pest: This chapter is written in a "mosaic" style that brings together short segments from interviews with several people. The names of the speakers follow each interview excerpt.

I stayed there for about six years. Once I came home for a while, because my poor father needed an operation, and I had to fill in for him in the store during it. I did the bookkeeping, I worked behind the counter, I did everything. It wasn't my goal to become a rabbi, but when the Germans took away the store—they came in in March '44, and by April they had already issued an order for us to close—I didn't have anything else to do. There was a shul in 48 Garay Street, I began to function as a rabbi there. Before the war, it was a well-attended place; on the High Holy Days the people didn't all fit, they stood out in the yard. After the war, many people didn't come back, they went abroad. It functioned at least until 1968, while I was there, and even a few years after that. There were hardly ten members, but in '73, when my mother died and I was in Pest for the funeral, fifteen or twenty gathered in the shul. After that, people didn't come anymore, the congregation had to disband and sell the building to some organization.

They took me away for forced-labor service, at the end I was liberated in Kópháza, near Sopron. I returned home to Pest on foot. My parents survived the dangers of Arrow Cross rule in the starred house[2] on Abonyi Street. In the meantime, the Russians unlocked our fabric store; maybe they weren't even the ones who robbed it, but the mob; the opportunity was there, so they took the whole thing apart. When I got home, all I found was twelve meters of canvas, and the only reason it remained was that they didn't notice it. My father reopened the store, but in '52 it was nationalized and closed, along with the house next to it, which also belonged to the family—since then it's been torn down.

Officially, there was freedom of religion, but our every move was restricted. Many of the Orthodox rabbis left. In '44 there were rabbis who left their congregations, and there were others who stayed with their congregations, even though they had the opportunity to flee. It was the same way in the fifties as well, not everyone wanted to leave Hungary, a few rabbis sacrificed themselves and stayed here. Others, however, didn't

2. starred house: Jews in Budapest were forcibly removed from their own homes and resettled throughout the city in "yellow-starred houses," where they were forced to live several families to an apartment.

want to remain in a Communist country. Whether this was due to cowardice or not due to cowardice doesn't matter. They saw that they couldn't maintain a religious life given the direction things were going. There were those who left because they didn't want their children to be raised in this mentality.

It happened that someone drew a swastika or a Soviet star on a Jewish store, but I don't know of worse atrocities. That wasn't the problem; the problem was that the system didn't make a Jewish way of life possible. Maintaining a religious life was very difficult, for example, making matzah and obtaining prayer books, bringing in *lulav* on the Feast of Tabernacles. This was sent in from abroad to Síp Street, and distributed very carefully, because propagating it wasn't permitted. Often you didn't know what was permitted and what wasn't. In those days you could get into trouble if you had more than a kilo of flour! It was very hard and in '56, when the Russians defeated the uprising, no one knew what would be the continuation. And when they opened the gates, whoever could, left.

Rabbi Sándor Benedikt

My father was enlisted in forced-labor service in '43—he was taken prisoner of war and only returned in 1948, almost among the very last. They deported my mother, and I was then altogether two and a half to three years old, so I know these things only from hearing about them; they took me to an orphanage, just to do something about me. When my mother came home, she spent a good two months looking for me, going from street to street until finally she found me in Buda, in Kapás Street. We lived with an acquaintance until my father returned. I don't have many memories. What I remember is that after the liberation, I went right away to the congregation's kindergarten; I remember Klauzál Square and that after my late father returned from prison, he was in uniform, and he bought me ice cream. That was when we moved to our apartment in Dob Street. I lived right there in the middle of the ghetto. Opposite us was Papper's grocery store, in the next house was Weisz's Sweet Shop, on the corner of Holló Street was the Jewish dish store. In the school on Kazinczy Street, a third of the children were Jewish, so in the upper grades we didn't even have to go in on the Sabbath. In '54 or '55, things were a little harder, then you had to go into school, but it could be arranged that we didn't have to write anything.

My father kept the Sabbath before the war; after the war he took his vacation during the High Holy Days, but he had to work on the Sabbath, otherwise he couldn't get a job and we had to have something to live from. Ever since I was a small child, I was the one in the family who went in a more religious direction; I was the one who made kiddush on Friday night, and I went for the wine, I went for the *barkhes* because my parents didn't have the time. I prayed in the Kazinczy; in those days it was full on the High Holy Days and three-quarters full every Sabbath. The Talmud-Torah was pretty well attended; I went there to learn, as there was a day-care part—I studied at Slomo Groszberg's[3]—we had two, three hours of religious studies, after which we did our homework. To spend our free time somehow, we played football in the yard a little, and there was ping-pong; we went home around six, seven o'clock. After I completed eighth grade, I wanted to study further, and I even enrolled in a vocational school, but I had some trouble there. The High Holy Days fell at the beginning of September, so I didn't go to school, and they said things behind my back, like "The *Yid*'s[4] turn to answer," so the mood was such that I switched over to a Sabbath-keeping company: I worked in the Small Vehicle Cooperative, on the corner of Csanády and Visegrádi Streets, studying to be a tool mechanic.

In '56, a few of my friends came over to our house and said we should leave, this was in the air then. There was no special plan, we just picked ourselves up, like everyone else; I didn't even take anything with me, I just went wearing what I had on, a loden coat; the others were a little better prepared. We set out one day, on foot, and with a little hitch-hiking, we got to Piliscsaba. We slept at some sort of workers' home that night; the next day one of my friends said that his stepfather was going to think he ran away because he wasn't good to him. Let's go home! My mother and father didn't know anything, they were very frightened; I promised that

3. Slomo Groszberg's: For Ervin Groszberg's narrative, see p. 46.

4. *Yid*: Slang designation for a Jewish person, often derogatory.

I wouldn't go away again. A few days passed, friends came saying that I should go with them, since I already knew the way from having set out once. There were three of us, one was a *yeshivah bokher* from Paks—him I only knew by sight, another was one of my friends, I hung out with his little brother. They talked me into it, and I went. This time, our trip was more successful. We didn't want to go towards Győr. At one point we swam across the Rába, this was pretty unpleasant in November, but my friend took off his clothes, jumped in and swam across, so I only met up with him in Austria. A tree trunk was lying down in the water; we stripped down to our underpants, tied our coats around our necks, and went across on it. The Austrian border was near, and they lit it from far away with a fire; it was cold, and there was snow, it was November 18. I've had a little rheumatism ever since. We warmed ourselves by the fire; they gave us a little to drink, and took us to the collection camp; we weren't there more than an hour or two before they came for us from Vienna, the people from the JDC.[5] They were looking for people who looked like Jews. They didn't spot me, but they did find my friend from Paks and asked him, who did he know here who wants to go to Israel. They took seven or eight guys away in their car; we were placed in one hotel, and the guy from Paks who wanted to go to America in another. The next day the JDC took us to a department store and bought us a change of clothes, a suit, a shirt, shoes, a raincoat; they took care of the ticket, I came to Israel.

I had two cousins out here, the letters that came from them weren't very encouraging, the atmosphere here wasn't very good either. The others I defected with all went to America, I was the only one who came to Israel. Except for the '56 revolution, it would have never entered my mind to emigrate, but I thought if I'm leaving because of my Jewishness, then I'm not going to America. The big immigration Aliyah was in '54. In '56 I was the first young child who arrived in Israel, there was even a story about me in the Hungarian newspaper here. The Jewish Agency had a

5. JDC: Acronym for the Joint Distribution Committee; it provided funds for those who wished to emigrate.

child-distribution establishment, a central gathering camp where the new *olim* came in. A distant relative of mine read the newspaper article, came there and took me to the yeshivah in Kfar Haroeh, where the cook was Mrs. Bauer, the daughter of Mr. Niszel, the restaurant owner. There were four or five among the children who spoke Hungarian. Mostly, though, they were *sabras*. At first it was hard to make myself understood, I had to learn Hebrew. I would have liked to stay here. In '57 more people came, acquaintances, friends, I met former classmates. My parents asked for emigration papers two or three times, but they were turned down. The reason I went back to Hungary after a year was that I was a minor, fifteen years old, and my mother wrote me a letter saying that she had found me once and now I had left her again. This spoke to my heart a little and I saw that I had to go. Besides, the director of the yeshivah told me that the Foreign Office had telephoned, the Hungarian embassy was threatening them with cutting off diplomatic relations because they were detaining a minor. He said he didn't want there to be complications because of me, I'd come back later.

—When you reached home, did the Hungarian newspapers interview you?

—No. Once, they called me in to the Ministry of the Interior and interrogated me, did I know who gave me the money for the trip back? They wanted to persuade me that it came from the CIA, but I said, no, it was from the JDC. I told them the story of how I emigrated, and after that I never heard any more from them.

I went back to the Small Vehicle Cooperative, but about a year later, something happened to my back and the doctor recommended that I leave this profession because the continual standing, sawing, and rasping wasn't doing me any good, and that's how I came to the congregation as an employee. They didn't pay very well, I got 800 forints. Bernat Moskovits, the director of the yeshivah at Paks, was the rabbi, and every night I went to his house to learn. There was something like a friendship between us, he had no children, at their house I was almost like the child. People came to ask about different things, but that was learning as well, because I sat there next to him, and he told me what it was all about; usually they spoke

Yiddish, and I didn't understand Yiddish. Or if there was something with poultry, was it kosher or not, he explained that this was good for this reason, that wasn't good for that reason. And we learned as well, I was with him every night from seven o'clock until nine. If he had to go somewhere, I was always the one he asked to accompany him—he didn't much like to go out alone at night.

—Did he want you to make something of yourself?

—I don't know: I was only fifteen years old then. In '58 I was the only young child there. There were some a few years younger, but my age group was very rare: Feri Raj, Tomi Raj, Imre Mózes were a little older than I.

Miklós Braun

From some villages all the children left, and the teachers remained, at least for a while, while in other places it was the opposite: the teachers all left, and the children remained. Mór Paskusz, then president of the Orthodox Division in Budapest, tried to place these children in a boarding school in Pest.

Sándor Benedikt

Social and Religious Life in the Orthodox Division

Parents and visitors took part in an edifying spectacle at the Orthodox Division's Mount Szabadság children's camp, where 200 children completed their summer sojourn on August 26 with due solemnity. The children, healthy, rosy-cheeked, visibly strengthened in body and spirit, bid good-bye to each other and their instructors, with plans to return to this blessed institution again in a year's time. The holiday program was organized into two groups: the girls' group of 100 in the month of July, and the boys' group in August, for four weeks each. Their provisioning consisted of five meals a day, with food provided by the Hanna kitchen especially equipped for this purpose by the Division.

During their holiday, the little people, the heirs of Hungarian Jewry's future, could gain mastery of much that is virtuous, beautiful, and good by following the example set for them by their instructors.

Új Élet, September 1, 1958

"I'm Going to Be a Real, Good, Decent Jewish Child"

MIOK's[6] daily mail consists of hundreds and hundreds of letters. Most contain requests or official matters. That's why those who encountered these letters in the daily mail looked up with shining faces . . .

György Szegfű,[7] a schoolchild from Miskolc, begins his letter thus:

> "Dear Mr. Editor,
>
> Please be so kind as to convey my warmest heartfelt thanks to those gentlemen who made possible my 14-day holiday in Fonyód. I promise that I will not be ungrateful for it—I'm going to be a real, good, decent Jewish child. I am going to spend every little bit of spare time I have studying the Talmud, because I am proud to declare that I am a Jew.
>
> With my hard work at studying, I want to become a public-spirited contributor to society. I am enclosing 50 forints for the noble cause which the Board turns over to the support of old people and the sick, and I promise to put together my pocket money and send it to your address. I ask the good Lord to grant you gentlemen long life to the greatest degree available to human beings. And I ask many blessings for your work. With deepest respect, György Szegfű."
>
> *Új Élet*, September 1, 1958

Miklós Rubinstein from the village of Kótaj writes in a page from an exercise book:

> "I consider it my duty, upon returning home, to give thanks for all the good and beautiful things which were bestowed upon me in my summer holiday in Fonyódliget. First I want to thank Mr. Gyuri, Mr. Laci, and Mr. Tibi, for being so good to us during our two-week holiday, and for taking care of us. My greatest happiness was that Mr. Laci taught us the prayers, which I can't take part in at home, because I am the only

6. MIOK: Magyar Izraeliták Országos Képviselete (National Representation of Hungarian Israelites). This body was founded in 1950 as the agency to administer all Jewish affairs, Neolog, and Orthodox.

7. György Szegfű: For another description of this student, see below, p. 123.

Jewish child in the village. And I want to thank Miss Rózsi and Miss Ilonka for all the delicious food they cooked for us. With deepest respect, Miklós Rubinstein."

Új Élet, September 1, 1958

NEWS FROM HUNGARY. YESHIVAH BEING ESTABLISHED IN PEST. (TAS) The Orthodox congregation in Budapest has decided to establish a yeshivah in the capital city—as came to light from a private letter sent to London by Mór Paskusz, the president of the Orthodox congregation.

The head of the yeshivah is to be Rabbi Baruch Moskovits,[8] the former head of the yeshivah at Paks.

The students of the yeshivah at Paks—as is well-known—left Hungary in the autumn of the revolution and some of them are now settled in *Erets Yisrael*.

Orthodox Zsidó Élet, Jerusalem, 5718 (1958) Ijjar 9

Work is proceeding busily in the building of the Division's boarding Talmud-Torah, which will start to function in September. The home is being built in the Division's headquarters at 35 Dob Street and will consist of two spacious bedrooms, a dining room, a medical center, the customary amenities, and the custodian's quarters. Sixteen students from the countryside who have outstanding academic records will win places with full board. Application for admission is now largely closed, although the selection process has not yet taken place, so if the institution has escaped the notice of anyone, they should make haste to apply by August 31st. Those concerned will receive separate notification by letter of the day of opening.

Új Élet, September 1, 1958

—Why didn't Rabbi Moskovits remain in Hungary?

—I don't know. He emigrated to Vienna, and his former students brought him out to America. Moyshe Weisz also wanted to emigrate and

8. Rabbi Baruch Moskovits: Above, Miklós Braun calls him Bernat Moskovits. Here *Orthodox Zsidó Élet* calls him by his Hebrew name.

they kept him at home by electing him chief rabbi in '65. I used to go up to visit him as well, and we talked, but more rarely. We corresponded for a long time; he always wrote as if he were writing to a good friend.

—Was he worthy of becoming chief rabbi of Budapest?

—In my opinion, he was worthy, and besides, there wasn't anybody else, as the whole Budapest *kile* was made up of seventy-eighty-year-old men, with only one or two forty-year-old young ones, so we didn't need anybody greater as chief rabbi. The secretary, Dr. Sebestyén, wanted to bring him up from Miskolc. I believe they did pretty well with him, because, the way I heard it, the *bet din*, the rabbinical court, had been a little neglected until then, and it worked pretty well during his time: they acknowledged its judicial decisions throughout the world, especially those concerning divorces and abandoned women.

Miklós Braun

My father and my uncle were both born in Dombrád; after the war my uncle was a *shokhet* in Tyukod, then in Debrecen, while my father was a *shokhet* in Dombrád, which is next to Kisvárda. I was already born in Miskolc on August 2, 1951. We lived in 7 Kazinczy Street, in the shul yard.

Izrael Weisz

I was a *mashgiakh*, a ritual supervisor, with him and he explained to me how to do things, what I needed to watch for. In those days, there were other rabbis: Jakab Berger in Majakovszkij Street, Jenő Groszberg, who was by then an old man. Moyshe Weisz was the youngest of them, the most agile. The Orthodox congregation also had to consider that kosher brandy, kosher wine, matzah meant hard currency to the Hungarian state. Moyshe Weisz was a *Szatmár Hasid*, and Szatmár is acknowledged throughout the world. Moyshe Weisz's *Hekhsher* was acceptable to everybody.

Miklós Braun

At first they didn't want to provide permits under any circumstances, and they didn't issue them, then finally they went along with it, that we would do it; they tacitly acknowledged that we would bring in twelve children to the little yeshivah. In the beginning, we really didn't bring but twelve children, and later we broadened it a little. Dr. Antal Sebestyén, the secretary, notified the congregation, and the children came and applied one after the other from the whole country. The greatest number came from Debrecen and Miskolc, after that from Nyíregyháza, Mátészalka, and one boy from Pápa.

Sándor Benedikt

THE BUDAPEST ORTHODOX DEDICATE A NEW TALMUD-TORAH SCHOOL

Sunday, November 30 morning—An intimate private ceremony marked the dedication of the residential Talmud-Torah school of the Orthodox Division of the Budapest Israelite Congregation, in which fifteen students will receive accommodation. The Claims Conference's[9] material support makes possible the operation of the school. Present at the dedication ceremony were members of the MIOK and BIH[10] leadership, the leaders of the Orthodox Denomination, and representatives of the Budapest rabbinate and the Orthodox rabbinate.

Mór Paskusz, the president of the Orthodox Division, set forth the events leading up to the foundation of the residential Talmud-Torah school and expressed thanks to the president of MIOK and to Marcell Steiner, the vice president, for their efforts in facilitating the fulfillment of the long-standing desire of Orthodoxy. President Endre Sós pointed out that nothing proved the realization of the principle of "a free church in a free state" better than the creation of this Talmud-Torah school. He thanked the Office of Religious Affairs for authorizing the establishment of the institution. Every branch of Hungarian Jewry looks with pleasure upon the new institution, because representatives of the most widely differing branches concur in the acknowledgment of the important role of Orthodox Judaism. The new institution, concluded the president of MIOK, serves to provide youth not just with religious training but also with the

9. The Claims Conference: The Conference on Jewish Material Claims Against Germany. This organization collected funds in compensation for the sufferings of the Holocaust and allocated them to assist survivors.

10. BIH: Budapesti Izraelita Hitközség ("Budapest Israelite Congregation"), the local association of MIOK.

love of country and with an appreciation of the social order provided by Socialism.

Új Élet, December 1, 1958

My husband had an estate in Kölcse, he didn't want to abandon it, so I went there to live. I'm the mimicry type, do you know what that is? I can get used to anything. After life in a war house, I got used to the village, and after the village I got used to the big city, after Jerusalem it was Netanya, after the big apartment it was a small apartment, and I never had a word of complaint, I fit in everywhere. But in '50 all the Jews left the little villages. It was not appropriate to be a Jew there. We received a notification that we shouldn't count on the estate anymore, because it would belong to the State Farm. The rest of it was taken over by the Agricultural Cooperative group, and the farm machines went to the equipment pool, without any compensation, of course. When we needed to do the threshing, we waited until we got a thresher from the equipment pool, despite the fact that our own thresher was there. After the nationalization, we still had twenty acres left of our estate, but the village wasn't suitable for Jews anymore. We never knew which moment we were going to be in for trouble, so we thought it was better to go to Pest. My husband found a job with the congregation: we could live out of the income from the twenty acres and his salary. He got sick in '51. Professor Haynal's opinion was that he couldn't get used to city life and that's why he's sick. We went back to Kölcse for a couple of months, but he got worse, so we went back to Pest again after that.

In 1956, everyone who could, fled the country. We longed for a quiet life, so we didn't have to live in terror anymore.

—Nonetheless, you didn't leave.

—And I'll tell you why: there was the prospect, they were talking about giving back the stolen land. And then, if we could sell it, we wouldn't have to start our new life with empty hands. But in '61 we even had to give up the land we had. We had to sign, that we accepted an exchange of alkaline, nonarable land in place of the arable land. And my husband, who knew the area well, said he didn't want it—he'd rather have nothing.

—Could you give the children a religious education?

—Yes. The yeshivah took shape when my sons were ten, eleven years old. We lived on Thököly Road, the corner of Thököly Road and Dózsa György Road; they went to the public school in Hernád Street, but they went to Talmud-Torah school with Benedikt, in the courtyard of the Garay shul. While the boarding school wasn't open, and until they got it furnished, they went to Dob Street every day on the bus or trolley. I, the mother, always watched from the window to see when the trolley came, so I would see them get off. And when they went to live in the boarding school, I traveled up to see them every night—I checked over their work, heard their oral assignments, because they only studied religion there and I wanted the children to be outstanding students in their other studies as well. That's what I was accustomed to.

Gizella Weiszberger

—At most, there must have been about forty of them studying in the yeshivah. They all lived in the residence hall and received their board—the JDC covered that part of it, and the Claims Conference, an American foundation, gave the money for the renovation and the furnishings. I don't know how much they gave, President Paskusz handled this. Besides him, Dr. Sebestyén and Herman Fixler, who was brought in as secretary in '64, also tried very hard, as far as their scope permitted: financial concerns and the like.

—How did the selection fall to you?

—There was no one else who would have done. We had already gotten the tacit permission, the yeshivah had been furnished, and there still wasn't a suitable teacher. I hadn't worked with children before either. The Hungarian Foreign Trading Company for Books and Newspapers had a store which bought up Hebrew books and sold them abroad—they used me as a *soyfer*—I appraised the books. In 1958 I was voted into the leadership of the congregation—I replaced Mózes Kornitzer as the director of culture, and from then on, educational matters belonged to me. I never thought, and neither did anyone else, that in the near future I would lead the yeshivah, but there wasn't anyone else. President Paskusz asked me to try to learn with the children, at least until they found someone more suitable. I was the temporary director, but then it stayed with me—later more people emigrated, the selection became even smaller.

Sándor Benedikt

Benedikt was much more suited to the task than anyone else would have been, because "these" boys weren't "those" boys anymore. He had to work with material that included every kind of child; he had to hammer them together, and in my opinion he did this very skillfully.

Miklós Braun

—We lived in Újpest, my father was the secretary of the Orthodox congregation there. We lived in a typical Jewish courtyard, there was a shul in the courtyard, the Müllers' prayer house, this was the name of one of the residents. Újpest was an Orthodox congregation. Until '56, a descendant of the rabbi at Vác[11] filled the job of rabbi. The Talmud-Torah was led by a man named Goldstein; there was a service in the shul every night. Even after there was no longer any locus, a prayer house or a prayer room, my father kept up an Orthodox minyan. At one time we went to Rákospalota to pray on the Sabbath, and then in the middle of the sixties, we succeeded at setting up a prayer room in a small office.

—Did your father want you to attend a yeshivah?

—Naturally. The child by himself doesn't decide where he will go. Újpest, given the condition it was in after '56, no longer provided an opportunity for getting a religious Jewish education outside of the home. Many people emigrated. Unfortunately, my father was seriously ill, and his illness simplified the decision that the only child should spend the whole week, though not at a great distance, but still not at home. This was around '58 or '59. I was admitted right at the beginning, among the first students. I had lived among Jews even until then. But the child, far from home, it's natural that he is frightened. For me this was resolved in a better way than for the others; I had an exemption which allowed me, out of consideration for my father's illness, to go home to my parents every other Sabbath.

László Herczog

11. a descendant of the rabbi at Vác: His name was Eliezer Weiser. See also pp. 73–74.

—We were the only Jews in Laskod. My father had a grocery store until about '53, '54, then it was taken away. My mom died in 1954, then my dad took me to Kisvárda, and I studied in the Jewish school there because I needed to say kaddish. We had a relative, I lived with him all the way until '58 when I got up to Budapest.

—What happened in Kisvárda in '56?

—I don't very much remember, I was eight years old. I only remember that it was break time, we were standing outside in the Jewish school, in the yard, and we saw the Russian tanks going on and on, and I remember that I got slapped by the teacher, because we ran across the road, between the tanks. In Laskod they called Jews names, I'm not saying they didn't, my dad told stories about it, but everybody liked him there, and many people stepped forward to support him. It could be, that if people didn't support him, then they would have done something to him. But my dad got along well with everyone. In 1960 he went in to Mátészalka; he was there, I think, about two years, and afterwards he moved up here to Pest.

—How did you become aware that there was a yeshivah starting in Budapest?

—Well, through the congregation. I think it must have been the case that a letter was sent to Kisvárda. The congregation at Kisvárda knew about the yeshivah. All of a sudden, my dad came, in the fall of '58, before the holidays, and said, "Do you want to go up to Budapest and study there? There's a yeshivah." I already had a little learning, I went to the Talmud-Torah in Kisvárda. I said that I wasn't at home anyway, and then he brought me up here. There were a good number of us, about twenty-five or thirty, I remember. Lautmann and I came together, he was from Mátészalka, the poor guy, a year or two later he died of jaundice. Mr. Weisz and Mrs. Weisz received us very kindly, so I immediately came to like being here. A year later, my little brother Kálmán also came up. Dad wanted us to receive a Jewish education.

Tibor Weinberger

—My dad was in Pest in '58—he was studying to become a *shakter* with Lazarovits and Friedman, the kosher butcher, and that's how we learned that there was a yeshivah. My dad worked for the Debrecen congregation, ours was a very religious family, our great grandfather was a rabbi, my grandfather's beard came to his waist, my father's earlocks hadn't been cut since he was three. Later he was in forced-labor service, but he didn't eat *treyf*. He didn't eat anything but jam, and his teeth fell out.

We are three brothers, I was born in '51, I was still a young child, I could have been eight years old, my parents said even at the railroad station that I could change my mind, because they were anxious about me, I was still very little, and you had to live there in the yeshivah, a seven- or eight-year-old child there in Pest, alone, it wasn't so simple. They said that I should wait one or two years, but I wanted to go, because Janki, my older brother, was there already.

—How long were you in the yeshivah?

—I was there for six and a half years.

—During that time, you never thought that you would stop, and go home?

—I never thought of it. I felt pretty good; you could be among Jewish children all day, and we could learn there. You know, in Debrecen there was no opportunity for that.

Mendel Deutsch

Here Jews lived in the whole house. When we came here, there were still fifteen Jewish children in this yard. Next to us lived the Leibler family, there were two boys, they went up first to the yeshivah, after them went the Bergers, after the Bergers the Deutsches and then mine went last. In the sixties here in Debrecen it was typical of the whole neighborhood that there were Jews in such large proportions.

We found it pretty hard to send our children to the yeshivah; before the revolution we were away from Debrecen for a good while, we lived in Kazincbarcika, there where there's the chemical factory. And imagine this, when we came back, we had been written off as having assimilated children, and that I didn't know anything about Jewish life. Even though my father had been an employee of the congregation, he collected the taxes, and so he was involved in everything, and he was a terribly religious man, not bearded and earlocked, just a very, very religious, God-fearing man, and that's how we were raised.

They hid the yeshivah from me. One woman said that I was a big *poyshe*—that means that I am terribly secular, I know absolutely nothing about Judaism, what do my children want in a yeshivah. My oldest son had already been up in Pest, in the orphanage. I was very sick then, and we placed him where we could place him, because he wasn't a very good child. That was a Jewish orphans' home, not Orthodox but Status Quo. We were visiting this son of mine when a neighbor woman sent a package to her own son. These were the Bergers. Well, so I took it up, I looked around a little, I asked how the food was; well, the place wasn't unacceptable. I told the boys, "Children, you're going to be there; if you come home, I'll take a look at you. If you lost weight, I won't let you go back; if you look the way you did, well, then we'll keep on trying the place; and if you were to gain weight, I'd be very happy." Well, that's a mother.

So I sent up my three boys, but only the two younger ones could stay there, the third one, I don't know why they didn't accept him. Benedikt told him to come home, because he wouldn't keep him there.

Mrs. Zoltán Dickmann

Then it was still this way: you could be there until you were in eighth grade. There were no children older than that in there. And he couldn't stay there then.

—Did you arrive there together?

—At the same time as my little brother, the beginning of August '63. Because we also went up to Mount Szabadság with them for a summer holiday. You see, Deutsch was up there, and Berger, and there were others from Debrecen, so that basically we didn't go among such strangers. Not to mention the fact that I adapted relatively easily enough.

Ervin Dickmann

—Who decided that the boys would go to yeshivah: you or your husband?

—I think I did. I'll tell you the truth, I wanted them to know something about their Jewishness, that they had been born Jewish, and their father didn't have time for that, and there wasn't proper instruction here, there wasn't a proper instructor. Earlier there was Reinitz, he taught the biggest boy, and Frankfurt, he was the *shakter,* but they all went away.

Mrs. Zoltán Dickmann

You couldn't study further in Miskolc, and in Pest there was the boarding school.

In Israel they don't send the child to another city at ten years of age, only after fourteen. And we didn't go home, except three times a year, and there wasn't a telephone, we couldn't call, and there wasn't . . . it was just letter-writing: how happy we were if we got a letter from home, we always took it to bed and read what they wrote about home.

—Did they make exceptions for you, because of your uncle?

—There was no difference. I had to be even more careful; if someone is related to a rabbi, he has to behave even better. He used to listen to my lessons on Saturday afternoon, what I learned the whole week. When I knew it, things were fine, when I didn't know it, he yelled. My father rarely came up, he wasn't much of a traveler.

Izrael Weisz

—What was your father's occupation?

—He was a shoemaker, but in '57 he got sick and couldn't work anymore. We lived in Szatmárcseke—we were the last Jewish family, and in '57 we moved in to Mátészalka. In those parts, one or two families still remained, scattered here and there, but there wasn't any serious religious life anymore. In Mátészalka, there was still a nice *kile,* serious people. Herman Fixler, Mózes Back, and my father functioned, so there were no such problems.

My father wanted me to stick with Judaism. I had a teacher in Mátészalka, Friedmann, he was from Fehérgyarmat, a good friend of my father's, an old man by now, he could be above eighty, he taught here in Pest, and he brought me up a day or two before September first, '62, for the opening of school. He didn't teach me here anymore, he was preparing to leave, and emigrated to America that year or in January of the next year.

—Were you glad to go to the yeshivah?

—No. They dangled carrots, that I would be among children, and candy and that kind of thing, they tried to make us swallow the bait, but when you confronted the facts, well, it wasn't that great: you were torn away from your parents at nine years of age, it wasn't a pleasant thing. Even today I suffer in some respects from the disadvantages of it. It affects me even today: when everything is said and done, what a man learns or sees in his parents' house is different. Here we lived under strict obligations. I envied those from Pest, who could go home every weekend to their parents, I wasn't allowed this; I could only be at home in the vacations, but that was too little. It was also different for those who had a brother here; they could get a kind word, or some good advice, or pour out their soul to somebody, if they had important concerns.

—You didn't have a brother?

—I had a sister, she stayed at home with my parents.

György Rosenberg

My husband's mother was very religious, but he was an actor and a member of the Party. He didn't like to display his Jewishness, but I for my part wanted my son to become a Jew. I told my husband that it's a very big thing, if a Jew has a son, because he'll still be saying kaddish a hundred twenty years from now.[12] I had a cousin—she sent her two sons, Yankele and Mikhele Berger, here into the yeshivah. Then the Dickmann boys and the Deutsches probably were already here. She arranged it that they took Tomi also as a boarder. The room and board was completely free, you didn't have to pay a penny, every child was there free of charge.

Mrs. László Szenes

Benedikt didn't want me to be home in surroundings that weren't religious.

He took up my cause and saw to it that I was admitted to the yeshivah. At first it was like a prison to me: you were locked up, you couldn't go home, you were completely isolated from everything, and there was a very strict daily schedule, praying and studying. Besides that, the others

12. a hundred twenty years from now: According to Jewish tradition, everyone lives 120 years, so your son will still be able to say kaddish until he gets to be 120 years old.

knew that I didn't come from a religious family, and they made fun of me and called me a *khazerfresser,* which means "pork eater," and it was a little disconcerting for a person. Here I really want to do this, from my heart, and then they throw it in my face, but not the instructors, only the children, they are always vicious, kids of the same age. Benedikt was strict, and he'd slap you in the face, but it was necessary, we deserved it, nobody ever came to harm because of it, no one ever died of it, at most we prepared our lessons better. Otherwise it didn't work. It wasn't pleasant, it wasn't any kind of dream at all. We lived nearby, on Rákóczi Road, and in the beginning, when I felt that now this is too much, a couple of times I ran off. They wanted to throw me out, and Mom had to beg so hard in the office for them to overlook it and take me back. But I'm glad I saw it through: with all the strictness, the religion took root in us, and something must have remained, because in my family as well, the two children go to yeshivah.

Tamás Szenes

My husband was a very talented actor, a skillful humorist, only he didn't have good luck. He was always surrounded by envious people. Árpád Latabár was always his partner, in the Rózsafa, in the Royal, and in the Corvin restaurant. I can still picture poor Latyi—not Latyi, Árpád was the taller one[13]—he always said, my dear Laci, where are you, where are you? oh I see, under my arm!

Mrs. László Szenes

He was an actor from childhood, a dancer and comedian; he performed in the Budapest Varieté and in the Kamara Varieté. And he was very much opposed to this yeshivah thing. You know, they shaved off the hair with a zero or two machine so you were bald, and he didn't like my becoming Orthodox, he didn't want to make an earlocked whatsis, a *chulent,* out of me—and I didn't become one, either. But the family conflicts

13. not Latyi, Árpád was the taller one: Here Mrs. Szenes momentarily confuses Árpád Latabár, her husband's partner, with his more famous brother, Kálmán Latabár, who was also an actor, and whose nickname was Latyi.

continued to grow, and he saw that it would be better for me to be in different surroundings, even if they didn't suit him.

Tamás Szenes

Among the Orthodox, Yiddish is the language of instruction, but many of them didn't speak Yiddish when they arrived. Most children hardly knew anything, but then each one upgraded himself, a little trace of the yeshivah remained in every child. No one left without that. The company was very mixed; there were some Budapest families where the parents worked on Saturdays, and the child, naturally, lived there for years, ate there in the boarding school, and didn't go home even on Saturday. He stayed there among the students from the countryside who always stayed in, they couldn't go home on Saturday. Then there were students from places where the parents came from religious families, but the children didn't live in an observant way anymore—I don't have any idea anymore what brought them here.

Sándor Benedikt

Back in our home every boy went to a yeshivah. Well, he said, but he was a Party member. "I don't care," I said, "who needs to know that, it's nobody's business. My son's going to be a Jew!" Previously, I took him to Kertész Street to the Jewish kindergarten, the teacher was that Tamás Raj's[14] mother. In '56 on October 23, when this revolution started, I saw the large crowd there. "Oh, Tomi," I say, "we'd better hurry home, something's going to happen here." Until that day, the child went to Jewish kindergarten. It ended because there was the revolution. The counterrevolution. Everybody was shouting, "Down with Gerő!"[15] I can still hear it from Tomi's mouth, he was shouting too, "Down with Gejő! Down with Gejő!" Well, what was he then, four years old?

Mrs. László Szenes

14. Tamás Raj: Raj was a rabbi and a representative to the Parliament. The crowd just happened to gather at Kertész Street (map 2 B3-C3) near his home.

15. "Down with Gerő!": Ernő Gerő was an unpopular Communist leader, Rákosi's second in command. He was the Party secretary at the time of the Revolution in 1956.

I was born in 1954. I belonged to the very last generation. When I came in here in around '63 or '64, I was by far the youngest one here. There were still children here then like Srulcsi Weisz or Mr. Weisz's sons. You could tell that for them, this was a lifetime ambition. It was eventually decisive in my life as well, since if a ten-year-old child breaks with everything familiar in his life until then and gets into a completely different milieu, then that's decisive for him. Well now, I see the stepped-up tempo which they required there as a positive thing or as a plus; and even until the present time I acknowledge that it shaped a person's style of endurance, and his way of understanding things.

My father was absolutely not religious. When I was two, he suffered a very serious car accident from which he ultimately died. My mother was left with two children and sought a way out. My foster father, who was a religious Jew, a Hasid, lost a leg after the war and it was precisely in order to raise her two children that my mother undertook this traditional Jewish marriage arranged by a matchmaker and bearing no relation to romantic love. My stepfather had a tavern, a famous cultural site.[16] Patyi's tavern was well-known in Makó, and it was the source of their livelihood.

In all my born days, I was never a good child, I was always causing problems for my parents. It must have been more my foster father who took the initiative in this thing, that here is this yeshivah; it would solve their problems if I wasn't making trouble at home but elsewhere. Besides which, they no doubt had a secret hope that I would turn toward a religious life and live in that spirit. Some of this worked out for them, and some of it didn't.

I remember that I cried when my mom first left me here; essentially until then I had never been far from her, in a school setting or any other way. She was a very simple woman, but she did a lot so that her daughter and son would grow up. She couldn't very well express this in words because she wasn't an educated, cultured woman, but from her deeds you could sense that she sacrificed a great deal to bring us up. I found myself

16. My stepfather: The stepfather's name was Márton Teitelbaum and his nickname was Patyi. To speak of the tavern as a "cultural site" is ironic.

in an unfamiliar milieu, among unfamiliar people, and in an unfamiliar situation. Everything was new, everybody was bigger than me—I remember clearly that I cried a great deal when my mom left me here.

This was in '64, because I know that I started the fifth grade in Makó, I must have gone for a month or two, and I came up here in the course of the school year.

György Budai

—Where was the yeshivah located?

—At 35 Dob Street, in the first building, on the third floor. From the stairs, the first room was the classroom, where we learned, then the bedroom and the dining room. There, where Ignác Weisz, the ritual slaughterer, lives today. He was my assistant, he supervised the children and went through their lessons with them. There were children who went in to him at noon, during lunchtime, telling him to come, because they already wanted to learn. It was his wife who kept the boarding school in order.

Sándor Benedikt

Yitskhak Weisz learned with us during the day, and his wife cooked. They brought him from Nyíregyháza, but he was from Nyírbéltek. As a young man he was a teacher, then a secondhand dealer; the war intervened, and he became a butcher, so by the time he came there, he had been through several things. He was a very decent, straightforward man. His older son emigrated in '65, he was training as an aluminum presser, there was a factory in Bnei Brak. Once I went to see him, I saw him, black to the neck with aluminum and he was going to high school at night to get his degree. I said, listen here, you studied at a yeshivah, this is not for you. But his father had told him to study a trade. A month and a half passed before I convinced him to go to a yeshivah. Today he is a rabbi and he teaches, he's a good instructor, and a very good speaker. The students at the Budapest yeshivah, even if they aren't Talmud scholars or rabbis, every one became a human being.

Miklós Braun

—Together with his wife, they were in charge throughout the day; Mr. Weisz taught, and his wife prepared breakfast and dinner; lunch was

5. "A portrait of Ignác Weisz, the ritual slaughterer who appears in 'Once There Was a Yeshivah in Pest.' This photograph was taken in the cellar of the Orthodox congregation in Budapest, during chicken butchering." Text and photograph by Sándor Bacskai.

brought from the Hanna and they distributed it. Mr. Weisz was far from being a *shakter,* he didn't even have a beard. In those days, he was an exceptionally simple man without anything like the learning he has today. He sat down with unimaginable diligence to learn with his elder colleague.

—In effect, did he later become a *shakter* out of necessity?[17]

17. out of necessity: That is, because everyone else who could perform this important ritual function had left.

—Yes. They came from a little village, when the yeshivah started, in that year, maybe from Nyírbéltek.

László Herczog

His wife looked after the clothes, the bathing, and the meals, and he took care of the instruction; he sat with us and learned. If the children asked a question, he answered them, he was responsible for the children. In '64, before I emigrated, he began to study to become a *shakter.* Mr. Krausz also studied *shaktering* then, because Lazarovits and Friedman emigrated, and first they trained them.

Miklós Braun

Mrs. Weisz used to cut our nails.

Izrael Weisz

Mr. Weisz struggled with us. In school I studied with his son, he was the same age I was, he was called Leibish. They came up from around Nyíregyháza and got a place to live; he and his wife kept the yeshivah going, they did our laundry the way you would for little children. I liked studying at Mr. Weisz's a great deal. When I said I already knew everything, he said that I should recite it backwards too, or that I should teach it to him.

Mendel Deutsch

Mr. Weisz and Mrs. Weisz really gave their hearts and their lives for us; they washed, cooked, and cleaned for so many children—there was so much work for them that it was indescribable.

Tibor Weinberger

Before he got up to Pest, he lived in Nyíregyháza, I believe, and he went down to Mátészalka to teach. He was hard enough too, enough of a fighting type. With him there was no forgiveness. I didn't have pleasant memories of him, and when I first laid eyes on him, that automatically influenced a great many things. In the first days, he didn't have a pleasant effect on me. After that I didn't have very much to do with him—I didn't learn with him—but they were in charge of the education, the two of them, he and his wife, and in addition his family lived there, so that we met every day, but he didn't concern himself with me. Today there are no such problems; we work together, he's forgotten things, and I too have left them behind. In their own way, they didn't mean any harm, it's just that when something is done by force, it's not a pleasant thing.

György Rosenberg

Oh, well there's no man like him! There's no way of describing how fine he is. He is such a dear man! He was just as courteous as he was religious. Kindly, and all heart.

Mrs. László Szenes

Mr. Weisz was a very good soul.

György Budai

◆ ◆ ◆

—At the very beginning, the Budapest Talmud-Torah and the yeshivah constituted a complete whole. To the student who was already studying in the yeshivah, the third floor was not only his place of residence, but also where he learned. This time period was preceded by different levels of training in Talmud-Torah. There was Mr. Mózes, there was an instructor named Krausz, and then later when I was already in the yeshivah, there was a tutor who could help with anything, but mostly in the preparation of school studies, and homework, he was called Lefkovics. For a short time there was an instructor named Sichermann. Kohn and Stern were later, and at a very basic level of knowledge, Friedmann. A gentleman named Steinberger was the principal, "Stea," he lives in America.

—When did the yeshivah come into its own?

—It didn't have a great ascendancy because, when the children reached that certain age of independence, many of them, grabbing at the chance, emigrated, and the numbers declined—of course, for a long time, it didn't decline, since it was always replenished from somewhere. But that was no longer the representative period.

László Herczog

The yeshivah wasn't tied to any age group, but there was a separate group of those who, no matter how old they were, were studying

Khumash,[18] and then a separate group of those who could study, let's say *Gemara*.[19] Later I got up to the so-called *roshyeshivah*,[20] where the whole thing was *Gemara*, Rashi,[21] and *Toysfes*.[22]

Tamás Szenes

There were three floors in use, and there were different teachers who taught the children at different levels. There were several rebbes, Rebbe Mózes, my little brother learned with him at a lower level. I learned with two rebbes, with Rebbe Friedmann for one year, he's out in America now, and after him I learned with Benedikt. He didn't live in the yeshivah, but he came in every day to teach a class or he came to hear our lessons. I know that he fasted every Monday and Thursday.

Mendel Deutsch

Instruction was in Hebrew and Hungarian. Among ourselves we spoke Hungarian. The children didn't much know Yiddish. We understood Yiddish, but we didn't much speak it, and the truth is, this was a problem. I learned it out in America.

Tibor Weinberger

I learned on the first floor, which consisted of two places; Mózes taught there and Krausz, and down on the main floor, where the Hanna is now, Rebbe Stern taught there. In the other was the sale of milk; in the kitchen at one time there was a *bet ha-midrash*, a small prayer house, Friedmann taught there, until the Hanna ended up there in '67. The yeshivah didn't

18. *Khumash*: Strictly speaking, this term is used to refer to the printed version of the Five Books of Moses, but it is more generally used to refer to the books themselves.

19. *Gemara*: Often used interchangeably with Talmud (see the glossary), post-Biblical rabbinic teachings.

20. *roshyeshivah*: Hebrew; this term refers to the dean (*rosh* means "head") of a yeshivah, but also, as here, to the program of study that he delivers, which represents the highest level of training at the school.

21. Rashi: Acronym for the work of RAbbi SHlomo Itzhaki, one of the leading commentators on the Talmud. See also the glossary.

22. *Toysfes*: Supplements to the commentary of Rashi compiled between the twelfth and fourteenth centuries. See also the glossary.

just mean those who learned there but also those who lived in the boarding school. We learned in the yeshivah, but we also lived there, so strictly speaking it was a boarding school. There were those who only went to the *kheder.* Rebbe Stern taught *alef-beys,* he just helped out if somebody was sick or was in the hospital; there was Krausz, the *shokhet*'s brother, he was the jumping-off point for the yeshivah. He died in the meanwhile, but in those days he taught, we liked him. There were only two in the yeshivah, Benedikt and Mr. Weisz. Later Mr. Weisz learned to become a *shokhet,* then his oldest son, Khaim, learned with the kids.

György Rosenberg

—When we got up to school, they started with four groups. Later there were three, then it decreased to two, you know, as the rebbes died. We were with Stern, that was the smallest group, he taught the beginners' course, that is to say, Moses' five books. He died right in that year, and the next year the small group was scrapped, and it all fell to Imre Mózes; I studied with him all the way through, Moses' five books at a higher level, and the songs, it was called *niggun.* Upstairs, Benedikt taught the whole *Gemara* completely, which assured us of an understanding equal to the level of a high-school diploma.

—Were these groups located in distinct places as well?

—No. Just because of the grade school, so there were lower level students, let's say we were in the lower grades, then there were upper-level students, some of these were like the Weinberger boys who were always upstairs, because they never went home, because there wasn't anyone to go home to. Well, first the mother died, I believe, then the father also. Gyuri Rosenberg was the same way, he also rarely went home—more precisely to Debrecen, his parents by then had moved here.

—Who was your favorite among the rebbes?

—I liked Rebbe Mózes, because I was with him all the way through, and also as a person.

Ervin Dickmann

For his thirteenth birthday he prepared him, but it was so amazingly beautiful, we held it here at home in Pásti Street, it was such a full house in the prayer house that people didn't all fit, they even argued about it.

And he taught him very well to say what he said. I was in trouble too, because I understood some of it, and the rest I just inferred from it. Because, after all, there aren't many of us who can speak Jewish.

Mrs. Zoltán Dickmann

I didn't know the *alef-beys* very well, I couldn't study the *Gemara* with the big kids, so I didn't wind up with Benedikt but with the teacher Mózes. He already had gastric disease; despite that, in his own way, and through his own devices, he loved us a great deal. I learned Yiddish and Hebrew from him, I only got to Benedikt in my last year. Mózes would also hit you, if you upset him, but he made a much bigger mental problem out of it.

György Budai

In *kheder* I studied with Mózes, from the first minute on. My first impressions aren't good there either. The first week, on Saturday morning was the *sedremaneroling*, the reading of the weekly text; I didn't go down, and when on Monday during the service I made a mistake, I got such a big slap . . . this was too much all at once.

—Did everybody fight here?

—No, but if there was a little thorn in somebody, at the next opportunity he pushed it out. In his own way, Benedikt wanted the best for us, but the punishments came if you got a bad mark or got into a scrape. When you needed a little encouragement, you got just the opposite. I don't want to run it down, because in a lot of ways I am still living to this day out of what I learned then. If a person wanted to live in a religious way, it gave the foundation, and the great majority remained on the side of religion.

György Rosenberg

—Did you have any connection with the National Office of Religion?

—We didn't, we belonged to Síp Street, and they maintained the relationship with the authorities. When they were negotiating about something that concerned us, or when it was necessary to bow down before somebody, then, once in a while, they summoned the Orthodox president as well.

—The Orthodox rabbis who spoke at MIOK general assemblies always said that there weren't problems.

—They didn't dare to say anything else. Everything was rigged and they were afraid that if they deviated from that, they would be relieved of their office, they would encounter inconveniences, there might perhaps be other unforeseeable harmful consequences.

—Was it dangerous to operate the yeshivah?

—We didn't think about that. We didn't want to think about that. You have to take some risks in such a situation. We remained quiet, we didn't create propaganda for it, and so they didn't bother us. We didn't have any other goal, except to study and to raise the children in the Jewish faith, to accustom them to a religious way of life. One afternoon I could only go in later. My wife said that she had been looking for me for some reason, and she saw that the children had sat down by themselves, and they were learning in the same way as if I had been there. When the children got out and went abroad, they didn't fall behind other children of the same age. Zalmen Brüll from Mátészalka, who at first hardly knew anything, is now an outstanding rabbi in Netanya. Pinkhasz Weiszberger teaches in the Talmud-Torah in Vienna. Srulcsi Weisz is a *soyfer* in Bnei Brak. At one time the son of Éliás Katz, the chief rabbi of Slovakia, studied here, and there was a child named Weisz from Pozsony, he is now a rabbi in Brooklyn. But the two Kleins from Miskolc, the Deutsch brothers from Debrecen and the children of Ignác Weisz were also intelligent boys.

Sándor Benedikt

—What was the proportion of students from Pest and from the countryside?

—Half and half, maybe. The students from Pest wound up in the yeshivah because of their earlier past in the Talmud-Torah. The whole concept was built on the idea of saving the children from rural congregations which were ceasing to exist. And the countryside wasn't just on the level of the traditional, well-developed congregations—Miskolc, Debrecen—but it included very small congregations as well: the Leipnik brothers came from Székesfehérvár, Brüll from Mezőkovácsháza, Gottesman from Salgótarján.

László Herczog

—Was there a barrier between the students from the countryside and those from Pest?

—There was nothing like that. All there was was that when I got there, when they said *"lóca,"*[23] I didn't know what that was. Or *"csupor"*[24] and suchlike, those country expressions, those I had to learn, because I had no idea what that was.

Tamás Szenes

—Disdain or such? There were one or two who looked down on the country students, but we got used to it, and later we developed a solidarity.

Tibor Weinberger

In my opinion, we weren't more at one time than maybe sixty. A few emigrated to Israel, that was ongoing, and then children came up from the country, from Kaba, from Mátészalka. We in the group from Debrecen were the greatest number, not always at one time, but at least eight: the Dickmann brothers, Gelberger, Reinitz, the Berger brothers, and us.

Mendel Deutsch

—When you got up to the yeshivah, how did the others receive you?

—I was nine years old when we came up, my brother was eight. Well, the few others that were from the country, they accepted us as well. The greatest number were from Debrecen. There were students from Székesfehérvár, Miskolc, Kisvárda, the Faragó boy from Böszörmény, the Rosenfelds from Kaba, but there were seven or eight of us from Debrecen.

Ervin Dickmann

—There were even a few kids who emigrated around then that I didn't even know. I know Janki Deutsch, he was still there for a year, and then I knew Mendu, I was in the same class with him, and Tuli Brach, and Leibish Weisz, who is now a *Szatmár Hasid*. He never wanted to be a Hasid. That's a good story: once I was in Williamsburg with my uncle on Shabbat, that's a religious neighborhood, and somebody shouts after

23. *lóca*: Hungarian, "bench."

24. *csupor*: Hungarian, "mug or an earthenware pot."

me, "Szenes! Szenes!" I didn't know who it was, so I looked around, well it was Leibish all dressed up—caftan, beard, earlocks, *biber* hat—I would never in my life have recognized him. And he, who never wanted to be a Hasid, because he was so hard-working, always just the work, the work, not goofing off in the sun.[25]

—Who were your best friends?

—The Brachs, to this day. There's the younger Brach, Itzu, but Tuli too, though he moved away, and there are family circumstances, so we don't see each other as often as we did before we married, and before we had children. In times past, we socialized a lot. You could say we got together three or four times every week for "sociality,"[26] that meant movies, tennis, such things.

—What kind of name is Tuli?

—He's Nátán Brach, later he called himself György, because he went to some kind of economics school and they made fun of him a lot. He's religious too, not a Hasid, but he has a beard, and he has some six children. He's sharp-minded, they were good students, Tuli was what we called him. He didn't have any kind of splendid childhood, his father was in prison.

—Was this hard on them?

—It didn't show. They were cheerful kids, but I don't know what was inside. Often people like that cry quietly. I don't believe it can help being hard on you, if your father's in prison. But we didn't talk about it. We didn't talk about such painful topics.

Tamás Szenes

He liked the Weinberger children, and Brach, him he likes even today. His father was in prison, and his uncle, it was very hard on them. In those days there was this currency—I don't know what trumped-up charges they used. They emigrated to America. Tomi said how clever Tuli was, he became a good businessman. He works with neckties.

Mrs. László Szenes

25. goofing off in the sun: The Hasid devote all their time to Talmudic study and this seems the antithesis of work to the speaker.

26. "sociality": The Hungarian speaker uses the English word here.

—His father was in prison, why, I don't know.

—Was people's opinion of Tuli Brach different because of that?

—No. They didn't talk about it then, we learned about it later.

György Rosenberg

—Did Rabbi Benedikt have children the same age as you?

—He had children of every age. For that matter, there were so many scrapes. There was a lot of fighting, usually among brothers. The Dickmanns were more close together, but the Benedikts, Robi and Khaim, and then the two youngest ones, Lemi and Tomi, were always killing each other, and the Brach children too.

Tamás Szenes

I have only scattered memories, as I wasn't in Pest very often from '63 to '68. I remember one or two children who were very weak in mathematics, and Dad asked me to go in and work with them. I considered this natural—even before that I always had students—mostly I tutored mathematics in the school on Hernád Street where Mom taught, and then also later in Debrecen, when I was at college, I made my living by tutoring. I went in anyway to my little brothers, the smallest of them was still in kindergarten then; I had to bring them home, and since Mom worked, I had to take care of them quite a bit. The bigger ones lived in the boarding school, Dad didn't make any exceptions, he was even stricter with his own children than with others. It wouldn't have been easy, getting up at four in the morning to get to Dob Street by four thirty.

—How many siblings were there?

—Seven: three girls and four boys. Two of us are blood relations: my older sister, Jutka, and I. She was born before the war, I was born during the war. In '46, our mother died because of medical carelessness. They treated her incorrectly. We already had our passports for emigration, but Dad decided that he would stay here and raise the children. Khaim—his Hungarian name is Gyuri—my oldest little brother, is four and a half years younger than me. After him came Robi, then Evi, then Lemi or Gabi, and finally Tomi.

Vera Benedikt

—Who were the best students?

—The Weiszbergers from Miskolc, the Kleins, who were also from Miskolc, Zalmen Brüll, Leibish Weisz, the Benedek[27] children. Everyone tried to keep to the level.

—And you?

—Not the best, but not the worst.

—And Kálmán?

—Kálmán too.

—Who were your best friends?

—Everyone. My closest friends were Herczog, and Leipnik—we slept next to each other. There was a boy named Szegfű from Miskolc, he was the most hot-blooded. We were a little afraid of him. He didn't fight, he was just the strongest.

Tibor Weinberger

—Was there a leader among the children, one the others looked up to?

—I didn't have a role model, everybody was different. I was little.

—And fighting or arguing, how about that?

—There's always arguing among children, especially when we played football, then we beat each other up pretty well if there was a goal or something like that, and the referee didn't award it. But there weren't big arguments.

Mendel Deutsch

Oh boy! The hierarchical order took shape right in the yeshivah. I remember that in the first days some big boy—and compared to me, they were all really big—had me on by getting me to believe that one child was the weakest one on the team, and everybody had to beat him up. They sent me there to start a fight with him, and it turned out he was the strongest.

György Budai

—How did those who had been there a long time greet the new arrivals?

27. Benedek: Weinberger means Benedikt.

—I don't believe it caused a problem for anyone. Rather, each person had to contend with his own ego.

László Herczog

—How long did it take you to get accustomed to the yeshivah?

—I never got used to it. You can't get accustomed to that.

Tamás Szenes

—Did the bad taste in your mouth remain for the whole time?

—Yes. I didn't like being here.

—How was your relationship with the children?

—Depends on who, how well we got along. I had some good friends, but there were those I argued with every day. I fooled around a lot with Kálmán, Leibish Weisz, and with Srulcsi. Srulcsi, when he was in the mood, was a fun guy; he was clumsy, but he liked to goof around. Mendu Deutsch was my best friend out of the later group, until he left for America. I clashed pretty often with Szenes and the Benedikt boys. I had kind of a nervous temperament.

—What does that mean?

—I'm that way by nature, unfortunately. Many things brought it out of me, I had a real dread of the punishments. The Sabbath was the only day when you weren't so uneasy. On other days, I was always in hiding from it.

—Did your father know about this?

—Not really. I would have liked for him to take me home, but he insisted on it, from a religious point of view, and besides, he was pretty old, so he wasn't able to work.

—You didn't tell your mom either?

—There wouldn't have been any point, she couldn't do much anyway. Once in a while, she came to visit, every other month or so when she could, given her time and their finances. It was a good feeling when she came up for a few days, it gave a person a little confidence.

György Rosenberg

—How frequently did you go home?

—Once a year. I usually went home for Easter. Sometimes for Hanukkah, but I always went home for Easter.

Tibor Weinberger

By the end of fifth grade I commuted alone, and that trained me to enormous independence, just the fact that I had to organize my life independently. My mother visited me once every month or two, as her circumstances permitted. They always sent money; it felt good that somebody was always coming up from Makó, like Mr. Markovits, and they always sent a fifty, which always ended up in the Trafik[28] across the street, where we spent it on treats like candy or chocolate—and just the knowledge that I had some spending money which I could budget for myself. And there was this man with a sort of credit system, where I could go and say that I needed ten forints now, and I got it. This trained me to enormous independence, and I am enjoying its benefits to this day. It's not a dumb saying, and I don't mean it in a conceited way, that this was "a mind ground smooth on the Talmud."

György Budai

—The day started at what time?

—Five a.m. We studied various religious foundational things until six thirty—the Talmud, the Laws, and moral subjects as well—that was the curriculum. At six thirty they had to go down to the little prayer house, the *Shas Khevrah,* to pray, and then they came up for breakfast. The children went to the public school on Kazinczy Street, one week the instruction took place in the morning, the next week it was in the afternoon. When instruction was in the morning, they went to school right after breakfast, they came back for lunch, and then from two in the afternoon to six we learned in the yeshivah. On the other weeks, we learned until twelve or twelve thirty, then lunch, and then they went to school. Every night at six came a tutor who went with them through the material they

28. Trafik: A small store selling tobacco items, candy, newspapers, and the like.

were studying in public school, or looked over their homework. When they finished, they had supper; bedtime was at nine.

Sándor Benedikt

At noon we went to the Hanna to eat—this was new, because before that it was in 32 Kertész Street, but the space there was too small. There was a curtain so we wouldn't have to look at the girls and women.

Izrael Weisz

—Did you do anything else?

—We played football here, that was the best. We had some good games in this area and we had a very good football team.

Tibor Weinberger

When they are able to force a ten-, twelve-year-old child to get up at five in the morning, study, attend the shul, go to school, have lunch at one, study the Talmud in the afternoon, daven in the shul, have supper and after supper get ready for the next day . . .

Looking back, what I think was a great mistake was that they didn't take school really seriously. I was decidedly a weak-to-middling student, but in Makó I had had top marks, maybe because of differences between the schools, but here they didn't pay attention to these things. Only one thing mattered, that I shouldn't get a warning or fail, because then Benedikt would take you to task and give you a good beating.

György Budai

"Stand on this stone!" and then from his backhand—his hands were bony—flew the slaps, it wasn't a pleasant thing, though people reacted differently. What I know, I didn't study with him, but many people put to good use what they learned from him. If I had studied with Benedikt too, I would apparently know more than I do now.

György Rosenberg

Benedikt was a big *talmid hokhem,* he knew very well how to learn, and he could keep the children in line. So it's not enough that a person can study and teach. There are teachers like that anywhere. But if there's no discipline, then it's finished.

Tamás Szenes

Our father still has a fine reputation. He attended the yeshivah at Galánta, he was one of the best students, they predicted a great future for him. They acknowledged him here as well, not just the very religious people but the rabbis as well, for example, Professor Scheiber. We learned a great deal on the Sabbath; I liked talking with him a great deal, but he's my father—I'm surely biased in talking about him. He was well-informed about worldly matters as well. It was taken for granted that he read the paper every day, that he followed political events with interest; this is not really typical of religious men today.

Vera Benedikt

—I liked him a lot. We truly owe him a great deal. He was a strict man, but you need a little strictness, because without it, it doesn't work.

Here it doesn't matter who is most famous. All that matters is to be able to handle children, and he was the most suitable for that.

—Wasn't his wife there?

—His wife wasn't here, but we were always going to his house at 48 Garay Street, and on major holidays, like New Year's and Yom Kippur, we always went there to pray in his shul. I loved to hear how he prayed—it was very beautiful, it still rings in my ear.

Tibor Weinberger

Benedikt gave punishments, that you had to write one hundred times, "I will not do this anymore," or you had to stand in the corner.

Izrael Weisz

As a parent, I want to say that I was very grateful to him, because he gave my boy the slaps he should have gotten from me. There was a rotten square in the paving, they had to stand there, and they had to show their report card, and if there was a problem, they got slapped.

Mrs. Zoltán Dickmann

That he was strict? That wasn't a bad thing. The children needed it. Because a child also needs to get strictness. You can't leave him to himself to do things the way he likes. The parents weren't there, so somebody had to bring up those children. I remember once I went up looking for Tomi. He said, "He's there, he's kneeling in the corner." You have to train a child and explain things to him, then he obeys much better than if you hit him. You have to know how to bring up a child. I never hit Tomi either, and he was always good and he respected me.

Mrs. László Szenes

—It's not possible to remember him without affection; it was different when someone judged him with a child's mind, because of the punishments he had been assigned, and considered him a bad man because of them, but this was actually to the benefit of the child. He worked with a harsh pedagogical method but evidently a useful one, because the children who came into contact with him are leading a religious Jewish life in nearly every part of the world.

—Did he make distinctions between the children?

—No. In fact, he punished his own children as severely, if not more severely, than the others. And he had to devote himself completely to working with the children, since one phase of the learning lasted from dawn until the morning worship service. He lived in Garay Street, he commuted with a bicycle, and certainly by five o'clock or quarter after, he was here for the learning.

László Herczog

I didn't resent Benedikt then either, I always respected him, because he was a good man, and he never beat me when there was no need for it. And today as well, looking back, I approve of everything he did. I can say that if it hadn't been for Benedikt, then maybe we wouldn't have amounted to much; not only me but also others.

Tamás Szenes

—What was your relationship with the chief rabbi and with the employees of the congregation?

—It was a closed world. They knew about us. Weisz, the chief rabbi, kept a file on us, and he recognized us by name as well; he knew who was who. In those days, there weren't more than twenty of us, they knew us.

György Budai

Sometimes he came up, it wasn't an everyday occurrence; he had other things to do, in those days there was still an extensive religious life;

he had duties to perform, kashrut and that kind of thing. If only it were like that today!

Srulcsi Weisz went on Saturday morning for kiddush, dinner, he was his uncle, he learned with him, he heard his lessons every week, on Saturday mornings. He was strict with him, he got in trouble.

György Rosenberg

—Who slept where, who decided that?

—As we arrived, they put us in, and we made friends.

—Were there bunk beds?

—No. There were iron beds, like in the army. There were built-in closets. We had some good games—we were always playing hide and seek—we hid there. So it was really great.

—Were there pictures on the walls?

—No. That there wasn't. There were placards, quotations from the Torah.

Tibor Weinberger

They put me in the outer room, which was closer to the first stairwell. There were iron beds, everybody had their own night stand; thinking back on it, it seems dreary.

György Budai

In beautiful, large rooms! There were rooms, neat, gleaming, clean, it was well maintained, the tables were set beautifully, lunch, dinner, everything, Friday night, Shabbat, it was very beautiful.

There was one long table, everyone sat around there, and they learned there, little and big, I can still see all the children in my mind's eye.

Mrs. László Szenes

There were two rooms, there was a large room, there were about fifteen of us there, among the big kids there were about ten or twelve. I don't remember the exact arrangement of the beds, I know in those days there were even bunk beds. By the time I left, there must have been fifteen all together.

Ervin Dickmann

Mr. Weisz and his family lived on the right side. On the left side, the first room was the so-called living room. When I came up, the little kids, who were in the lower school, slept in that room. One or two were in the upper school. Sometimes the roof leaked when there was a big snow, and you can still see the signs of that on it. The bigger kids slept in the so-called bedroom—that was the smaller room—the middle room was the dining room, and we also studied there, and later when there were fewer students, and they didn't use the living room, then there were the two bedrooms and the first room, where the studying and the eating took place.

György Rosenberg

The Weiszes had a separate apartment opposite the yeshivah; the wife did our wash, and cooked, and Yidesz also lived there, their daughter. She was very beautiful to us, but she was the only girl.

György Budai

We were cut off from many things; we didn't watch TV, so if we were allowed to go somewhere to look at a match on TV, that counted as a thrill. We experienced little. We weren't involved in worldly things. On Sunday afternoon, if we weren't under restrictions, we could go out. During the week there wasn't much time for it; you needed special permission if you wanted to go out. On Sunday we went—there were group outings—there was a kid, Miki Braun, who took us places. He's out in Israel; he emigrated in '64 or '65. He went out to the slaughterhouse—he worked as a *mashgiakh* for the congregation—but besides this, he undertook to take us on outings.

Later there was pressure from the father of the Brach boys and Fischer's foster father for us to get some fresh air. Also, we got bananas and fruit, they fought for it. In those days, twice a week there was poultry for lunch in the Hanna so that there wouldn't always be beef. Fischer liked to stir up trouble; we children laughed at him because he argued a lot. They looked out for our interests in a lot of things, so it should be better for the children. We got fruit, bananas, oranges, which was a big deal at that time.

—Did your parents have to pay?

—They didn't have to pay, nobody paid. They got money from America, from the JDC. They wouldn't have been able to support so many children.

—It was interesting that when Americans came—America must have sent "support"[29] with them—then they had the children recite. In my day, they asked me to recite the *Gemure*, you know, the *Gemara* that they study, because they wanted to show that we learn things here so they should continue to give us more "support." In America, I met a man who brought great numbers of children out from Czechoslovakia, Romania, Russia; he brought them money and he tried to save Jewish children from Communism so they would continue to be Jews. I met him there and got to know him; he told me that in those days he used to come here to the yeshivah. He remembers that I recited from the *Gemure*.

Mendel Deutsch

—How were the children's meals?

—They were good. The cooking was fine. I ate there myself a couple of times because Mrs. Weisz invited me; she served their food. She worked hard for them. And lots of children were fresh to her on top of it; the poor woman had enough to do with so many children. Children are always making trouble, playing pranks, being fresh.

Mrs. László Szenes

We didn't get fruit very often—for the most part there wasn't money for it, everybody had to buy it for himself—but the food was pretty good. Once a month my mom came up; I was very thin, I had scarlet fever a year after I went up, probably from the meat or from some spoiled food. Chief of Medicine Dr. Barta looked after the children, he was a very religious doctor, a keeper of the Sabbath. I don't know if he received any money, or if he did it for free because he felt involved. If somebody got sick, they called Dr. Barta.

Mendel Deutsch

Oh, Dr. Barta! How I adored him! Well, he was such a dear man! There's no one else as warm-hearted as he was! He was all heart and

29. "support": Deutsch uses the English word in reference to the funding provided by these donors, doubtless echoing the language of the donors themselves.

unselfish—he didn't even get paid by the yeshivah. He examined the children out of kindness. Really, the people were like that, all goodness!

Mrs. László Szenes

—I have very good memories of him. Of course, I am influenced by the fact that we pray together to this day. He's not the doctor of the Orthodox congregation, just a very good Jew, and a man of deeply felt religious feelings who was completely able to reconcile his medical profession with the strict regulations of religion. He was a remarkable person; as to how we children were able to pull the wool over his eyes, that's a different matter.

—There was a boy who died of jaundice.

—I don't know, the way I remember it, he died of something else, something much wilder than jaundice. It's a fact that when his illness started and they quarantined him, there was some danger of infection. Mr. Weisz's family had an apartment laid out so there was a completely separate room; this was the only time I remember that they lodged someone there. But only for a short time, because he wound up in the hospital and died in a very short time.

László Herczog

And we always went to bed late, because we had to do our Hungarian homework until eight or ten at night.

Mendel Deutsch

No television, no radio, no books. There wouldn't have been time for it anyway; if we had fifteen minutes, then we preferred to play soccer in the yard, or you wrote a letter, but they didn't much leave time for us to think about the things a ten-, twelve-year-old child thinks about. I don't know if this was intentional or not, but we certainly didn't have the opportunity to spend time on anything else.

György Budai

Ping-pong on the second floor, soccer in the yard; just yesterday I took the children there, to show them where their father grew up, where I spent six or seven years. There was no television; sometimes we went over to Mr. Fischer's if there was a game.

Tamás Szenes

—Were the yeshivah students Pioneers?[30]

—I'm sure I wasn't, insofar as they asked me at my university entrance exams why I was never a Pioneer, or a KISZ[31] member. I don't remember anyone among us who was.

László Herczog

—We were always locked up in 35 Dob Street. We didn't go out in the street, just as far as the Kazinczy Street school. It was pretty bad for the constitution, we were tucked away inside the walls. They let us out once a week, on Sunday, to go walking with someone named Miki Braun who lives in Israel now. You had to study all day.

—Were you boys interested in other things?

—We played soccer, we had a team, the country kids played the city kids, I kicked an enormous number of goals in that yard; the goal posts are still there, I visited there this week. That was the only recreation, there was nothing else, no movies, we didn't read anything, just what we had to study in Hungarian school. We were bald, our hair had been shorn off, it was a religious yeshivah.

Mendel Deutsch

—It didn't feel like a closed world. The class schedule was looser on Sunday afternoons and on the afternoons of school holidays. There were small outings in the Miki Braun period. Besides this, there were of course children's shenanigans; we went to soccer games, but I was no MTK[32] fan. I only went once in a great while, for the heck of it.

—Did no one ever flunk?

—Sure they did. In that case, they couldn't go home, they couldn't meet with people, if visitors came or relatives or parents.

László Herczog

30. Pioneers: member of a Communist youth organization founded in 1946.

31. KISZ: The Hungarian Young Communist League (Hungarian: Magyar Kommunista Ifjúsági Szövetség, KISZ), was a Communist youth movement in Hungary, founded in 1957.

32. MTK: Magyar Tornaklub, a national soccer team which had the reputation in the 1930s and 1940s of being a "Jewish" club because of a number of Jewish members.

—We should really have been sleeping, but we always snuck out somehow, so Mr. and Mrs. Weisz wouldn't notice, and we got back in time for prayers. The very first time Dudi Guttstein was with us, the poor guy had problems, he had his little flaws,[33] he was the Honvéd[34] fan.

—When you went out into the city, did it show that you were Jews?

—Of course. We had earlocks, and we went around in caps. And also because of our neatness.

György Rosenberg

—Did you sneak out to soccer games too?

—Not to soccer games, I snuck out for water polo games, several times. Alone. There's a reason for this, as there is for everything. I loved to swim; in school I met up with a teacher who had a great effect on me, in an interesting way. Interestingly enough,[35] his name was György Patyi; he was a gym teacher, a water polo coach. I felt that he paid more attention to what I did, how I lived; on Saturdays, if I snuck out of the yeshivah, he put me in the junior team, which absolutely no one knew, right up until now.

György Budai

We went out every Sunday with a guy named Miki Braun, he took us, it seemed to me, just out of kindness. There was something every Sunday afternoon, often we went for an outing on Mount Szabadság, or we rode rowboats in the City Park, or we just went out to play soccer in the City Park.

Tibor Weinberger

On Sunday mornings, Berger heard our lessons, what we had studied all week, but the afternoon was free.

György Rosenberg

33. he had his little flaws: This is a passing reference to the mental problems this student was experiencing.

34. Honvéd: A national soccer team.

35. Interestingly enough: By coincidence, the nickname of this student's foster father was also Patyi. See pp. 111, 174.

—They were kept busy all the time, that's why once a week, on Sunday afternoon or on holidays, April 4, May 1, we had to take them out to relax a little.

—You didn't see them during the week?

—I saw them when I went to shul, but I didn't have any contact with them. I took them for walks; in the winter we went out to look at the skating rink, or if it was raining, we went into a museum or the Vajdahunyad castle, always somewhere else. They were pretty good, there was rarely any trouble with them. There were ten, twelve children at once, sometimes more, sometimes less; I always worked to get them to walk in an orderly way. One of them told me that once I slapped him so hard when he got out of line that he still remembers it today. But I have been on good terms with every child right up to the present day.

I was on good terms with all the children, I was the big boy. Sometimes a couple of children from the Talmud-Torah also joined us, when we were planning some better outing, to Csillebérc or Hűvösvölgy. In summer the days were longer, so we went further.

—When you were walking, was there name-calling in the street?

—Rarely. It happened, but you can't say it was the rule. During the Communist regime in Hungary, they didn't much dare call Jews names. They would make comments pretty quietly, but there were no conspicuous incidents. Before '56 it was more glaring; there were more Jews living in Hungary, and they really did go around in caftans with earlocks, mostly around Dob Street and Kazinczy Street.

—Do you know that the children snuck out to go to soccer games?

—Now I do. Once there was some telephoning, Laci Herczog was involved in it, and three other children, they telephoned someone, the police caught them, and Stea[36] sent me to get them out. But for the most part they were good children.

They tell stories that I was a little harsher with one or the other of them. This is an accepted thing in a yeshivah. The Talmud says that

36. Stea: Jenő Steinberger, Ervin Groszberg's successor as director of the daytime program at 35 Dob Street (map 2 [04] C3). See pp. 57, 65, 115.

whoever spares his children walloping doesn't really love his child. This doesn't exist in the yeshivahs of today, but then it happened.

Miklós Braun

Everybody had a cap on; you could tell we were Jews. They often called after us. You could hear, "Here go the Jews." There were one or two boys who answered back.

Tibor Weinberger

They called after us even more than now. Even my classmates called me names because I was a Jew. It was painful—I was the only one in the class, there wasn't anyone from the yeshivah with me.

György Rosenberg

We most often met up with Gentiles in school, because except for that the schedule was tight. I didn't much feel the anti-Semitism, at least not physically; also I was considered a strong child and if there had been anything, we would have retaliated.

György Budai

In the summer, I took my vacation and I went up to Mount Szabadság with them for two, three weeks, when they had their summer holiday.

Miklós Braun

Every year we went somewhere as a family for summer vacation. With seven children, the only way you could do this was for my parents to rent a place somewhere on Mount Szabadság, and we moved up there for two months. Several times we spent the summer in Óra Street, but it also happened that for some reason we couldn't go back where we had been the previous year. I remember that many times the two of us—my father and I—went and looked at several places. I'm not sure, but it seems to me that when Dad became the director of the yeshivah, he looked at the same time for a place for us and for the yeshivah. We took everything up with a small truck; this was the most exciting part of the summer; it was preceded by several days of packing, then we used a truck taxi to take up the clothes, the beds, the bed linens, the dishes. And we moved down the same way. One year we lived quite close to the house where the yeshivah had its summer holiday, and then we brought the food from there. That was much more pleasant—I got out of doing the dishes and other unpleasant tasks. At one time, there was a kitchen lady—I don't remember her real name—she cooked for the children.

Vera Benedikt

—What went on in this camp?

—Studying, of course, supplemented by playing. Prayer in the morning, then studying, eating, playing, studying again in the afternoon; essentially the same as in Dob Street, only in a little freer circumstances.

László Herczog

I remember the street name: Hűvösvölgyi Street?

Tibor Weinberger

It was up on the Svábhegy, on Óra Road—I could still find it today from Lóránt Road, this was a little, old house, and there they furnished it with bunk beds, and we lived our everyday lives in the same way, the studying part somewhat more loosely, and perhaps the community life was different. I remember that Srulcsi slept above me, they were worn-out old beds, you could rock them back and forth; I slept below and if he dropped his blanket at night, he rocked the bed until I woke up and then called down that I should pass him up his blanket.

György Budai

It was in a great big, long building. It was so long ago that I wouldn't recognize it anymore. I believe we got off at Gyöngyvirág Road, the road led you between bushes—it could be that I might find it after all—there was a big wood nearby. They rented the same house every year. They were many, two groups didn't fit in the house at once; half went in one month, they had their holiday in July, the other half in August. My son was there the whole time, because Rabbi Benedikt loved him so much—he didn't give a two-month holiday to anyone except Tomi. He was always a dear child, Tomi, a charming child, and obedient and dear and good-hearted. He's the same today—he can't hear this now, or else he'd interrupt that I shouldn't praise him. I adored him, I didn't just adore him then, to this day I still adore my child.

Every day Mr. Weisz brought the lunch from the Hanna, however, I brought everything up for Tomi, I took home the dirty laundry, I put clean clothes in the bureau, I sewed on his buttons. You know what he always asked for? What should I bring? Carrots. He longed for carrots, that I should bring up to the mountain, not candy or chocolate, but carrots, they were what made him happy. He cleaned them for himself and chomped on them. When he was a schoolboy, we were assigned to Nyár Street for dental work and once they informed us that they wanted to see Tamás Szenes's mom. I go in and say, well, what's wrong with the child's teeth that you're even calling me in. Please be so kind as to explain, what do you give this child to eat? We're asking, she says, because he's the only one who has healthy teeth.

Mrs. László Szenes

◆ ◆ ◆

—Did your children succeed at becoming outstanding?

—While I was there, they held their own in their studies. It didn't last long: the older one completed six grades, the younger one finished four.

—Why did you make this decision, to leave Hungary?

—Because it was almost impossible to keep the Sabbath. And since we gave the children a religious upbringing, it was up to us to make provisions that they would be able to manage in this respect. There would have been only one possibility for them to continue their studies, rabbinical school. But that wasn't entirely suitable for us either, because we were Orthodox and the Orthodox spirit was not predominant in the rabbinical school. At first my sons studied together with Schőner at the yeshivah, he's the same age they are. He actually went into the rabbinical school to study. Whoever stayed there didn't have any other solution.

—Where did you settle down?

—For a few months we lived in Bnei Brak and then we came here to Kiryat Zanz. The children went right into the yeshivah of the rabbi of Kolozsvár.[37] They were young boys, and the environment, because of

37. Kolozsvár: (Cluj-Napoca, Romania) (map 1 C6). The rabbi of Kolozsvár was Yekutiel Yehuda Halberstam who founded Kiryat Zanz in Netanya.

the influence of the rebbe—the rebbe had such an extraordinary effect on people that those who heard him speak felt nearly as if they had been enchanted—they promptly got used to life here. My older son is a rabbi at Netanya, the other received a job offer in Vienna: he teaches at the yeshivah there.

—How did you become a writer?

—I'm not a writer. I only write a bit for my own satisfaction. In the women's group in Pest, I held a reading of my work every week. Once I wrote a poem, "The Mourning Widow," and recited it to the women's group. It was very successful. They asked me when did I work on my writing. I said, while I am doing the laundry or the dishes. I didn't make a big deal of it.

Gizella Weiszberger

—I worked as a *mashgiakh*: we slaughtered the merchandise and sealed it; it was put aside until it cooled, and we distributed it among the meat markets. There were Orthodox meat markets in three places: Dob, Visegrádi, and Hernád Streets.

At first we brought in twenty, thirty, forty calves a week. Even in the worst times, I brought in three or four for the Szeretet Hospital and Alma Street. We always got beef, but later on there were problems with veal. And there was a time when every liver couldn't be released as kosher, because of the need for export; they released the meat as kosher but withheld the liver. Usually Berkovits brought in the internal organs, the lungs and such, for sausage. At one time we exported kosher tongue to Switzerland, as the animal rights groups there wouldn't permit kosher slaughtering.

—Did Lazarovits and Friedman slaughtered the beef?

—Yes. There were already smaller *shakters*, I don't remember who, but there was only Lazarovits and Friedman for beef. They certainly slaughtered beef in Debrecen and Miskolc. My wife's father was a butcher in Kisvárda; there was regular slaughtering there until '62. In Budapest there wasn't enough beef in the marketplace; Gentiles also came into the store, people came from the Arab embassies, they stood in line for veal, and the congregation sold it because it made money on it.

I had time left for study and I made use of it; I attended high school through a correspondence program and passed my exams in '62. I knew that there would be no chance to go to university, as I had defected, and I work for the congregation. I attended the rabbi seminary[38] occasionally, with Rabbi Weisz's tacit consent, mostly when Samu Szemere taught Talmud or philosophy at the basic level. I didn't take any exams, as a member of the Orthodox congregation,[39] I was careful about this. In the meantime, I worked with children.

Feri Raj and I had two groups to whom we taught the fundamentals of Hebrew in our apartments. This wasn't looked on favorably, but in '65 the situation was more liberal. Jewish youth gathered at my house or at Feri's, usually at my house, as my parents didn't put restrictions on me, and I lived in the center of town, so everybody could come and go. In '65, when I got my passport, this broke up a little. Feri Raj wanted to study on at the university—I think he went into Persian studies—and I heard that he was called in and talked to. If he wanted to be admitted, he should discontinue his Hebrew classes and there shouldn't be much hanging around in groups. But this warning wasn't in earnest. We also noticed that we were being followed in the streets, but we didn't take it very seriously.

Dr. Sebestyén would have liked it very much if I had stayed, jobs were recommended to me, he wanted me to study to become a *shokhet*. Others recommended that I should marry, or suggested that I would be elected secretary. I can't say that I wasn't happy, those were my best years, but there was patriotism in me; once someone has lived in Israel, his heart always longs to return.

Miklós Braun

—Those who emigrated, 70 percent of them had well-to-do relatives supporting those who emigrated.

38. the rabbi seminary: The Rabbinical Seminary of Hungary, 27 József Körút, Budapest (map 2 C3).

39. as a member of the Orthodox congregation: The Orthodox regard the use of seminaries to train rabbis as a violation of the traditions of the faith.

—You didn't have anybody?

—We didn't have anybody. My sisters also started at such a level, at the most basic level. They went into a kibbutz; that's where they started. My oldest son emigrated; he wanted to go into a kibbutz, so he could work there and be provided for. They said, we're sorry, but you're too old—he was forty-six years old.

Poor Laci went back to the yeshivah for a while; he didn't want to go, I felt sorry for him.

Mrs. Zoltán Dickmann

But by then there was hardly anybody left; I think there were three or four. Then we already knew, as we had heard it within the congregation, that Benedikt was preparing to leave. When he left, the yeshivah was finished, at least as far as I know.

László Dickmann

—Poor Mrs. Weisz cooked separately for my Laci, so he wouldn't leave, so he'd stay there; well, she really would have done everything to please him. And I came in crying, my Lord, that my Zoli doesn't want this child to leave. Besides, he would have done better if he had stayed; he had great difficulty studying, and while he was there, he never failed a grade even once. Here he went through almost every class twice, but this can't be considered his fault. He studies the lesson, and recites it beautifully to his big sister, afterwards I also hear the lesson, and he knows it completely, totally well. The next day the poor child comes home with this little puffed up face and doesn't look either right or left, ay-ya-yay I say, there's trouble here, he got an F. Well this is a horrible thing, there's something wrong here. I didn't bother him, I just cried with him. A very good pediatrician named Dr. Szabó lived in the same courtyard, and I said to him that my child was sick when he was very small, and wasn't that connected to this. I should have given him into remedial instruction, but, you know, a person isn't eager to do such a thing with her child, especially if she doesn't know that he belongs there. I thought he would grow out of it, but no. As soon as he came home from the yeshivah, he flunked a grade.

—And was he a good student there?

—No, but he passed.

—I told him, head to the Sabbath-keeping cooperative and tell Jóska Rézmovits that you are Éva Deutsch's son and he will certainly give you a job. And really, he's been there since then. But there are no Sabbath-keeping people there anymore.

Mrs. Zoltán Dickmann

The older ones left, with regular emigrants' passports. Them I never even knew. Later whole families left, and that I remember. That Szenes was related to a family, the Bergers, who lived in Debrecen, with four or five children. They were the same way—the children didn't go to school anymore, and when the High Holy Days were done, they emigrated.

There were a few still upstairs, not many. Laci Horovitz was still there, and Sanyi Rosenfeld—a few years ago I used to meet him from time to time: he was going to high school, he was studying a trade, chemical engineering, I believe. But I don't see him these days; I don't even know if he's still here. He had an older brother who defected to Israel back in '64, I haven't seen him since. The students left, they petered out, and there wasn't much replacement, especially not in those days.

Unfortunately, this was the fault of the parents. In most places, the parents were young, around forty, not like my father. There were those who hid their Jewishness; I didn't know this as a child, but I have heard since then what went on in those days.

György Rosenberg

—We had no future. We didn't know that Gorbachev was coming. They couldn't advance, they couldn't go on with their religious studies at a higher level. But it wasn't up to me whether they emigrated; it was to their parents that they belonged, not to me, after all.

—Why did you emigrate?

—Well, because of the children! As long as it was possible, we kept them there to learn, but we knew we had to leave. When I left Hungary in '68, Rabbi Weisz continued to direct the yeshivah for a while longer. But there wasn't anybody to do it for, there were hardly any children left.

Sándor Benedikt

Clearly, they emigrated because of the children. He felt that their studies were problematic. One of my brothers, Khaim, was out in London for a year, and then came back, but couldn't go out again. The two biggest boys were eighteen and nineteen, and they would have been drafted. There were hardly children in the yeshivah, their further studies were problematic—it's clear that this is why they left.

The second floor of 48 Garay Street was one apartment. There were two spaces downstairs, the big shul and the little shul. There were beautiful glass windows; they are now in 35 Dob Street: how they got there, I don't know. In '69, when Dad and the family left, I had the apartment divided. The smaller part became mine; the Fülöp family got the two other rooms, precisely so they could keep the shul going. It was still going in '72; after that they went out too. Since then I've only been in Garay Street once, and I felt miserable.

Vera Benedikt

—After Benedikt emigrated to Vienna, they would have cut it off, the population began to scatter, things became a little looser. I studied to become a furrier. I didn't sleep in, we were already older—I spent my twentieth birthday in Vienna. If I hadn't left then, I would have been a soldier in a month. I would have emigrated sooner, since my cousin lives abroad, and I always said I was going to go where Gyurika was. I always felt that I wanted to go to America, but military service is two years, and then you aren't allowed out for another three years, so you won't carry out the Great Hungarian Security Secrets. And even after that, it's not certain that you'll be allowed out. It's a complete miracle that I finally succeeded.

—Did you defect?

—Yes, I defected. I snuck across the Yugoslav-Austrian border. It made quite a story—I had to go get permission from the military. The guy responsible came over to me—he must have been some kind of officer—he looks at my file and says, "You have a military obligation." I said, well, I know. Well, they hadn't fallen on their heads either. Why do I want to go to Yugoslavia? Have I been to Czechoslovakia? I said no. Had I been to Moscow? I said no. Nor to Romania, and he listed all the Communist countries. Now why do you want to go specifically to Yugoslavia, why don't you take a look at the other countries? I was so lucky, I had just read an article in the paper about the nudist beach, I called him over and said, I didn't want to say this in front of your secretary, one of my pals was in Yugoslavia and there's this kind of beach there full of gorgeous chicks, naked women, I have to go there! The guy began to laugh, okay, he was already signing the paper. That's fine he said, when you get back, come tell us what it was like.

—When I said goodbye to my parents, I said, listen here, if you see me within two weeks that means either that I was forcibly deported or that you'll see me dead. I won't come back otherwise.

Tamás Szenes

—How long did you attend the yeshivah?

—Until 1963. In '63, it officially stopped being a yeshivah, but there were still one or two children after that. I lived here in the dormitory up until I married. I was permitted to do this because I worked in Verpelét in the wine cellar. They really wanted me to go down there; there wasn't anyone else. I went down every week on Monday and came back on Thursday night. We made kosher wine—there were three of us, Mr. Domán and a guy named Guttstein, he's dead now. The three of us made the wine, and at harvest, when it was harvest time, then five or six others came with us from Budapest to help. I was twenty-three years old when I married. After that we moved to 16 Kazinczy Street.

Also, there wasn't much of anybody to learn with. Many people emigrated. My little brother also lived here, and another two or three people, the two Brachs and Szenes. I believe that's how many of us there were.

—Did you know that you were going to leave sooner or later?

—It wasn't possible to know that—we took things one day at a time. Many people left with their parents, and many people emigrated on their own. It was clear that there wasn't much future for Jewry.

—But, well, it would have been precisely you who provided that future. If your age group were here now . . .

—That's true. Nobody gave us a foundation. Nobody concerned themselves with saying, "Stay. We'll set things up for you, so that it will work out for you."

I made the wine for ten years. I got married, and my wife and I thought it would be better if we emigrated. We went to Vienna; we had to wait there for around eight months.

Tibor Weinberger

For a person to obtain a passport for emigration, it was necessary to have a permit for settling somewhere. I asked for permission to settle in both the USA and Austria, and I got it from the Austrians first. We turned in our passports right away. Then we were stuck in Vienna, I was a ritual supervisor in the slaughterhouse.

Sándor Benedikt

He invited us several times. In those days, he had a meat store; he always gave us chicken and frankfurters, and Tuli Brach worked for him in the slaughterhouse. We went out about the same time as this Brach boy, with only a few weeks' difference.

Tibor Weinberger

Benedikt treated everyone very decently, he was fair to the greatest extent. I got together with him frequently, I was often at their house for dinner.

Tamás Szenes

I left in '69, because of military service. I didn't want to become a soldier, because in the army you can't keep the Sabbath. I talked over everything with my parents; they didn't want me to stay. I wasn't the first: there were others as well who fled abroad. I tried to get out through Romania—Israel had diplomatic relations with Bucharest—but they wouldn't let me do anything. The restrictions were even tighter there than in Hungary; even though the connections with Israel were there, Ceaușescu was much stricter in internal matters than Hungary. I went to the embassy in Bucharest, but they said they didn't know anything. I came back to Hungary. *Shokhet* Katz, who had been sent from Israel to Hungary for slaughtering animals for export, told me that the Belgrade congregation would take care of this. First I asked for a passport to Yugoslavia, but my request was denied. Then I asked for a passport to Bulgaria. The train passes through

Belgrade. It stopped for half an hour, I had no right to get off, but I got off. I went in to the congregation; they could tell from my manner that I wanted to get away. There, there was somebody who helped. He worked for the Belgian embassy but had been placed clandestinely there by Israel. My Hungarian documents were taken away and I was given a paper stating that I am an Israeli citizen, I lost my passport, and I am on my way back here. If, God forbid, I had been forced back to Hungary, I would have had to serve a bunch of years.

I had to stay there in Belgrade for a week while they arranged the ticket. I had a little trouble when I went to the airport and showed this paper. They stopped me and didn't want to believe that it was genuine. I indicated that I didn't know English. I didn't want to indicate that I knew Hungarian, because then they would figure out that I had fled. I didn't have any Hungarian papers on me; they had all been taken. They went into the office and telephoned the embassy, asking whether my paper was true or was it a fake. I was so afraid, I thought they would make me go back. I was between life and death. They said it was in order and let me through. I went to Athens, and there was a man from the Jewish Agency already waiting for me at the airport. I slept one night in Athens, and the next day I was already here. During that week I was in Yugoslavia, I couldn't send any kind of notice to my parents; it wasn't possible to phone, because my calls were monitored and they were very frightened because they didn't know that it would take a week for me to travel. So they had to wait another two weeks until they got the letter. And even then I couldn't describe what happened openly, I had to give a sign. They were called in by the police—it wasn't easy. My parents said that I was over sixteen, they weren't responsible for me anymore, I had run away and they didn't know anything about me. I was sentenced to ten years in prison. For ten years I couldn't go to Hungary. I couldn't meet with my parents for three years; they also weren't permitted to go abroad. I had to travel to Romania—I had an aunt in Kolozsvár and we met there. When I married, my father wasn't permitted abroad, and neither was my mother. She went to Vienna, the embassy there gave her false papers, so nobody knew that she was also coming here; they didn't even stamp her passport that she had been to Israel.

Izrael Weisz

In Vienna, the Americans sent me to the Israeli embassy. There they wouldn't leave me alone, and talked to me for hours, trying to sway me. I said that if I had come out a little sooner, in '67, then certainly I wouldn't have gone anywhere else but Israel. It had been so much a part of me that I wanted to be a soldier there, fighting for Israel. But I had gotten some sense by then and said to myself, why die. I'd rather go to America. And then finally they resigned themselves to it.

Tamás Szenes

I traveled to Vienna, and there of all places I ran into Szenes—he had fled then too, but he didn't want to go to Israel. There wasn't anything else for me: you couldn't escape to America from Yugoslavia, they said they couldn't pay my expenses if I went to America.

When I arrived in Israel, to where the immigrants were, and the Jewish Agency organizes them, I said that I wanted to go among the religious. They didn't want to let me go to a yeshivah; they wanted me to go work in a kibbutz, but I stuck to my guns. For four years I studied in Jerusalem at the yeshivah from Eger, because it was Hungarian, and I had once met the rabbi in Budapest when he was visiting. The rabbi received me gladly. The greater part of the *bokhers* was Hungarian; in those days the children there still spoke Hungarian. I studied there until I married. After that I was a *mashgiakh* in a slaughterhouse in Tel Aviv; four or five years later I trained as a *shakter*—that also is a religious profession.

Izrael Weisz

—Why did you remain here?

—When the revolution took place, I had no intention in the world of leaving with five tiny little children. Anyway, I had already lived for two years in Germany—my oldest son was born there—but I nonetheless broke my neck to get home; my homesickness was so great that I thought I would lose my mind. After that, we tried to leave as a family; my husband went in to the Interior Ministry, as he had a very good friend—his name is Seifer, but then he was called Szívós—and he asked his help in getting us our passports. But it didn't do any good, we were refused. He said, Zoli, how many sons do you have? He says, four. Well, you see. Does Israel want your four sons for soldiers? Well Hungary does too! And we didn't get passports. We were completely beside ourselves, because quite a few people had wound their way out to Israel; this one had left, that one had left, dear God, am I really going to be the only one who stays here? It had just been two hundred years that the first Jew was admitted to Debrecen, and the council room was chock full, and I just looked at them and thought, "Thank God, I'm not the only Jew after all." So I'm here, aren't I? My oldest son went to Israel, but he's a mother's boy and so he came back.

Mrs. Zoltán Dickmann

—I think I left the yeshivah, because he hit me once and I said, that was the farewell smack, goodbye and I went home to Debrecen. I didn't come back anymore—my older brother and I knew that we were going to emigrate. My little brother was a lot younger; we couldn't take him with us into the world. My older brother was always trying to make us leave, but my dad was a *shakter*, a rabbi, in Debrecen, he didn't want to leave Jewry behind. All America knows that my father went to the villages to slaughter so that Jewish people could eat kosher; my dad was a very, very religious man. They know all about my dad in America today. My dad was very much loved, he had a very good name, no matter what they say. Even the Szatmár rebbe knew him.

—Nearly every country rabbi came up to Budapest.

—He didn't come up. He worked for three thousand forints a month, but he didn't want to come up to Budapest, he wanted to be in Debrecen. In 1969 he was out in Toronto, and he was offered a job as a *shakter* for a thousand dollars a week. That's a gigantic sum of money, but it was still the height of Communism and he had been given a passport in such a way that we had to stay here, and he didn't want to live abroad without the children.

My dad didn't get involved in politics, he was just very religious, he studied day and night. And he kept Jewry going for twenty years in Debrecen and its vicinity: Miskolc, Nyíregyháza, Kisvárda, Mátészalka, Nyírbátor, Hajdúszoboszló, Tiszafüred, Berettyóújfalu. Whatever is in eastern Hungary, he went there to slaughter. I remember, sometimes he put up for the night when he went to Miskolc; he left on Tuesday and came home on Thursday from somewhere. They hardly paid anything.

Mendel Deutsch

—After getting my high school diploma, I applied several times to medical school—I was an honor student throughout high school, but in those days the entrance examination didn't take place in such a way that they evaluated only your school record. In '68 it wasn't expressly an advantage to have gone to high school there—in '67 a person's chance of getting to university was minimal. I worked in several places; between two university entrance exams, I worked in a hospital, after that in a number of positions with the congregation. I was at the meat-processing plant that is today near Kővár; in those days Berkovits was the owner, before that it was the Rebenwurtz factory. Following that I directed the poultry business; meanwhile at the same time I took care of the congregation's administrative work in Újpest. My father was no longer living, I was seventeen years old when he died. I lived with my mother in Újpest up until I married. After many, many other positions, I became the director of the Síp Street congregation's Ritual Department, and after three years passed, I got to the Orthodox Division.

When Chief Rabbi Moyshe Weisz, may he rest in peace, began to be in poor health at the beginning of the seventies, and could no longer fulfill the function of *moyhel,* then we succeeded at solving the problem of circumcision with the help of an English gentleman. The issue was raised of whether someone would take over this function—I had intended to go into the medical profession, and I felt that I would have some talent for it. I studied in London with this gentleman—I lived at his house, and with the passage of two months I received my diploma. At one time, it was possible to study in Hungary, but nowhere else in the world have such high standards been implemented as in England; Israel and the United States, so I have heard, are far from achieving the English level.

—Why didn't you go abroad?

—My dad's illness unequivocally decided why not; after that, unfortunately, my mother had a similarly serious illness. I couldn't.

László Herczog

—How long did you remain in the yeshivah?

—Until I was an eighth grader, so until '68. Again, this was the parents' decision, not mine. My foster father must have had some idea that

I would come home and work in the tavern. My mother in her simple way saw that the tavern wasn't the surest means for the development of a fourteen-year-old child. Therefore, after a family agreement I went into a Jewish-founded organization, the Peace Cooperative, as an industrial apprentice, with the stipulation that I don't work on Saturday, I go to shul. With four years of yeshivah behind me, I became a reliable member of the minyan—I knew how to pray, if there was need for it. I went off as an industrial apprentice.

—Were there only Jews in the organization even then?

—Oh! There weren't five of us Jews out of one hundred twenty people. I got into an environment I was predisposed to: we began to be involved in KISZ which had been very much forbidden to me until then. For example, in public school, we were the only ones who were not Pioneers. At the same time, the Pioneer life was an interesting thing to children, whether it was full of ideology or not. I got very heavily involved: I started on that road and that aspect strengthened and the religious aspect weakened. The decline of the Orthodox minyan greatly contributed to this, and I came face-to-face with those problems which are the problems of otherness: why don't I work on Saturday? There were no anti-Semitic remarks—it was just that I functioned in a given community where "we cry together, we laugh together." This closed community had a great effect on me after the yeshivah, and these people taught me what I couldn't learn there and experience there. This was the time period, the seventies, when I became distanced from religion. This caused a conflict with my parents, and I said I couldn't square it with myself that let's say one day I go to a Party meeting, and the next day I go to shul.

I learned the toolmaking profession, I took my exams, and after that my father's dream came true, I worked there for a while in the tavern, but we didn't get along well with each other. I went back into the organization, and from there into the municipal KISZ board where I worked as an independent "paid revolutionary." I enlisted as a soldier, but by the time I was discharged in '79, my workplace had closed down. I took the exam for the Juhász Gyula School of Education folk art program, after which I worked in a cultural center and then went over to the council. After five years, I created a private company which dealt with tourism. In recent years, I am the person within the company who handles Israel. We are the national leaders in Israeli travel.

—How do you look back on your past in the movement?

—Similarly to the yeshivah: it was a formative period in my life, and I can't imagine a situation in which I would be ashamed of it. Through several terms, I was a member of the National Pioneer Council, for many years I directed the junior leaders. I treasure experiences from this time period which I couldn't have gotten elsewhere. In '87 I left it behind; I didn't support the upcoming party organization. There are strong agendas here, and I had to realize that the most important agenda is my own: this is what I had to represent and to defend.

György Budai

—There are many other people in Budapest who live on the same religious level as I: golden-mean Orthodox, not in externals but in the realm of feeling and its non-showy manifestations: the management of a strictly kosher household and family life of an Orthodox nature. A truly religious, Hasid lifestyle is practiced by Mr. Weisz and Srulcsi Weisz.

—Is there any chance that Orthodoxy will spring to life again?

—The possibility arose particularly when I myself began to direct a Talmud-Torah, six or seven years ago.[40] Those children must have lived through exactly the same things we did, though they didn't have as many restrictions, but they came here directly from school, they ate here, we studied all afternoon; there was a tutor in addition, with whom they did their homework. That host of children also had a strength of around twenty-thirty. Today they are studying abroad.

László Herczog

—How did I come to stay here? How do I know? I studied glassmaking in Majakovszkij Street. I was there a year, and when it came time for the second year, and I would have had to go to school on the Sabbath—my father wouldn't allow it, and my mother arranged that I was hired at a building trade company in Debrecen. Let's say, I was happy about it,

40. seven years ago: This interview took place in 1993.

too, but if I had known, I would have rather stayed in Budapest. In '68, I went home between the holidays—sadly, I was away a lot, there were no leaves, I was an apprentice at a company, and I had to go to work whether I wanted to or not, they wouldn't let me have time off—I had already been out so much. And then the message that I should come home, I don't find anyone at home, I go to the shul, and there I see that my father is dead. At *Shemini Atzeret*[41] they had called him up to the Torah as *maftir*, he recited the *maftir* and collapsed. I was left with my mother and my little sister, who was still a schoolgirl.

I didn't go abroad? A little bit, I didn't dare to go, to start off blind into the world, I don't know in what way it would have been possible to set out, there wasn't anybody I could have asked for help. Because of the draft, I didn't dare ask for a passport because it was always my bad luck that if I reached the age limit, it was always raised just then. When I became twenty-three, it was raised to twenty-five, and then from twenty-five to twenty-eight. I was happy to get out of the draft, I didn't have to go be a soldier. Unfortunately, I had good reason, and for this reason I didn't dare ask for a passport: I didn't want to call attention to myself. For precisely this reason, I also didn't travel abroad.

—You didn't have relatives abroad?

—There were some, but we didn't have any personal contact with them, only a letter-writing relationship until the seventies. My uncle first came here in '77. Another uncle already wanted to bring me and my sister out to America thirty years ago, but my mother was talked out of it. If it had come to that then, now I would surely not be here, and I would have been dropped into another world. What it would have been like, I don't know.

In '83 I got up to Budapest, first to Kővár, where I learned *treibering*.[42] After that I worked at the congregation and when Kálmán left in '85 I began to do it, I am a *mashgiakh*, a ritual supervisor, in Visegrádi Street and in the slaughterhouse. Besides that, it is my job to go out to the hospital

41. *Shemini Atzeret*: A holiday following the celebration of Sukkoth.

42. *treibering*: Porging: after the animal has been killed in accordance with Jewish law, this process removes the carcass's veins, *chelev* (caul fat and suet), and sinews.

for *treibering* and, when there's free time besides that, to go to the matzah bakery, and if wine is being made, then there also.

—You can't perform slaughtering.

—There's no chance of that! God forbid! *Shaktering* is a serious profession.

—You didn't want to become a *shakter*?

—No. They made me an offer that I should learn it, but, well, I felt that I couldn't master it. It needs to have a serious basis in learning—you can't shuffle pages and look up in books what the rules are. You have to decide that second whether something is kosher or not.

I learned many things here, I don't deny it. I lament many things which I didn't learn then, but I didn't like, well, I'll tell it honestly, I didn't like being here. I make very good use even now of those things, and moreover it wouldn't have hurt to know more. For me, the fifteen years I was down in Debrecen was a big loss. I worked for a company, I wasn't my own boss, I went out to the country to work; for years, I left in the morning, I came home at night, and in the summer there were mostly ten-hour workdays in the building industry. I was too tired to learn.

György Rosenberg

—My brother Kálmán went out only seven years ago. He lived in the courtyard of the Dessewfy shul, he was the slaughterer, he was the rabbi in the shul. There are these books of Jewish photographs, he is in every one.

—Where does he live now?

—Now he's in Williamsburg, in New York. About half an hour from me.

—What do you do?

—I remained with the profession. I work at a wine company, it's called Kedem, a very famous company.

If somebody comes, we always get together a little. I keep my connections with everyone, or at least I try to.

Tibor Weinberger

We were twenty years old when we got out to America. I work at one of the biggest publishers, Simon and Schuster, I am a credit manager there.

Without me this company can't sell any books. There are 9,200 people working there and I am the only religious Jew. Janki has a baked goods factory, thirty-eight people work for him. Therefore I believe that we are the ones who did pretty well in America.

Mendel Deutsch

It's a nice memory for me, and for the children who studied with me. I think the students were very loyal. One of them wrote the kind of letter that says he remembers the olden times, and he owes a debt of gratitude. Another, whom I haven't met in a good long time, sent me a message, that I should visit him. If somebody came to us once or twice, it was always a joy, like when a man meets up with his children.

Sándor Benedikt

◆ ◆ ◆

And I want to say that Benedikt wrote my *droshe* for my bar mitzvah, even though he was very busy then; I think his son was just getting ready to leave for London.

Tamás Szenes

About two weeks before his bar mitzvah, Tomi said that he still didn't know his *droshe*, what the child recites in the shul. I say, well tell Rabbi Benedikt. I told him, he said, but he doesn't have time. He asked me to speak to him. I said to him, "Mr. Benedikt, Tomi is complaining, that he doesn't know his *droshe* yet, and he's afraid." "Pay attention to me! I know your son. Better than you do. He's going to know the *droshe* so well, so you can relax."

Mrs. László Szenes

We were bald in the yeshivah; I had to cut off my hair to zero, and my *foter*[43] took me to the hairdresser, but said he didn't want to make my head bald; instead he had it styled. Benedikt was insulted by this, and he didn't come, even though he wrote the talk. Except for that the bar mitzvah was very pleasant, in the Kazinczy; there were many rabbis there, just

43. *foter*: Yiddish for father.

not him. Garay Street was also far away, but that wasn't the problem. This hurt me, I could even say it hurts me to this day.

Tamás Szenes

Rabbi Weisz congratulated me, I received a great deal of praise at how well Tomi spoke the *droshe*. Everything was beautiful: the table was set beautifully, the child gave the speech beautifully, kosher wine, kosher pastries from the kosher bakery, many boxes of grapes, Mrs. Weisz provided the tablecloth, we borrowed the dishes, there was a Jewish dish store in Király Street. It was a beautiful bar mitzvah. And he ruined it with that haircut. It doesn't matter.

My son—I'm not allowed to praise him to his face—is very learned. He is a great Talmud scholar. It's just that now he doesn't follow it. But here in the Akácfa Street shul he *leyned*, and that's a great thing, if a person knows how to *leyn*, he has to know a lot. For this you have to have a special understanding, and he always *leyned* in the shul, and moreover, also he was always taken up to Balatonfüred to pray on the Sabbath, even when he was just a child; I waited for him at the train when he came back from Balatonfüred and I shouted, "Tomi! Tomi!" I was so afraid that he went alone, and he came back alone too.

I worked there in the Klauzál market, in a small private stall. I couldn't stand to go home without stopping in, I never went with empty hands, I always brought something he liked. He loved bananas—in those days it was still interesting to get your hands on some—well, as a worker there, I was always told when there were bananas, and I'd say, put away four pounds for me, and then I'd run up to him, in those days I ran up the three flights easily. And he didn't want to let me go, "Mommy, stay here. Sleep with me!" I'd often sit there for hours. He was the kind of child who'd make friends with anyone, and he also saw that his mother was always visiting, so he relaxed.

Mrs. László Szenes

The Minyan at Kassa

The Kazinczy Street[1] Orthodox synagogue is cold, even though this is the end of May. The building was unheated all winter, and the sun has been working slowly since then to warm the thick stone walls. The shul is open only on holy days, or not even then. Sometimes they greet the Sabbath in the small prayer house on Harang Street. Next to the prayer house is another Orthodox synagogue, but this is no longer a house of worship; it doesn't even belong to the Jews. The city uses the worn, hundred-year-old building for book storage: most of its disintegrating piles of paper have been chewed by rats or destroyed by dampness. At night, the books and the ancient synagogue wail together, raising their moans in Hebrew, Yiddish, Hungarian, Slovakian, and German, though there is no one around at that hour, no ear to hear them.

For now, Kassa's minyan meets every day. Morning and night, as many as thirteen or fourteen old men pray together. There are those who arrive promptly; others are sitting around well before the service starts, waiting for the eighth, ninth, and tenth man. They talk together or they just watch quietly, nodding on occasion when they hear something especially sensible.

"And you, sir, where have you come from, that you speak Hungarian so well?" one of them asked the night I first strolled in.

"From Budapest." And then they all looked at me, because strangers hardly ever turn up here, not even half strangers from Budapest.

"I hope you're for the MTK."[2]

1. Kazinczy Street: Now called Puškinova Street.

2. MTK, Fradi: MTK stands for the Magyar Tornaklub, a national soccer team that had the reputation in the 1930s and 1940s of being a "Jewish" club because of a number of Jewish members. Fradi is a nickname for the Ferencvárosi Tornaklub, another football team.

"No, I'm a Fradi fan."

"Well, I heard what those guys were up to last time, as usual, throwing stones at the clubhouse and shouting, 'Dirty Jews.' They're a bunch of fascists. Decent Jews don't root for the Fradi."

"But after the war they were the first to give jerseys and balls to get the MTK started again. Anyway, I'm not a Jew." Then I had to explain what I was doing there, that I was going to what used to be a world-famous yeshivah at Hunfalu where there would soon be the *yortsayt* of Chief Rabbi Sámuel Rosenberg.

"What! You say you're not a Jew, but you know what a *yortsayt* is. If you know what a *yortsayt* is, and you know about the Hunfalva[3] yeshivah, then you must be a Jew. I don't care what you say, as far as I'm concerned, you are," he said, looking at the other men. Several nodded silently.

As the time for evening prayer approached, the numbers in the little prayer house grew. Miksha Reisman was the last to enter. Two fingers together, he caressed the mezuzah fixed at an angle to the doorpost, then raised the fingers to his pale, narrow lips and kissed them. His face too was narrow, and his skin very white, revealing blue veins around his eyes and at his temples. Stubble grew on his chin; he had buried his third wife only a week ago, and he could not cut any of his hair during the mourning period. The law stipulates that a Jew must not only mourn inwardly but must also give outward signs of his grief. In fact, under ordinary circumstances he was supposed to be at home, sitting on the floor, until the shivah, the first week of mourning, was over. But the death occurred just before Shavuot, the feast of the Giving of the Torah, and the obligation to keep the feast absolves the bereaved from "sitting shivah," so he came to pray, but hadn't touched his beard, as that restriction applies for the entire thirty-day mourning period.

"I hear you're from Pest. What part of the city do you live in?" he asked me later in a weak voice. He was the third one that night to name streets in Pest, asking did I know where they were, because the questioner

3. Hunfalva: Known as Hunfalu after 1902; today Huncovce (Hunsdorf), Slovakia (map 1 A4).

had once been there, or had relatives and acquaintances, maybe no longer living, whose faces and voices could be evoked merely by mentioning the melodious names of streets in the city.

"My little brother lived in Nagymező Street," the old man said quietly in a very tired voice. He was cold, too, though it was still warm; the sun hadn't set. On his shriveled ninety-two-year-old body, the long black coat flapped as if it had been left forgotten on a broken, dried-out tree branch.

The next day, after morning prayer, everyone gathered to eat a little cake and throw back a shot of brandy. Mr. Braun, the assistant chairman, filled a glass to the brim and held it out to me. Ferdinand Glück, who used to learn at the Hunfalva yeshivah, brought a book with him. Except for the rabbi's name, he remembers nothing, but here is this book—*The Master and His Student* by József Guttmann—it contains everything that I am interested in knowing about. Mr. Reisman waited until we were alone, and then took out an envelope with a few photographs and the copy of a letter.

"Allow me to point out my son, this one here." He indicated a Jewish boy standing with three others in some kind of school corridor. The photograph was published long ago in the 1943 newsletter of the Jewish high school at Munkács.[4] With a trembling finger, he caressed the paper, touching his son's face, his hair and his hand.

"And then what happened to him?"

"Well, what happened to Jews? I sent this picture and the newsletter to the Yad Vashem museum. I wrote a letter with it to explain everything. Also, I once wrote an article for *Új Élet*,[5] 'Eyewitness to the deportations at Munkács,' I called it. Tonight I'll bring that too."

◆ ◆ ◆

The one-story house behind the prayer house was once the residence of Orthodox Chief Rabbi Moses Jungreisz. Today, the main floor is occupied by the office of a small business while a family lives upstairs. He works in

4. Munkács: The people in the ghetto in this town (now Mukačeve in the Ukraine) were deported to Auschwitz-Birkenau in May 1944 (map 1 A6).

5. *Új Élet*: The official paper of the Hungarian Jewish organized community. See also the glossary.

a factory; she has charge of the keys to the prayer house and the houses of worship, as well as cleaning the congregation's office area. When I ask, she brings down the keys to the mikveh without a word and opens the door of the ritual bath. A narrow staircase leads down into the depths, each step seemingly colder than the one before. At the first level, two twelve-foot, white-tiled pools await the arrival of the bathers who will immerse themselves, head and all, in the clean, cold water, until they are completely clean. The old ritual bath beneath our feet no longer waits for anyone: it has been disfigured by heaps of old furniture, boards, and dusty rubbish. Here even the lightbulb doesn't work. You can make out the circle of changing rooms around the dead bath, but the water beyond isn't visible. The woman leans across the railing and drops a small pebble into the depths. Two, three seconds pass before it reaches the bottom with a plangent, lazy plop.

Beside the building extends a low fieldstone wall with an iron door that leads to the congregation's courtyard. The offices of the community are here, along with the slaughterhouse and the kosher kitchen. These facilities are not functioning now, as the raw, bumpy surface of the courtyard is littered with piles of sand and rubbish; the renovations will take until August. The project's cost is half a million korona[6] and an extended interruption in the meat supply, but the work couldn't be put off any longer, because in Czechoslovakia,[7] you couldn't spend money on this until now.

At *Pesakh* they received matzah from Hungary, and not long ago the JDC[8] sent Israeli canned goods which are being given out just now. The program has been going on for a week and a half, but the supply shed is still piled high with brown cartons of canned meat and fruit. Mr. Spiegel, the congregation secretary, is very busy; someone always drops in to his

6. korona: The pre-1927 Hungarian currency: these Hungarian Jews use its name instead of *koruna*, the Czechoslovak unit of currency.

7. Czechoslovakia: This interview was done in 1991, before the breakup of Czechoslovakia.

8. JDC: Acronym for the Joint Distribution Committee; it provided funds for economic rehabilitation of shattered communities.

office and needs to be given supplies, but at the same time he has to keep the distribution equitable. To make it worse, there will be a funeral this afternoon and the *shames* is out sick, so the secretary has to do the inspection as well to make sure that the grave has been dug deep enough. In the cemetery he finds everything in order. After exchanging a few words with the groundskeeper, a big strapping man who looks like a village blacksmith, the secretary takes the trolley back to the congregation offices; the washers of the body can proceed.

The cemetery groundskeeper lives with his mother. The handful of vegetables grows just as well here, the few chickens scratch as successfully here, the assigned apartment is no more run-down than one they would get outside the fence.

The mother works along, keeping herself busy; she is the one who assembled the coffin of rough wood. She lays down the shovel, hoes, rakes a bit, and then brings a bucket and fills it to the brim with water from the tank on a wagon parked in the yard. For the anticipated mourners she sets out a clean towel; an observant Jew washes his hands before leaving the cemetery.

They can't use the pump in the garden because oil seeps into the ground from the neighboring bus garage and pollutes the water, making it undrinkable, complains the woman in Slovakian; I wouldn't be able to understand her if she didn't act out what she is saying with her hands. With gestures, she invites me to view the deceased if I want, there's nothing frightening about it. I wouldn't like to see the body laid out, naked; I gesture back that I'd rather take a look at the graves of the rabbis, and I start up the gradual slope to the Orthodox part of the cemetery: somehow, their plots always wind up in the back.

Jews were allowed to settle at Kassa and found a congregation only after the National Assembly of 1840 passed a law extending their rights. Before that, only three or four tenant innkeepers[9] in all could spend the night inside the city walls. After the ban was lifted, the majority of settlers

9. tenant innkeepers: Since the Jewish Laws did not permit them to own property, Jewish innkeepers rented their establishments.

came from Rozgony, four miles away, in those days the site of a well-established congregation. Márton Kohn, the first rabbi of Kassa, also came here from a position in Rozgony. The prayer house in Harang Street was built in 1842, and by 1866 the new synagogue had been completed, although many did not cross its threshold. In fact, the year before, a rabbinical congress had held a meeting at Nagymihály which was an important step in self-definition and codified the six criteria for the observant in synagogue building and liturgy. Even a passing glance revealed that the new house of worship at Kassa failed to meet two of the six regulations: its builders had fancifully adorned it with towers, and they had not centrally located the *almemor,* the platform used for reading the Torah. The prayer house had been closed upon the dedication of the new synagogue; the Orthodox at Kassa requested that it be reopened for their use, but the Neolog wouldn't hear of it. At that time in Hungary there were similar disputes in a number of congregations, and their adjudication was usually entrusted by the government[10] to well-known rabbis. Márkus Hirsch, the rabbi of Óbuda, was delegated to resolve the issue at Kassa, but the Orthodox did not accept his decision prohibiting further use of the prayer house. From then on, there were those who preferred the open air, meeting for prayer in a garden on Szepsi Street, and thereby expressing more than incidental devotion to their beliefs.

In 1871, the Orthodox group at Kassa withdrew from their mother congregation formally as well. In a few years, they established more educational and charitable societies than the much bigger and financially more secure congressionals. In addition to the *Khevrah Kadishah,* which was fundamental to their constitution as a congregation, they established, despite their financial problems, the *Shas Khevrah,* the *Bikur Kholim,* and the *Gemilat Khasadim* societies, all functional in the first year, as well as a Talmud-Torah and an Orthodox grade school. Following the break, they

10. the government: In 1868, the Hungarian government called a congress to try to establish a single bureau to govern Judaism, so disputes of all sorts would be adjudicated by that body in the manner described here. However, the Orthodox community withdrew from the congress and rejected all forms of external centralized authority. See the Introduction, p. xvin6, for details.

built their own synagogue in Harang Street, and in 1888 they began to operate their own cemetery separated by a fence from that of the Neolog.

The doctrinal disputes are long gone, but the wall still stands. It has sunk a little, and ivy runs along its top, but the stones are sound. The Orthodox cemetery extends across two hills; in the valley between them runs a little stream with a small bridge across it. A bit to one side, the ruined mortuary is on its last legs; eyes poked out and *kapedli* knocked off, it waits for someone to take pity and recite the prayer for the dead over it.

On the hilltops, substantial little houses[11] rise above the cemetery. The *ohel* covering the resting place of the Jungreisz family[12] is on the near hilltop, right next to the entrance; on the other side of the stream stand the "tents" of Chief Rabbi Brach,[13] the *gaon* of Radomyshl,[14] and the rebbes from Sztropkó and Biecz:[15] thus the learned men surround and oversee their by now eternally faithful flocks.

There are no burials here anymore. There is only the very occasional visitor with an entreaty from Brooklyn, an imprecation from Bnei Brak and a pebble or two which he does not toss, though this would be the place for it; stray dogs circle the motionless white stones in the "house of life."[16]

The man who is being buried this afternoon converted to Christianity before the war, then became a Jew once again in the sixties. They say he painted his own self-portrait in a prayer shawl more than once. He is Lajos Feld, the famous painter and graphic artist; in those days, his artistic abilities saved his life. Mengele himself wanted to conduct experiments on his

11. substantial little houses: See the glossary, *ohel*.

12. Jungreisz family: Rabbi Moses (Moshe HaLevi) Jungreisz who became chief rabbi in 1889 and his son Rabbi Ignác (Yitzchok Tzvi HaLevi) Jungreisz who succeeded him in 1906, serving until his death in 1933.

13. Chief Rabbi Brach: Shaul Brach.

14. the *gaon* of Radomyshl: Shmuel Engel was born in Radomyshl in the Ukraine, and came to Kassa (map 1 A5) during World War I: *gaon* is a Hebrew word, an honorific for a great Talmud scholar.

15. the rebbes from Sztropkó and Biecz: Rabbi Avraham Shalom Halberstam was from Sztropkó in Slovakia and is buried near Rabbi Ahron Horovitz from Biecz, Poland.

16. house of life: Translation of the Hebrew for cemetery, *bet ha-khayim*.

dwarfish body but was disposed first to sit for a portrait before the little Jew. After that, the other SS summoned him, one after the other; he had to trade his bread ration for paper and charcoal, but at least he didn't become a specimen for the enlightenment of German medical science, and the secret of his nonconformity in stature was kept from the uninitiated. Later, in the seventies and eighties, prizes and commendations were awarded to the painter's students, while Lajos Feld received nothing at all, because, in those days, Czechoslovakians didn't like religious men, or Jews.

"The country had three great enemies: South Africa, Chile, and Israel. Of course there was no anti-Semitism, just anti-Zionism: the newspapers were full of it, you could hear it everywhere," said Pál Foltyn, a member of the Jewish club, a few days later. For some time now, the young people at Kassa have been gathering once a week in the congregation. Sometimes thirty come, sometimes even more; there were at least seventy on the day the American consul visited them.

"In those days it was very difficult for a Jew to get the better jobs," continued Foltyn, "because you had to declare your foreign relatives in your autobiography.[17] I never denied my relatives in Israel, why would I have, they knew all about it at the police station. A whole separate department dealt with Jewish matters; they were always watching us. So in the seventies we would arrange it so that we went skiing in Ždiar,[18] and we regularly met our friends from Budapest there."

Pál Foltyn is a young man. He doesn't keep mentioning the names of Sándor Pohl, Csatáry, and Horváth the chief of police, like the old men. He doesn't talk about the brick factory at Kassa from which they deported those 12,000 Jews, among the first in the nation. Between the middle of May and the beginning of June, five shipments left Kassa, but the city also saw the other 130 Hungarian transports, as it was a point of junction in the railroad line between the country and Auschwitz.

17. autobiography: The Communists required workers to describe their life experience in a biographical document, as in a resumé or *curriculum vitae*, but the narrative was intended to reflect their conformity to the goals of the Party.

18. Ždiar: resort town in northern Slovakia, then Czechoslovakia (map 1 north of A4).

There must be 200 people at the Sunday morning ceremony commemorating the martyrs. Dr. Juraj Czikk, the young president of the congregation, is conducting his speech in Slovakian; I understand only the place names. Mr. Frankel is standing beside me, in his hand the latest issue of *Rosh Chodesh* from Prague. He just came home from Israel, he gained a little weight because of his sister's fine cooking. On Friday night when he got back and headed immediately for the prayer house, he told everyone how many kinds of fruit he saw at the market, and that even on the coolest day it was 25 degrees warm, and that nobody called him a Jew—at this everyone began to nod.

"There were eight children in my family," he says. I lean closer to hear him over the speech, "We had a little store. Well, that little *kreizlerei* made just enough money to feed the ten of us. Now all I have is this one sister and a brother in America, that's how many of us are left. And some Slovakian 'democrats' say it's all just a children's story, that all they did was take Jews to Germany for a labor exchange. Well, I lived through this children's story."

The martyrs' ceremony continues with kiddush at Kazinczy Street. In the synagogue, there are only a few old men listening to the rabbi, the young ones are out in the courtyard talking.

"They don't understand Yiddish, and I certainly can't speak Slovakian in the house of worship!" bursts out Sámuel Groszmann, the rabbi, cantor, and kosher butcher at Kassa. Until he was twenty years old, he learned at a yeshivah; in 1942 he fled to Ungvár to escape the Slovakian deportation. He hid out there until '44, but when the Hungarians too started the deportation, there was no place left for refuge. Afterwards he went home to Nagymihály: from '56 to '72 he was in the service of the congregation, leading the Talmud-Torah group until it was banned. By then there were so few members left anyway—they had died or emigrated—that he too went to live at Kassa.

"Then I worked only at Kassa, but that was enough. Then the rabbi at Eperjes died, and then the one at Pozsony, so that eventually I had to supply the entire Slovak territory. Today I am the only one in all Czechoslovakia: next week I have to go to Pozsony, though I am seventy-nine years old and my wife is seriously ill. At one time, I used to make the circuit to

Prague, but I wouldn't have the strength for that now. I have no backup, even though I miss it very much, because I am tired, and I can't endure it anymore."

"Why don't they call someone from Israel or America?"

"No one wants to come here. We couldn't pay the person in dollars, and he certainly wouldn't want korona. There is no one among the younger ones who could be trained. The learning has to start when the child is young, and the forty-year-olds here don't even know the alphabet. Now it's permitted to go to temple, it would be permitted to learn, but it doesn't interest anyone. Two thousand Jews live in Slovakia, but they are completely scattered. Maybe if we were together, we could do something about it—but as it is, there's no escape."

◆ ◆ ◆

The door keeper at the city hospital was just having his coffee break.

"Excuse me, sir, would you happen to speak Hungarian?"

"Me? Why, I do everything in Hungarian! I can't even run in any other language," he responded, and I was sorry he showed me where to go while sitting down, because I never saw a stunt like that.

Mr. Reisman was assigned to a three-bed room; he looked up from his bed near the window, across from the door. The towel across the window was no curtain, and the sun shone right on his head. I had asked the doctor in charge what the problem was; they suspected pneumonia, she said, and he was a little weak, but he should be able to go home soon. The old man still had the IV in his slender white arm; we smiled, when we said goodbye, at having to shake with our left hands.

"I set out the *Új Élet* for you, but they brought me in here because I was very weak." I promised to look it up in the library. I brought a kilo of oranges; in exchange he offered me tomatoes. The others watched TV while he told me about the magnificent Lonyay estate and about the theater at Munkács where, as an art-loving journalist, he had always been welcome. I was sitting there beside his bed, leaning quite close to him, but still, I barely heard it when he said, "Life was good."

Downward

I first went to Dessewffy Street because I heard somewhere that the old men who went to shul there still spoke Galícian Yiddish.

A man with a shaven face stood in front of the Orthodox synagogue. He was born in Csorna or Sárvár, I don't remember which, and he learned Yiddish there long ago. But here, he said, nodding toward the synagogue, they only speak Hungarian nowadays.

The second time, I was looking for Berkowitz. He lives in Brooklyn but is often found in Budapest, and whenever possible he prays in the Dessewffy every morning. I waited a while, sitting on the badly planed bench worn smooth and shiny over the years. I made a mound of the hard, dry, *barkhes* crumbs left over from who-knows-what morning. From time to time I looked out the window. Berkowitz didn't come, and I just sat on, looking at the dawn-rising, threadbare old men as they shuffled here and there, unwinding the rolled-up straps of their tefillin, then raising the leather case of the phylactery to their lips and kissing it, afterwards fitting the straps to the dry skin of their anguished foreheads with fastidious, thoughtful movements, and beginning their bowing prayers.

A wall clock ticked next to the Ark. Water dripped into the sink, monotonously, the way it does from those old faucets—there's no point to going over and turning them harder—you can only dismantle them, not turn them off. I began to feel the tap was answering the clock: if the drops of water didn't thud on the chipped enamel at the bottom of the sink, neither would the wall clock strike any more.

I go there often.

The arched doorway opens onto a tiny open square. Dingy firewalls molted to gray rise on either side, their grayness unrelieved by the green of a slender little sumac with roots sunk God-knows-where. But below, the tiny courtyard is magically transformed to fairytale splendor by a tiny secret door, gallery steps vanishing into darkness and the red-brick, Norman-windowed building of the shul.

The best time to be here would be when the first snow falls.

On a summer morning when you sniff the air and know right away that today will glow even hotter than yesterday, and that even if there will ever be rain again, it won't get here any sooner than fall, Mr. Helfer, one of the leaders of the Dessewffy shul, said, "There won't be a minyan today." There was a quarter hour or so until the start of the prayers, and only three men had come: Helfer, Béla Grósz, and a bespectacled, baseball-capped boy who spent his workday carving up raw beef in the kosher salami factory in Kővár.

More people could have come, but Mr. Helfer had already at home counted up those who weren't worth waiting for. Some were in America or Israel, others were vacationing at Balatonfüred. Two had fallen sick, and one had business to take care of. Later there came three lightly dressed, tan-skinned French Jews; they retreated instantly, but Helfer succeeded at explaining how badly they were needed. "Maybe we can pray after all," said Béla Grósz, and he began to count. "Seven," he said at last. Don't count me, I said, so six remained.

I was looking at a notice on the wall when Mr. Vas arrived. I didn't hear him enter, or offer a greeting, nor did I notice the new round of counting instigated by his arrival, although all these things must have taken place. It was only when I turned away from the wall that I noticed a bony-faced old man with thick spectacles sitting behind me. In his hand he held a cord-bound shoebox; he was already loosening the strings with his thick, horny fingernails and sighing sharply from time to time. He put the lid beside himself, reached into the box, began to draw out *kapedli*, scarves, and bobby pins, and then addressed Grósz, who was sitting a little further away, "My dear Béla!"

At that time Béla Grósz sold devotional objects in Kozma Street; he used to sit at the entrance of the cemetery with *kapedli*, picture postcards, and three-week-old copies of *Új Élet* on his table. Once an American journalist didn't ask for change from a dollar, though he was buying a postcard. Béla Grósz told everyone this story; I had heard it several times.

When Vas addressed him, he had already rolled up his shirtsleeves and was already holding his tefillin in his hand. Others would hardly allow their attention to be diverted at such a moment, but Bélá stepped readily toward Vas, and even waited patiently while he looked for a piece of paper for him to write down what he said. "Pay attention, my dear Béla, I wouldn't like to repeat what I said. Sell the silk *kipah* for 300, the velvet one for 320. Two-twenty of that is mine, that's what I bought them for. This ladies' scarf, let that be 150. Or you can sell it for 100. Sell the bobby pins for 20 forints." "That'll be too much"—remarked Grósz. "Eighteen then." "Even that's too much; it's 5 forints in the store, I can't ask for more."

They finally wrote a 10 on the slip of paper, next to the word "pins." From now on in Kozma Street, the black and white postcard representing the Buda castle would cost 15 forints, the German-language guide to the Jewish Museum would be 30: Vas had bought them long ago for the same price.

Together they put the whole kit and caboodle back in the box. "Look after this," said Vas. "It has considerable value. Shall we check through it again?" But Grósz only shook his head from under the prayer shawl spread over himself: everything will be fine.

Mr. Vas doesn't pray, doesn't put on tefillin, and doesn't cover himself with a tallit. He himself is not sure whether he believes in God, he is just the kind who likes to round things out, the man who should be tenth: when he sees that there are too few even with him or that there are enough even without him, he looks at his watch and sets off about his business. "I'm not a *tsadik*," he says at such times, although he is from Tőketerebes in Zemplén, and so comes from one of the most Orthodox regions of the country. However, we should take him as an example that even there everyone is not born to be a rabbi. "I'm not religious," he explained once. "I clean the house for the Sabbath, I cook the green beans. I say the *Shema Israel*, and that's it. Gyula Gózon never prayed either, just when he was taken to the hospital, he was visited by the congregation, and then he said the *Shema Israel*—that calmed him down and he died well."

"I don't want a religious woman," he muses. "She should light candles when needed and what she cooks should be kosher. I don't want any more than that, I'm not the Gerer rebbe."[1]

One Friday morning, Béla Grósz brought up an acquaintance, a sixty-year-old widow who has a house in Zugló, and a car and a garden-plot in the country besides. Vas had him repeat the most important particulars several times, and got him to describe the woman›s appearance, asking for the details again and again; presently, they agreed that Grósz would talk to the widow at the charitable residence on Városmajor Road, where he would be spending Shabbat.

On Sunday morning, Mr. Vas put on a clean shirt, tied his necktie, and—which hadn't happened much until then—was among the first to reach the shul. Grósz only came later, and he was preoccupied with something. Vas stared at him for a while. "It's not urgent," he said a little offended, and when the other man didn't respond even to this, he asked impatiently, "Well, have you no news for me?"

As I said, Grósz was preoccupied just then and what was wanted of him didn't quite sink in. "News? I only have this one," he said, absent-mindedly drawing a ragged-edged, last-week's copy of *Új Élet*[2] from his shopping bag.

◆ ◆ ◆

Jósika Street 4 is entirely different. Perhaps its only resemblance to the Dessewffy synagogue is that this apartment house in Erzsébetváros is just as surrounded by its taller, more bulky companions. It's as characterless, and nondescript as the street, as the whole neighborhood. It's gray, summer and winter.

It's already a hundred years that a family, the Kattlers, lived upstairs; the house was theirs, along with the hat factory on the first floor. One day,

1. The Gerer rebbe: Ger (the Yiddish name for Góra Kalwaria, Poland) was the location of a notable Hasidic community. The expression means "I am not so strict."

2. *Új Élet*: The official paper of the Hungarian Jewish organized community. See also the glossary.

their little girl was playing on the balcony, rolled over the railing, fell down and died. Her parents established a prayer society in her memory, and they turned the premises of the hat company into a shul. They even named it after her, "Erzsébet Kattler Prayer House." Every shul needs a name.

"I'm going to the Kattler to clean," said Mr. Helfer one morning when he had thought through his agenda for the day, and he considered how many sacks he would need for hauling the dishonored books and devotional articles to the cemetery. There had long been no Torah scroll in the prayer house; the two homeless men who had broken down the doors one night had found nothing but heavy, seemingly unsellable furniture and moldy-smelling books with stuck-together pages. They had had to make do with these: they selected several of the more elegant prayer books with metal-inlaid covers which they thought must be more valuable than the others, put a couple of candleholders under their arm and set out. Either the antiques store was closed or the books weren't wanted; they went on to Dob Street, where they asked for the chief rabbi. "Fine," they were told, "he'll be there in a minute, sit down meanwhile." And while the two homeless men dreamed of money, Mr. Herzog, the congregation's secretary, phoned the police.

Mr. Helfer nailed up the street door with a few boards and put things in order as well as he could. Next time they broke in from the courtyard.

When this happened, there hadn't been services in the Kattler for years. The rabbi had died, Mr. Berger went to the Kazinczy, even though he lived next door here. The early eighties were long gone! Back then there were regular services not just here but also in the prayer houses in Akácfa Street and Vörösmarty Street. Budapest had a Hungarian chief rabbi then, and you didn't have to bring in a ritual slaughterer from Vienna. There were more learned old men who had studied with famous rabbis and fewer unclaimed prayer books forgotten on the cooling seats of the shul.

But that was nothing in comparison to the sixties, when there were still shuls in Garay, Dobozi, and Majakovszkij Streets, when Ausster the butcher still weighed out kosher meat in Hernád Street, earlocked children still buried themselves in the Talmud in the little yeshivah in Dob Street, and summer was unimaginable without the Orthodox camp on Mount Szabadság.

And even then the fifties were long-gone, with their rabbis, slaughterers, and cantors who had remained faithful and devout even in the repressive atmosphere, the fifties with their Sabbath-keeping cooperatives, with the Budapest Talmud-Torah's six hundred true-born Orthodox children, and with synagogues full to overflowing morning to night with men and women who, having survived everything, thought it conceivable that they would die at home.

By the end of the Kádár regime, there were only crumbs left of all this, and the shuls had turned into old-age homes and hospices.

In the final days, only one little old man sat for an hour or two in the Kattler on Sabbath mornings. Breaking the prohibition a little, he would plug in the wall clock, light a lamp, wipe the dead flies off the table, take a prayer book in hand and quietly begin to murmur—I still saw him. Since the door was broken in and he can't come here anymore, he stays at home: he doesn't go to another shul.

Gyula Weisz's family lived in a courtyard apartment next to the prayer house. If they looked out the window, they could see a red Lada that was parked there day and night; beyond that were the wall on the opposite side, some dusty windows, and their own washed-out reflections in the glass. They didn't like to look out; they were afraid of the noise; they lived behind a locked door and closed windows.

Mr. Weisz moved with difficulty, Mrs. Weisz could hardly see and her feet hurt; their belated marriage could better be explained by their interdependence than by the enormity of their love.

The doctor came every two days, Helfer when he could, and I, when I remembered. The doctor rubbed ointment on Mr. Weisz's feet which had been frostbitten in the Ukraine, bandaged them, and left. Helfer brought this and that, he reported the news, and sooner or later, he too had to leave.

In the end, the old man came to expect me, too—he kept mentioning me if he didn't see me for a long time. When I went to see him, we discussed what the radio had said. He took out his photographs, we spread them out on the oilcloth like cards, and he marched his finger along the illustrated life's journey like the solitary playing piece of an inexhaustible board game. I looked a little longer at the picture of him as an earlocked *yeshivah bokher* than at the others. He noticed: "What is your opinion then, how old would I be?"—and he told me. "I don't believe it!" "I am very happy, that I have met with such kind and intelligent company as you, sir!"—he recited solemnly, squeezing my hand; at length, I said goodbye and went home.

At other times, we didn't look at pictures, he knew a few jokes, and he told them. He was no good at telling jokes. We laughed. Then he told stories about the Warsaw ghetto, where he cleaned ruins, or about the Ukraine, where he almost froze to death and where the Hungarian soldiers set fire to the hospital he was in, where they had taken him when he rolled off the filthy stretcher. Sometimes I asked him about it, sometimes he just remembered it suddenly, but whether it happened this way or that, he always had to get the Ukraine out of his system, with his frostbitten feet and the military hospital set afire around them, smelling of burning grease.

Miss Helénke, the Jewess from Máramaros with swollen feet and weak eyes, looked in on us from time to time. Otherwise she sat in the kitchen cleaning the menorah, she salted down the chicken, cleaned carrots or shelled peas, raising each one to her blinking, near-blind eyes before she dropped it into the bowl in her lap.

"*Git shabbes, Helénke*!"[3] I said, taking my leave of her in Yiddish one Friday afternoon. "No one has said this to me since my girlhood," she cried out, leaning against the doorframe.

Then I moved, my son was born, and, though I remembered the aged couple occasionally, I didn't pass that way for a long time. When I came to Jósika Street for the first time in half a year, it still wasn't because of them. I had a meeting with Helfer in front of the synagogue. But I looked into the yard, I just stuck my head in, and I would have already pulled it back if I hadn't seen something white move: Mr. Weisz was standing in front of the window in night clothes; he looked at me, smiling. "I'll come soon," I waved, and turned to go out the door.

He must have died a few days later, outliving Mr. Vas by several months, and Béla Grósz by somewhat more than a year, if my calculations are correct.

3. *Git shabbes*: Yiddish, "Have a good Sabbath," the greeting at the start of Sabbath.

One Step toward Jerusalem[1]

At the very end of April 1944, Mr. Gy., the suddenly unemployed Christian porter of the Makó[2] Jewish School, knocked on the door of the local police commandant to announce that, according to his observations, Moses Vorhand, the learned chief rabbi of the Orthodox congregation, had received enemy spies in his house. The next day, May 1, the police escorted the chief rabbi, together with his granddaughter, to the station. They slapped the young woman, and yanked the beard of the eighty-two-year-old rabbi and boxed his ears. Since the old man still wouldn't reveal his clandestine contacts, they knocked him down and jumped up and down on his stomach. Some of his students managed to convey the half-dead old man, writhing in pain, to the Budapest Orthodox hospital, where, conscious of his impending death, he prophesied the dreadful times which would come upon his people and pledged to intercede with the Creator: Makó's Jews would not perish.

After a month and a half of German occupation, it was counted as miraculous that the rabbi's body was successfully transported home and buried with respect. But the real miracle occurred when, of the three trains setting out from the sporting complex at Szeged, two turned toward Vienna instead of their original destination of Auschwitz.

◆ ◆ ◆

Miss Rózsika lives in Deák Ferenc Street, once called Little Jew Street because here and on the parallel Eötvös Street lived half of Makó's Jewry.

1. One Step toward Jerusalem: The title is based on a Hungarian saying describing a great, unbridgeable distance: "As far as from Makó to Jerusalem."

2. Makó: A town in southeastern Hungary, near the Romanian border (map 1 C5).

Back then the Feig family lived here. It was long ago; Rózsika was still far from being old enough to be called an old lady, and the girl with the pretty name who lived in Aknaszlatina with its scent of pine trees may never even have heard of the Hungarian plains: it was only after '56 that her second husband, "Patyi" the tavernkeeper, brought her here.

Of all the Jews still living here, she is the only one who keeps kosher. Beef gutted in Budapest gets to her by mail; and from time to time, Mr. Weisz takes the train down to her to kill a chicken in the longish yard of the erstwhile commercial building. In '64 Miss Rózsika sent her son to Dob Street in Budapest—it wasn't her fault that the adolescent boy who returned after the closing-down of the yeshivah first abandoned his ear-locks and then his religion and in time became a KISZ leader.

On the door frame is a mezuzah—I'm ringing at the right door. "Perhaps she is watching TV," helps a neighbor lady; I should knock on a street-side window.

"World conference!"—I mouth to the woman's face appearing in the window. Magical password. Miss Rózsika nods and waves, smiling from behind the glass.

A guest is sitting in the kitchen, an old acquaintance; Simon Rubinstein used to come home regularly from Brooklyn even in the days of the Kádár regime. The heart attack caught him here at home, and he was treated on Amerikai Road—after his recovery, he vowed that if possible, he would visit his birthplace every year. He hasn't come alone—his cousin, the bearded, bespectacled Leibish, had been bustling about for days, negotiating, taking care of things. This minute as well, he is in Budapest, ordering a bus to Ferihegy to receive visitors arriving tomorrow on flights from New York and Tel Aviv.

Simon Rubinstein is getting ready for dinner. A decent Jew wouldn't touch a spoon in the Korona, where he is lodging. Instead he has entrusted the purity of his meals to Miss Rózsika, whose pantry is at the moment the only place in Makó where kosher can't get mixed up with *treyf*.

Icy matzah balls sit frozen in a plastic tray. He asks for two, but the woman warms it all, and, taking the third dumpling out of the cabbage broth made bright red by ketchup, she places it on a separate plate for me.

"Go ahead and eat," Rubinstein taps the edge of my plate. "This stuffed cabbage has come straight from Boro Park!"

The matzah flour makes it a little sweet and there's no paprika in it—only its name is Hungarian.

Six Jews live in Makó today, but the keys of the synagogue and the cemetery are kept by László Fodor, a Christian blessed equally by local patriotism and philo-Semitism. Enough work comes his way. On Thursday morning he gets on his bicycle and rides to the shul on Big Jew Street. The long-unused Orthodox synagogue is only half a minute from his house; it's not a big trip, he simply has to ride through the place where the Hasid prayer house was torn down after the war, sown with grass, and christened Petőfi Park. Also not far from here towered the Neolog shul whose strong walls, erected with firm knowledge, outlived the stormy lives of Szálasi and Rákosi but didn't escape the slower currents of city planning in the sixties. The dilapidated, perilous building could fall down at any time, according to the order of condemnation pasted on the domed structure resembling its sibling at Szeged. But later, during the demolition, the walls, bricks, and mortar would yield only to the aggression of the jackhammer.

Mr. Fodor walks his bicycle into the courtyard of the synagogue and throws open the doors of the shul.

The May sunshine streams in the narrow window above the Torah cabinet and, roaming the walls, strides across the peeling layers of paint spread atop each other over a hundred years, the spiderwebs of indeterminate age, and the marble memorial tablets rescued from the demolished Neolog shul. The light touches a name here and there, then marches on and warms another, itself a voiceless memorial service recurring daily, a liturgy bowing its head before them all.

The local historian also gazes at the marble blocks; to him the inscribed names mean former buddies and neighbors, and he, like the sunlight, could not go about his routine and overlook their untimely deaths.

He has brought two velvet coverlets from home—he spreads one on the table in the *bimah*, the railed platform from which the Torah is read. The other is the curtain of the Torah cabinet—this has survived from the ruins of the Hasid prayer house—he himself dragged it from the rubble. There is no Torah: the "rebbe of Makó" will bring his own from Israel's Kiryat Ata. A red runner is still needed: it would liven up the shabby shul—he will go with a truck taxi to fetch one from the mayor's office. Two carpenters arrive—they are going to fix up the broken or cracked seats and fasten them to each other with long boards, so they don't sway during the repeated bowing of the prayers. Yesterday the electricians were here—a row of newly affixed glass globes runs around the walls. The cemetery grass was cut and arranged into stacks several days ago. Behind the synagogue stand brand-new privies—the shul would be in order now too, but the cleaning woman hasn't come. At last, the carpenters agree that, for 600 forints, they'll sweep and wipe the soft dust covering the rows of benches, the thousand-year-old dust.

The taxi from the old age home to the Korona is a hundred forints. I count it out ahead of time and clutch it in my fist, but I keep offering it to the chauffeur in vain—my traveling companion, ninety-five-year-old Mr. Ernő, won't let me pay. He has been getting ready for the world conference for weeks. It may be his last spectacle at Makó—a few more days and he'll be moving to the Jewish residence in Szeged. It's not that it was bad here—he got a bed and dinner, and the caregivers loved him, perhaps for his short stature and his childlike, ever-smiling face. But, for all that, it'll be different in Szeged—a two-bed room, other Jews, kosher meat on his plate.

We sit in the banquet-hall at the Korona, listening to a fly; we already know the essentials about each other and neither of us wishes to chatter. It's hot, the street-door is open, we can see Ehrlich house, the clothing store which long ago belonged to Mr. Ernő's family, and the monotonous noise of border-city traffic permeates the room. A sound distinguishes itself from the general whirring: a bus rolls into the parking lot in front of the hotel and comes to a stop with a loud huff.

The excitement of arrival overcomes the tiredness of travelers haggard from the heat and from many hours of sitting in one place. They lug into the hotel the ponderous suitcases meted out from the depths of the elegant bus and put an end to their long journey. Some haven't been here for two years. But others have been away for forty-five years and are searching for something to latch onto in a cityscape preserved in their

6. "Friday morning prayer in the former Orthodox synagogue in Makó. A prayer service in a church or chapel that has not been used in a long time is always a great joy for visitors returning home, requiring as it does that at least ten adult men come together. The worshipper without a tallit is an unmarried man, a *yeshivah bokher.* The building itself was cleaned in honor of the world conference, but it was in bad repair, therefore the drop cloths on some of the pews. Later, money was raised and it was repaired and repainted." Text and photograph by Sándor Bacskai.

heads, but not exactly like this. They can no more distinguish between the buildings descending on them than can we, the spectators, sort out the black silk coats, the burning eyes, the brown wigs and all the earlocks.

The hotel, quiet until now, begins to vibrate; everyone walks about, makes small talk or murmurs prayers. As one sits down, another rises to his feet, wanders elsewhere, and looks for a chair; but even if their legs aren't in motion, their hands surely are: they stroke their beard, wind their earlocks, adjust their head shawls. Mr. Ernő contemplates the scene cheerfully; between brief, nervous greetings, Miss Rózsika is looking for five pounds of beef promised on the telephone—it was supposed to be sent with this bus. Maybe it will come in the other bus, the American one—they'll be even blacker and more bearded, as they'll lack the flashing splotches of color provided by the occasional shaven faces and summer shirts in the Israeli group.

The descendants of the martyred chief rabbi have come: Zeev Vorhand, the "Prague rabbi" from Manhattan, and the Lemberger boys, Simon, Mendel, Efraim, Avram, Shlomó, and Asher, all rabbis like their father, father-in-law, grandfather, and great-grandfather. Besides the rabbi of Makó, they can also count among their ancestors the *tsadik* of Csenger and the *gaon* of Balassagyarmat.

Unmarried *yeshivah bokher*s swarm; balancing suitcases and pointing right and left, they run around and make arrangements, they take and pass on instructions in Yiddish—this is their day. The soldiers of a holy army—if the rebbe said so, they would empty the entire city in half an hour, not just two measly buses.

With the exhaustion of the suitcases, they carry in the half-prepared foods; the hotel's kitchen may well not have seen so many paper boxes, disposable plates, and plastic cups since its opening. Brand-new metal plates are affixed to the cooktops, aluminum foil gets wrapped around the faucets, plastic sheeting is spread on the tables—the work can only start after this. Leibish Rubinstein's wife is the lord of the kitchen—she won't sleep much until Sunday. Her son Benjamin works in white gloves. Like his mother, he is no cook, but he enjoys puttering around in the kitchen. While the others are looking around in their rooms, unpacking their suitcases, or resting for a while, he is boiling eggs, taking them out with a long-handled strainer and putting them in cold water. He then ladles boiling water into a glass. You'll burn your tongue, I think, but he's only taking it to one of the very religious for handwashing.

Before 1944, Makó's two thousand Orthodox didn't count for much in the country. But the congregation had long been considered among the significant ones in the light of its renowned rabbis and famous yeshivot. Makó was the most secure enclave for the religious Jews of south Hungary, flanked as it was by the region's Neolog settlements. However, with the return of a relatively large number of Jews after the war, it became one of the most important communities. The city had already been liberated in September '44, and people trickling back from here and there immediately rebuilt their congregations. In 1948, there were more Orthodox residents than here only in much larger Budapest, Miskolc, Debrecen, and Kisvárda. In addition, many children and young people were included among Makó's nearly five hundred souls, so that there were three synagogues in operation, as well as a *kheder* and a Talmud-Torah: for a time, Nándor Lemberger, the chief rabbi after the war, even directed a yeshivah. The nationalized Jewish merchants and craftsmen established a Sabbath-keeping company and the religious youth were able to organize Agudist Youth Days on a national level.

After 1948, Makó's children also attended government schools. To some extent they were lucky, says Rachel Lemberger, the daughter of the chief rabbi who is buried in Kiryat Ata: in theory, they were supposed to attend school on the Sabbath as well, but when the Jewish school ceased operation, its director was hired as assistant director; he arranged that the children would stay home on Jewish holidays—with the stipulation that they couldn't use their absence as an excuse the next time they were called on. It made no difference: often they didn't get good grades even for perfect lessons. "You children have better brains, you have to know next year's material too for an A!" declared one of the teachers, drawing out the information by lingering over eminently tuggable earlocks.

"There was continuous Jew-bashing, we acquired all kinds of nicknames. Some of the teachers were real anti-Semites; for example, I remember a Russian teacher, she was horrible," complained Gábor Gombó cheerfully. He grew up in a time of change; he was born in '41 in the Hungarian plains, but by the time he was three years old, he had seen the world as far away as Bergen-Belsen; he was taken from a land besieged by one country and returned to one besieged by another country. He went to *kheder* in a republic—by the time he was in grade school it was the People's Republic. When he got to the yeshivah in Soltvadkert, where he arrived in '55, it was at 9 Stalin Road, but a year later, the street signs were knocked down, and then the revolution toppling them was knocked down as well.

"Oppression, servitude / This was the order of life for a thousand years," he sings. Zsuzsanna, who arrived with her older brother and sister, directed the girls' Talmud-Torah back then, conspiring in the little house behind the shul. Their father, while he lived, tried to hold together the people from Makó scattered throughout the world, and they supported the yeshivah newly revived in Kiryat Ata from the donations pouring in at the yearly gatherings they organized. Before the war, the older Gombó, like everyone from Makó, was involved in the onion business. It was Makó's Jews, the Iritzes, the Landeszmanns, the Montags, the Paskeszes, the Strauszes, who familiarized the world with Makó's onions. They exported 75 to 80 percent of the crop; there was no competitor on the world market from December to March. In successful years, a hundred pounds of onions were worth two hundred of wheat.

The post office operated day and night because the big transactions were conducted by telephone and telegraph; families sent their eldest sons to Hamburg or London to indicate instantly if favorable prices developed. When they loaded the cargo at home, the horse-drawn wagons stretched from the thirty-five-platform train station to the center of town, and the hired seasonal workers loaded four or five trains a day. "I used to tell stories about this to my children—they thought it was a metropolis, but when I brought them here, all they saw was a dirty, quiet, dying little town," broods Mr. Klein. Coming home from the war, people again tried their hand at onions. The Jewish merchants drummed up $25,000 worth of merchandise which they wanted to sell in Budapest, but at Rákosrendező, the Russians shot at the cars. Not much later, Mr. Klein took his bride by the hand and emigrated to Palestine by way of Constanta.

"Are there any onions here at all?" He exaggerates, "I didn't find them in a single store."

Interesting-looking customers come in the store door; most are looking for paprika. "Look out," a well-informed man raises a finger, "they adulterate it with milk powder. It will turn the meat into *treyf*." Mr. Strausz, a shaven, muscular man who manages his own farmstead near Tiberias, bought raw pumpkin seeds. If they flourish, next year he'll eat baked pumpkin and roasted pumpkin seeds for the first time in forty years.

◆ ◆ ◆

Friday promises to be long. First Moses Vorhand's *yortsayt* in the cemetery, then the mayor will greet the world conference participants, then the main event, the Shabbat, at one table with the rebbe.

7. "During the world conference in Makó commemorating the fiftieth anniversary of the death of Orthodox chief rabbi Moses Vorhand, all the participants went to the cemetery, praying there not only at the tomb of the chief rabbi but going to see their grandparents' and relatives' graves as well. Most of the older participants were returning to their hometown for the first time since childhood. Like many other visitors, this gentleman was using black paint he brought with him to outline the hard-to-read letters on the memorial. I saw many others repairing and repainting long-unvisited gravestones. He is not wearing typical Hasid attire and thus must have been from Israel. The gravestone bears the name of Sara Alte Chaya, the daughter of Avraham Chaim, probably the visitor's mother or grandmother." Text and photograph by Sándor Bacskai.

After morning prayer, many people set off for the large, whitewashed building at the end of Eötvös Street. This was the Béke Cooperative. Here they manufactured slide projectors, satin pants, and teddy bears, often surpassing the quotas and making up for the Sabbath holiday with efficient work practices. One person cut out the pattern, another stuffed it with straw or sewed the eyes on it. The rabbi lived here, the *kheder* and the yeshivah were here, the mikveh and the slaughterhouse were a little further on.

They would like to go in—even if it's been rebuilt since then, they would like to look at the place where they spent most of their time in the first half of their lives. The gate doesn't open; through the keyhole, a thin slice of the courtyard is visible, but this is too little for those standing in front of the unoccupied house. "Help us open this somehow," asks a tall, big-bodied man framed by a grey beard; looking at his sharp-featured face, I think he is Sephardic. He once went to *kheder* here. Would he be reassured by what he saw in there? There is no key. It looks as if there won't be one either; the neighbors don't know who is renting the building. In any case, there isn't much time; we have to set out for the cemetery; one by one, we start back to the hotel. A few locals stand in front of their houses, murmuring; they eye the black procession; some invite an acquaintance in here and there. Others walk back and forth in front of the Korona; they are looking for classmates, or they are just standing agape. The Jews tell them more than once to come inside, but in the four days, I don't see anyone cross the threshold.

I move comfortably among the Hasids; they are really good spirited. I sit at their table, I eat their gefilte fish, I reach into their boxes of pastries, I drink the cola from a plastic cup. If I don't understand something, I ask them; if I don't like something, I tell the ones I am sitting nearest to. If I hit up against a wall, I stop, and if it can't be dismantled, I try to back down without taking offense. There is no five-minute interval when somebody doesn't address me, and, although my presence is more unfamiliar to them than theirs is to me, they soon share with me one chapter or another of lives which abound in tragic developments.

Mayer sets out on a walk; a Dixieland band plays in the square; a little girl hands out small political flags. We are among the first to receive one of them; we listen to the music for a minute, and while we stroll in a leisurely way during the speech, Mayer, the bearded, earlocked poster boy, waves the liberal party's paper flag about. He has an inquiring temperament; on the way here, on the airplane, he had his neighbor explain the political situation and the probabilities of the election. We study the candidates smiling from the SZDSZ posters: Jew, not Jew, we try to guess.

The country appeals to him, everybody here is calm and friendly, they greet him first in the street; the next time he comes, he'll bring his children as well. We cut across the square toward the house recognized from a photograph. The Webers are also headed this way; his parents were the neighbors of Mayer's grandfather; there was a passage between the two lots; it has been walled up by today. I notice something else as well: on the street side of the fence, a six-pointed star has been painted, hanging from a gallows. It wasn't here yesterday, but the Jews have already been in the city for twenty-four hours, so it was time the right-wing nationalists should formulate an opinion. I wouldn't mention it, but it makes me angry that the mayor, at the end of his luncheon speech, asked for ten thousand dollars for the renovation of the synagogue—the Jews would take advantage of it once a year, if that. In ten minutes, six thousand dollars was collected, and the rest was promised as well. It would therefore be appropriate to paint out the graffiti.

Béla Weber's stomach contracts, at first he doesn't even understand what I am saying. He paces agitatedly, his face made angry by his thick, furrowed eyebrows; over and over, I regret not staying quiet. In half a minute, I have ruined his pleasant impressions.

"Pleasant?!" he snaps. "Do you think it's pleasant to come home after fifty years and find nothing?! That is anything but pleasant!" From now on, he'll walk the streets with the feeling of not knowing when he'll be knocked on the head.

"There are stupid people everywhere, there are anti-Semites everywhere," says Mayer calmly. "You shouldn't let them bother you. If I hear 'stinking Jew,' I don't even hear it, I don't even look, I just keep going." He was born after the war.

On the morning of the Sabbath, the gray synagogue becomes colorful, black-garbed Jews are bowing in snow-white tallit. The married men have pressed *shtrayml*[3] on their heads. White stockings are stretched onto the legs of the rebbe rocking in the corner. Cantor Deutsch is singing on the

3. *shtrayml* (Hungarian Yiddish for *shtreimel*): fur hat worn by married men among Haredi Jews, the most conservative Orthodox.

bimah, Mr. Ernő is listening below—who knows when he last went to shul? *Bokhers* take turns standing in the open doorway, not as if to send away the people staring through the fence; rather they are angrily observing those whispering inside. K., who lives here, was born a Jew and is one today, although he has been a Catholic priest in between as well. Liking the synagogue full of Hasids, he reaches into his jacket, takes out a compact camera, and, before anyone can stop him, flashes right into the middle of the Sabbath observance. The disturbed congregation is a swarming beehive, but the anger fades quickly, and those standing around K. explain pedantically why it is forbidden to disturb the sanctity of the law.

The local paper has published pictures of the cemetery visitation, I observe innocently while walking towards the hotel. Since they can't handle money on the Sabbath, I am charged with buying every copy available in the city. Not just those forty copies, but even one hundred, two hundred, would be too few. I should go to the newspaper office, I should go to the press, I should get a thousand, I should get as many as I can, says Gombó excitedly, who would have thought that the Szeged press would be closed on the Sabbath?

The *sholet* reaches our plates, and a thigh, and a breast; of the three main meals of Shabbat, lunch becomes the longest. First one, then another Lemberger boy stands up and begins an explanation of the Torah. The rebbe, reb Simon doesn't give the *droshe,* he leaves the opportunity for his younger brothers. When his great-grandfather was beaten nearly to death, he was a two-and-a-half-year-old child, now he is a man in his prime; his sister Rachel says he looks most like their father. He is up until dawn and, after a brief sleep, awake again while it is still dark. Now he rubs his forehead and, eyes closed, tugs at his graying beard. Trunk rocking, he stamps his feet: where does his spirit wander when it is not leaping up from his swaying body? His voice rises: his followers pray with him, clinging to his hoarse lamentations.

Simon Rubinstein, who has already fed me once, brings me cookies from the rebbe's plate, turns, and comes back with wine: "Drink this, it has already been blessed." He brings *sholet,* fish, I can't starve to death while he is in sight.

A little rest, studying, noshing from the cake boxes, and night is well underway. The *havdole* candle, woven from different strands, separates weekdays from holidays, but more than a simple Shabbat is coming to an end. Mayer dips his fingers into the wine dripping from the filled goblet, draws them across his forehead and his pockets: may he have as much brains and money as there is wine in this bottomless silver goblet. He extends it to me, so I can be blessed too. Flustered, I don't imitate him but instead start to explain, the time spent with them has convinced me, instead of following the laws of others, to look upon my own as sacred.

A man in a gray suit comes to pay a visit, the city's representative in Parliament. He breaks the zealous spirit of the group a little, talking about his party's achievements. He pronounces the presence of the Jews as the first sign of reconciliation; everyone nods, then he gives voice to hopes that others will follow this first step and that there will be those who move back. All at once, the Jews cry out in protest: for the second time today, I feel myself in a beehive. The representative did not expect such great resistance; he stops here and there to chat, but doesn't distribute his present of photo albums published about the burial of the late prime minister. He leaves them instead on a table; in the morning, the *yeshivah bokhers* who have stayed up all night will page through one, puzzled at what the heck it could be.

"Freedom! Long live the Popular Front!" Gombó squeezes his hand into a fist; I can't help laughing, but I can't shake the melancholy descending on me.

Mr. Béla stands in front of me. There was a little pressure here, he says, pointing to his stomach, but it has subsided. They painted out the hanging Star of David. I bring him a chair. I touch his arm. He didn't find much of the old Makó, but stepping from the high school building, he counted out where his father's tropical fruit and candy wholesale store stood. He remembers clearly the names of his one-time classmates and teachers, as well as the dates of leaving Hungary and arriving in Israel. It's a wonder he still knows Hungarian: after he returned from Theresienstadt without his mother and his younger brother, he wanted to forget the language.

"You heard the representative? I remember his every word: he said he wasn't the cause of what had happened. I have no problem with him: he may even not have been alive then. *Aber*[4] my feeling is that there isn't much here for me."

"Then why did you come, sir?"

"I came because of him." He places his hand on the shoulder of his son. "He wanted to see where I was born. I wanted to a little myself. I don't want it anymore."

In the afternoon, he walked a little with his older brother; they struck up a conversation with some teenage girls. "And what are you gentlemen doing in our city?" inquired the girls. While his brother set about explaining why they were here, he stormed off. "I would have you know that this is not *their* city, it's my city. My great-grandfather was born here, they even buried my great-great-grandfather here," he mutters, face reddened by anger.

"I was driven away! What else do you want? That I am happier for being here? Sadder!"

What I wouldn't give if I could peel off some of the crust which has been deposited on his heart.

"The people here are very fine," says Mayer. "I'll come here another time, and again and again," he rhapsodizes happily. "I want to get to know Hungary. If there's a fat boy among us, you say about him, 'He's not attractive, why does he eat so much?' But if you know that a car ran over his papa, and he's fat since then, you look upon him differently. It's wrong to prejudge; the only thing that counts is whether a person is good or not."

I look at Mr. Béla.

"What else are you curious about?"

"You haven't spoken Hungarian for fifty years, sir?"

"But we have, at home with my wife."

"Strange."

"You see, that's a little strange for me as well. What can I do, it's my native language."

4. *Aber*: Yiddish, "but."

It's still dark when the first bus leaves for Budapest. The other will leave in the morning, but it's not worth going to sleep 'til then. I take a walk to the shul and linger on the ditch edge. The early risers hurry along Eötvös Street.

Jew Street was never so desolate, I think.

The Jews of Pápa Go to a Strange Place

On a day in early March, Moyshe Rubinstein, the young owner of Brooklyn's One Stop Kosher restaurant, packs up, is driven to the airport, and flies from New York's winter to Budapest's early spring. Leibish, his uncle, awaits him in Kertész Street. They pile the car with the glatt kosher foods mailed from America and the set of dishes for meat borrowed from the Budapest congregation. The trip to Pápa[1] is three hours. The rain begins to fall, stops, sprinkles again, and goes on like this for a good while. When they park in front of the Platán Hotel, it is hard to say whether it is raining or not.

Moyshe puts on a white apron over his dark gray sweater, adjusts his black velvet *kipah*, and takes his place in the kitchen. He begins to open the brown boxes. "Let's see what-all we have": cocoa Danish, Landau cookies from Brooklyn, milk from Ramat Hagolan. The head chef of the restaurant who, as the only male employee, assists him, is cleaning celery root. As yet he has no idea how much he will be paid for three days' work as a kitchen boy, but he has been assured that he won't come off badly. It doesn't matter—he is accustomed to working through the weekend in any case.

Majse knows exactly how much he will receive for undertaking three days' work as a chef in Hungary instead of Brooklyn—he didn't ask for a cent; in fact he has even paid for the plane ticket and hotel out of his own pocket. To him, it is worth anything to be with his friends and his beloved

1. Pápa: A Transdanubian city which developed from a medieval market town (map 1 B3).

rebbe at Pápa. The most important thing to him is that the rebbe and his Hasids feel as comfortable as if they were spending this extended Shabbat in Williamsburg or Jerusalem, not here! Or at least, if they are to be in Pápa, it should be prewar Pápa, a town which, they say, could hardly be surpassed in Jewishness.

He scatters corn flakes into a little pan, uses a wooden spoon to stir egg barley softening under a lid, and waits for the rebbe.

Leibish is also waiting for him. He doesn't exactly know when the rebbe is coming. He and his group arrived by airplane in Kiev five days ago; they got on a bus there and have been rattling from cemetery to cemetery across the Ukraine. Yesterday they were in Belz; in the morning they were in Huszt and Szatmár; by now they should be in Hungary. From time to time, they call the hotel on a cell phone. First they predicted their arrival by morning, then by evening, then ever later. Leibish, the president of Brooklyn's Hungarian Jewish congregation from Pápa, isn't the quietly sitting type, he paces up and down in the entrance hall of the hotel. Sometimes he sits down, glances at his papers, writes something or browses his room assignments, then springs up at the first ring of the telephone and hurriedly rushing to the porter's desk, tries to piece together the sounds filtering through the crackling.

At the table in front of the TV, a nun in a white headdress, "the missionary of love," talks to Ilonka, the hotel director; Leibish settles next to them. "The Jewish religion is contemplative," declares Mother Theresa's follower. "It prays forth the good for humanity." Ilonka reflects on this—it's all the same to her, which religion, just let there be love, and peace. For a while they listen to the pounding of the rain, then they turn on the lights, and everyone tends to his business.

At nine p.m., the first bus pulls in, with a "Rusland" sign on its windshield, the driver is Ukrainian, the only foreign language he understands is Russian. Perhaps ten people traveled with him, exhausted men and women, en route from time immemorial. For five days, this bus has been their living room, dining room, house of study, and sleeping quarters! The center of the world, through whose windows villages, cities, plains, and mountains flow together, the way the car traffic flows together when you look out of the windows of a house by the road.

An older man drags his burden toward the hotel; I spread the double-leaved glass doors open before him. "Well, sir, are you here as well?" Joseph Weber and I look at each other familiarly; he is a Jew from Makó, a student at Pápa, and a resident of Brooklyn. Panting from the weight of his suitcase, he flops down into an armchair and his eyes slip to Friderikusz[2] jumping around on the TV.

Everyone doesn't go to sleep, several sit around the table in the entrance hall and make merry with a large tray of cocoa Danish. Goldberger, the distinguished-looking focus, jokemaster, and spokesman of the small group, pulls the tray a bit closer. "A little heavy," they pat his stomach. Goldberger also puts his hand there—"not heavy, just strong." His strength is a job requirement: he is the rabbi of three thousand Jewish policemen in New York. He reaches into his suit-coat pocket and pulls out a silver police badge, flashing it in the lamplight and in the awe-stricken quiet which suddenly comes upon the group, he solemnly helps himself to another Danish.

Several vehicles arrive, rented cars with German license plates, Hungarian taxis; the hotel fills with muddy-booted, cemetery-visiting Jews. Although they can't eat much because of their fatigue and excitement, the long trip draws to an end in the restaurant, which is most suitable for socializing, since you can best discuss what has happened so far and what can still be expected with a glass in your hand. A bluish flame holds the warmth of the cooked egg barley, hot water drips from the simmering samovar onto Nescafé sprinkled in plastic cups, the tea bags are soaking—the American Jews, like the Russians, just bite a sugar cube with it. They eat a little pastry, then—it's already tomorrow—they go to their rooms or to apartments rented in town—each goes wherever good fortune makes his bed.

The noise dies down, the hall empties; only Mandl, the *yeshivah bokher*, remains, leaning over a long table, his red earlocks unfurled, brushing against the piece of paper on which he is keeping his journal. His father, a teacher in Brooklyn, has written some five children's books. Perhaps

2. (Sándor) Friderikusz: popular television news reporter and anchor.

one day, Mandl's works will be published as well, but for now, this is not important: his hand is guided by the joy of writing. He likes being able to recall his experiences with ease.

He pushes the notebook aside, pulls another toward him, and taking care to pronounce them correctly, he repeats the words written down at home: *"köszönöm," "utca," "Ez jó!"*[3]

"Mówisz po polsku?"[4] he then asks. Several Polish mechanics and repairmen work in the yeshivah where he lives; they don't speak English and have not mastered more than a few words of Yiddish, so to communicate, the *bokhers* have learned Polish. *"Nie wiem,"*[5] says Mandl, *"Bardzo dziękuje!"*[6]

He tears a page out of the notebook and draws New York. Manhattan is only a line, Bronx and Queens aren't interesting, we're just familiarizing ourselves with Brooklyn; maybe he hasn't seen much more of the city either. He draws five lines, these are the avenues cutting through the neighborhood of Williamsburg. Ninety-five percent of the people living between the twenty streets crossing the two outermost avenues, Wythe and Harrison, are Jews, and the greater part of them of Hungarian extraction. Mandl uses tiny circles to designate the shuls and important buildings, and so that everything should be clear, he cross-hatches those from Pápa: the rebbe lives on Penn Street, the congregation, with its shul, mikveh, and a twenty-five-member yeshivah, stands on Bedford Avenue. The smaller children from Pápa study in Harrison and Wilson Streets; the bigger boys, for whom a thousand dangers would be lurking in the big city, attend another yeshivah a good hour away in Kiryat Pápa built in Westchester County. The rebbe makes the forty-mile trip three times a week; the *bokhers* cover it somewhat less often—they are only allowed home at Easter and the Feast of Tabernacles.

At one a.m., no sooner had the patrolling police inspector said good night than those keeping vigil on the chairs suddenly spring up. A white

3. *köszönöm, utca, Ez jó!*: Hungarian, "thank you," "street," "This is good!"

4. *Mówisz po polsku*: Polish, "Do you speak Polish?"

5. *Nie wiem*: Polish, "I don't know."

6. *Bardzo dziękuje!*: Polish, "Thank you very much!"

Mercedes stands in front of the hotel, its top shining from rainwater. Mr. Hernádi, the chauffeur from Budapest, opens the doors. One of the three passengers—a bespectacled, leather-booted man in his fifties—pulls together the wings of his lapels as if he fears the cold, and, smoothing his beard, stands hesitating beside the car, a little smile on his lips. The Jews rush to him. He won't sleep here—his room has been arranged in the little house beside the shul—but he is nonetheless ushered in and welcomed from room to room in his passage through the hotel. Stepping out of the kitchen, he walks past me, looks at me, and nearly comes to a standstill. He is told, *"Er iz a tsaytungshrayber."*[7] His hand is as soft as a child's. Later he is left to himself for a while and strolls along, looking about. I step up close and address him. He looks surprised, or rather scandalized, then he slowly turns his back and moans once, quietly. He looks at the wall until they come for him.

They say he hasn't slept for two days and he hasn't eaten. He has hardly arrived and he is already looking for his chauffeur to take him to Csorna. The lamentations of the *rebetzen* are in vain, he doesn't want anything except a little water, and a little milk, he doesn't want to sleep; he'll rest when he has come back, he'll sleep in Brooklyn, he'll lean back when the Jews' suffering has come to an end. Now he would just like to pray. The men arrive running, shaken awake from their dreams; as they reach here, they are pulling on their black overcoats. When there are ten of them, the rebbe steps to the eastern wall. As if a signal had been given, the Platán's restaurant falls silent; only Wieder, who happens to be the leader of the prayers, can be heard; when necessary, his creaky voice is answered in unison by the Hasids from Pápa.

Since his master has arrived, Mandl the chronicler has drawn his eyebrows closer together and has been pacing with hands behind his back in the teeming entrance hall. The rebbe has chosen him as *shames* for the trip to Csorna: it will be his responsibility to rap at the door for the cemetery key, to open the gate and to proffer water for the washing of the hands. Until the departure, to keep his eyes open, he sets out on a walk toward

7. *Er iz a tsaytungshrayber*: Yiddish, "He is a journalist."

the main square, he stops in front of shop windows, peers into doorways, his shoes touching places where, long ago, his father walked every day. At home he promised that he would telephone; he looks for a booth and calls America.

◆ ◆ ◆

An older woman walks around the puddles in the parking lot; she has heard from somebody that the Jews have arrived. She freezes at the door; inside eighty people are waking up, walking, talking, and eating breakfast at once; the hotel is full of running, gesticulating people, full of unknown young faces. They are red-haired and black-haired, tall and smaller—but the woman from Pápa sees none who look like her storekeeping neighbors of happy memory. Those bustling around inside don't look at her, they don't even see that she is standing around in the door. In particular, it occurs to no one to speak to her. Only little Deutsch goes over, the son of big Deutsch, and the almond-eyed Grünbaum. It's easy for them, they were born back here, they have come home now, and they find the woman's sentences comprehensible even after so many years. Little Deutsch's father was a milkman in the market, it wasn't only Jews who stood in the line in front of his stall, recalls the woman, and she can still picture him there. Grünbaum steps forward, he would show her something. In the ragged-edged picture you can see a classroom, a row of seats, boys; in the corner a young woman in a cape, beyond the window a chestnut or poplar tree; where, he wonders, would he find that kind teacher? The picture gets to Ilonka, and from her to the cleaning woman; the wooded courtyard seems familiar to them, the teacher doesn't. They only have advice about where to look for her—with their words, they add something to the picture, but take even more away from it, as I see on Grünbaum's face.

Petőfi Street must be a few hundred meters from the hotel, below the level of the gates on Fő Square; in the pedestrian precinct it can be reached in minutes, but through the alleys it is even faster; it is in this direction that the Jews hurry to their prayer house. There stands the large 150-year-old synagogue of the mother congregation, once the shul of hundreds, even thousands, but the Jews with prayer-sacks don't ask for its keys at the Fidesz[8] office. The Hasids are headed for the *bet ha-midrash,* the little prayer house lying on the neighboring lot. They recognize its peeling walls, its swaying benches, as their own; if it was good enough for their fathers to pray in, it is good enough for them as well. Soon only the first seat is empty, but then that one is taken too: "*Der rebbe kimt,*"[9] the *bokhers* run in. He stops in the doorway with his head turned to one side, pulling at his beard; no one speaks, only the feet shuffle as a path appears in front of him. He waits a moment, looks around once more, then suddenly he moves and then is there, bowing in his place, worshipping his God in the place where his father prayed, and his grandfather before him, Jákov Jehaszke Grünwald, the great rabbi of Pápa, who is due a little more mention.

He was born a hundred fourteen years ago in Csorna, where not many Hasids lived in those days, but by the time he had traveled around Hungary as a rabbi, and returned to Transdanubia, he was hailed as a rebbe. He studied with his father, the rabbi of Huszt, and was a rabbi on the northern border, in western Sopronkeresztúr, and finally down in the southeast as well, in Bánffyhunyad in Kolozs county. It was from there, after the country fell apart, that his followers here called him home, to move his well-run, well-attended yeshivah to Pápa. He did not direct the Orthodox congregation but the "Adasz Jiszraél," the prayer society which was more Orthodox than the Orthodox. The yeshivah at Pápa was held to be second only to the one at Szatmár as the greatest of the time. Even after Rabbi Grünwald's death, it did not give way; rather, his son Reb Joszéf was able to maintain its level for the three years remaining until spring 1944. A few months before the Germans crossed the Hungarian border, the alumni society at Pápa laid the foundation stone for a new classroom building to be erected in the future. József Grünwald survived the war, his wife and eleven children did not; he married again, wedding a Weber girl from Soltvadkert. First they lived in Szombathely, then they also emigrated, and although a couple of hundred Jews remained at Pápa until '56,

8. Fidesz: At the time, a center-right national political party: today it has moved further to the right.

9. *Der rebbe kimt*: Yiddish, "The *rebbe* is coming."

the very famous "*Puper*"[10] yeshivah was already rebuilt in Williamsburg. The rabbi died in '84; the oldest boy, who received his granddad's name, Jákov Jehaszke, is the current rabbi.

The Hasids pray for a long time, the planned schedule slips—the agenda can wait, the Creator can't. Nonetheless, by one o'clock it becomes possible to conduct everyone to the restaurant of the Platán. The mayor receives two rounds of applause, one from those who understood his speech, and those who learn from the Yiddish translation what it was he said: he will do everything in the city's power in the interest of unhampered cooperation in the future as well, and he feels he can promise this in the name of the whole city. He receives great applause and the gift of a middling computer. Afterward, Mr. Wollák, the president of the congregation at Veszprém, speaks, and he presents the rebbe with a Hebrew-inscribed ornamental vase. He too receives great applause.

The joint program continues in the old cemetery. The buses full of Jews rumble across the city, and they stop in front of a house along Városlődi Road. Leaving the summer-kitchened, tied-dogged, chicken-cooped yard, the path running alongside the vegetable bed and the vine stakes runs into a stone wall. The Kohanites stop;[11] gravestones gleam beyond the opened gate. It came to light recently that the 250-year-old graveyard does not, to this day, belong to the congregation—so far, they have only the right of use, not ownership. The city would gladly give it up—this is a cemetery and not a lot; if they ever planned for a race track or a shopping center, they would not build them here—it's just that they are very poor, their expenses are also great, a few dollars would come in handy for the municipal government.

The brush has been exterminated, the toppled stones stand anew. The local TV is broadcasting, the reporter and cameraman support each other; the residents of Pápa can view their Jewish cemetery from their armchairs. The mayor looks at gravestones, he asks about customs. Leibish explains

10. *Puper*: Yiddish, "from Pápa."

11. Kohanites are members of the priesthood descended from Aaron, the brother of Moses. They are prohibited by the Orthodox from most contact with the dead, including participating in funerals or entering cemeteries.

8. "Jews reading Psalms (Thilim) in the Jewish cemetery in Pápa at the *yortsayt* of Rabbi Grünwald, that is, the anniversary of his death. The reading of Psalms is an important part of visiting the cemetery. The worshippers who are looking up paused in their prayers at the approach of the photographer." Text and photograph by Sándor Bacskai.

enthusiastically, the rebbe is also in good spirits—they consider the matter of the cemetery settled.

◆ ◆ ◆

On Friday afternoon the asphalt gleams, the sky clears, the clouds scatter their fine mist elsewhere. The late lunchers stand up from their chairs and scrape their *sholet* remnants into a pail. Jews with tote bags hurry towards the sports center swimming pool, the gray pile of concrete has changed into a mikveh: the essence is the running water, not the designation. Twilight comes suddenly. Being late for the Sabbath is not very virtuous; the alleys swallow the men taking rapid steps.

You don't see such things in America, says Schiff in the alley, and points to a house wall worn down to the bare brick. There this would immediately be plastered, here people only come to their senses if the house falls down. He moved to Israel four years ago—he doesn't provide information on the situation there. Behind a wall, a dog yips, the Hasids give it wide berth, their coats scrape the opposite wall. Schiff doesn't change direction, America is rich, poor Hungary will be a long time catching up. His father was born in Burgenland, his mother in Makó: until '57, Rachel Ehrenfeld was an activist in the Orthodox youth movement, then the family knocked the dust from its suitcases and took a look at the Atlantic Ocean from above. Schiff began to study in Williamsburg, at the Tselem[12] yeshivah. Later, the educational institution, which had once seen better days, became depopulated, and the boy who longed to learn moved a few doors over. From one day to the next, he became a *bokher* in a flourishing school—in the course of time, he turned from an Ashkenazi into a Hasid, but that was the result of a longer process.

Yesterday he got stuck in the mud in Makó; it was from there that a tractor pulled him out. He could have gone with a "foot bus,"[13] he laughs at himself. Later he headed southwest from Makó, and, for the sake of the cemetery at Magyarkanizsa, he hopped over to a country at war.[14] He didn't hear gunfire, he didn't see any victors; in war the losers face off against even greater losers, he sums up wisely. For a week, he traveled Hungary's cemeteries in his rented car; his arrearage was great: this was his first trip home since he was six years old. He gave thanks that he was

12. Tselem: the Hebrew name of Sopronkeresztúr or Németkeresztúr, now called Deutschkreutz in Austria (map 1 B2).

13. foot bus: The feet are ironically described as a vehicle. See p. 27n7.

14. a country at war: Serbia.

able to get to so many graveyards, and he asked for forgiveness from those he didn't have time for.

I would go with him to the prayer house—it's good to talk to him, but I can't. "Reach in here, please." Grünbaum stops me and spreads his coat-pocket opening with his finger. I fish around in the pocket; the two coins which I come across can't remain with him on the Sabbath. "There has to be one more!" he says meticulously, and peacefully tolerates my rummaging around some more in his bottomless pocket.

Gombó also finds me, he doesn't have his *sider*: but how can he pray without his book? The Sabbath has set in, so he can't carry burdens. It is good fortune amidst his troubles that he lives two houses away. I get to the first floor on clattering wooden steps: clothes tossed on top of each other, gaping suitcases, the nighttime accommodation of teenage boys. I grab up the *sider* and take it over to Gombó, but he waves me off immediately: he can't take it from my hand, that would be forbidden, I should put it on the gas meter—he lifts it up from there.

The religious women accompanying their husbands light a candle in the hotel. A hundred twenty men cram the prayer house; more would have come, but the New York bomb scare held twenty men hostage. By the time it was called off, the risk was too great; they preferred to go home rather than having to say *"Git Shabbes!"*[15] to each other on an airplane. So now they don't see the rebbe's *"tish"*:[16] after the dinner, in the prayer house's smaller chamber, the hundred twenty men sit on pushed-together benches. The area around the head of the table has been left free; only Halpert, the previous *gabe*, can stand next to the rebbe. The rebbe bends his head to one side; his soft fur collar brushes against his *shtrayml*.[17] He picks at a *barkhes*. He pushes it aside. Halpert distributes the remainder, then he serves chicken and egg barley from dishes which have been kept warm and places the plate on the table with a fork. A hundred twenty

15. *Git Shabbes*: Yiddish, "Have a good Sabbath," greeting at the start of Sabbath.

16. *tish*: Yiddish, "table."

17. *shtrayml* (Hungarian Yiddish for *shtreimel*): fur hat worn by married men among Haredi Jews, the most conservative Orthodox.

people watch as a saint eats. He stops from time to time, sings, swings his body. He eats a bit again, morsels from the pile of barley, grapes from the bunches before him; it is not hunger which gnaws him, he is honoring Shabbat in this way. He raises his head, looks around, puts his arm on the chair back, and slowly turns around. Two boys are arguing over a piece of *barkhes*—their hushed whispers can be heard pretty well in this great quiet. They are shushed and poked until, finally, they jerk up their heads to see the rebbe's face in the circle of Jews, his suffering eyes, his unsmiling face. The two boys look first at the floor, then at the tips of their shoes, and although such incidents are everyday things for them, the redness of their faces only slowly loses its color.

The rebbe gives his dinner a final poke. *Gabe* Halpert pulls away the plate, peels off a little piece of chicken from the thighbone, drops a little barley between his fingers, and, pressing it into the outstretched palms, distributes it. There are more palms, and less leftovers, but everybody gets some; the *gabe*'s sense of proportion can only be praised. He may be the only one who hasn't eaten. But at the end of the banquet, he, like the others, licks his fingers.

◆ ◆ ◆

Something has happened to the *sholet*; at noon Saturday, Moyshe has the suspicious-smelling dish thrown out. "Do you want a little fish? Or do you want a little chicken?" He fills a paper plate, packing onioned eggs, horseradished beets, and *barkhes* alongside; if it's all gone, I should let him know. The two waiters can't keep up with the work; the youngest of the *bokhers* joins the ranks of the servers. They haul in enormous trays with the fish soup and the chicken, the beets and the kugel. They sing the Hasid songs along with those making merry inside, and, although they can't, because of their burden, embellish the tune, if it fits the rhythm, they loudly stamp their feet.

At the end of his work, Soscher, the six-foot-tall lad, puts down his tray and settles next to me. Even though his dad was born in Soltvadkert, he doesn't have any reason for knowing Hungarian. Two flounderers clinging to each other in the sea of language, we conquer the yards-high waves. Our conversation doesn't flow, but it is amusing: Hungarian is to him what Yiddish is to me. I give Slovakian answers to his Spanish words, and respond to his French greeting with Romanian. Finally he asks, *"Mówisz po polsku?"*; he too has learned a lot from the Polish workers.

Mr. Soscher is an international linguist and an American sportsman: he takes a banana out of the brown boxes, backs up several steps, and, as if throwing a well-curved three-pointer into a basket, lands it in my lap. He waves that I should now throw it back to him and kneels down in the pose of a baseball player awaiting the ball. He catches skillfully and, straightening up, becomes a football forward, an American one, of course, and hugging his banana-scented ball rumbles out the door. I could wait for him to dance back in time and feint or juggle the ball a bit, but in vain: the Hungarian arts don't speak to him.

Like him, the majority of those traveling here grew up in America or were already born there; what ties them to Hungary can't exactly be called roots.

Mendel Kolman, the volunteer paramedic from Brooklyn, speaks with a little accent, but this is completely understandable, since he left Hungary in '56 as a few-months-old baby in his mother's arms. But his nine children would be at a loss if he spoke to them in this exotic language. Wassermann, Löwenstein, or Joel Weber, who lives in Jerusalem, are more or less the same age as he and understand Hungarian, and can even speak it, more or less, but they would consider the transmission of the dead language unnecessary, even if they married a Hungarian girl.

On Saturday night Nachman Elbaum, the organizer of the trip, directs his drivers: whoever wants to can go to Pozsony, anyone who doesn't can remain in the hotel—the group will pop in for them around midnight, on the way to the cemetery. The buses start toward Slovakia; by the time they return, the day would soon be breaking. With such a large group, no matter how much care is taken, the strict schedule easily begins to collapse.

In the Platán it is now possible to relax a little, to take a nap, or to grab Kolman: now tell the story of how you became a paramedic. He doesn't know, he says, it was in his blood, it seems. Like every child, he too was afraid of blood, but when, in the yeshivah, a boy ran into a glass door, and everybody ran away in fear, he pulled off his shirt and pressed it against the cut body until the grown-ups got there. He is in the building-supply business—after work he goes home and, if he can, spends time with his family, but if the cell phone rings, he throws himself into the car, and by the time the municipal ambulance arrives, he has already for the most part done what he can: he performs CPR, he sets broken legs, he brings back heart-attack victims with his ten-thousand-dollar machine. He doesn't expect gratitude, he doesn't accept money. One of his colleagues, Mr. Tauber, is speaking quietly with Elbaum at the restaurant table. A few minutes later, when I look in again at the loud singing, they are already in each other's arms, dancing the Hasids' dance. "Do you want something to eat?" asks Moyshe, and then joins the circle, his eyes gleaming, his mouth breaking into a smile of shared rejoicing.

A little group surrounds the "strong"-stomached Goldberger, he has told some sort of joke, the silver star gleams in his hand. Now, knowing that there is a police rabbi and a paramedic in their midst, great misfortune can't strike the Jews of Pápa.

The March night has disappeared, and midnight has passed, as happy days usually do, in an instant. I was still up at three in the morning, someone had left open a door, I spread my coat over me, and stretched out on some pushed-together armchairs, I was listening to the almond-eyed Grünbaum, as he talked to the two policemen! One was bearded and a practicing Catholic, he keeps the commandments; for example, he gives wide berth to women with their periods. "Whoever believes that someone is keeping an eye on him does not murder, does not steal," I still heard Grünbaum say. After that, all I remember is that the air under my coat seemed warmer and warmer.

At 5:30 somebody passes beside me, steps over a bag, and kicks the metal ashtray; I hear the clanging which wakes me for some minutes longer. The door is open; I have already gotten more of the screeching wind than I would like. The bus is puffing out there in the street—it has already deposited the Pozsony travelers at the Jewish cemetery; now it is waiting to do the same with those who stayed here.

The new cemetery, like the old one, also begins in the yard of a one-family house; spotlights show which way it continues, how far there is chicken yard and where the cemetery starts. Behind the mortuary there's a black March dawn, the Jews bow their heads, the sleet which the wind scatters in our faces cruelly highlights our bodies' lack of sleep. At the fence in the distance, the *ohel* has been illuminated; the string of bulbs hangs on a wire. I can still see where we are headed but not so much how; it's a big help that more people are walking ahead of me than behind my back.

First the sleet leaves off, then the darkness lifts, and, though you have to keep moving to prevent the toes from freezing, the cold also abates. In front of the *ohel*, clear sheeting wards off the wind—a plastic tent in front of the *tsadik*'s "tent"—and those standing in the iron doorway can already feel the warmth. The inside of the building is heated by *yortsayt* candles; as we move toward the gravestone, the mourners themselves and the sunrise warmth increase by degrees.

The rebbe also stands there by his grandfather's grave, the Brooklyn Greenwald next to the Hungarian Grünwald. The name on the gravestone is at once his name as well, and when he reads the *kvitel*, he places his hand on the stone, and rests his forehead on his hand; the two burden-carrying rabbis of Pápa plead together.

◆ ◆ ◆

The Jews have gone away.

Mandl waved, I saw Soscher salute, before he got on the bus, I said goodbye to "little Deutsch" at least three times. Tauber got into a car and, so that we could talk, took me with him to Győr.

Moyshe remains alone, packing up. Whatever belongs in Budapest will end up in boxes. A van has been promised—he shuts his eyes while he waits for it to arrive. The next day he flies home and unpacks; if things go as planned, he won't take his suitcases out for a while yet.

Glossary

◆ ◆ ◆

Bibliography

◆ ◆ ◆

Indexes

Glossary

Agudah. The *Agudah* or *Agudat Israel* ("Israel Association") was a worldwide Jewish organization established in 1912. The *Agudah* aimed to preserve Orthodoxy in the face of trends toward assimilation and Reform movements. Some Hungarian Orthodox rabbis viewed it as unnecessary because in Hungary, unlike other countries, there was already an Orthodox organization. See Orthodox Congregation.

Alef-beys. (Heb.) The Hebrew alphabet.

Aliyah. (Heb.) Literally, "to go up." To "make Aliyah" means for a Jew to "immigrate to Israel."

Almemor. (Heb.: *baal emor,* speaker.) In a synagogue, the platform used for reading the Torah.

Arrow Cross. Hungarian National Socialist Party, an extreme right-wing faction characterized by the wearing of a distinct "Arrow-Cross" symbol, called Nyilaskereszt in Hungarian. Members of this party occupied strategic positions in Budapest on October 15, 1944 and launched a reign of terror in the capital that lasted until the Russian occupation on February 13, 1945.

Ashkenazi Orthodox. Refers to Jewish communities with a Germanic or western tradition of pronouncing Hebrew. The ritual life of Ashkenazi communities is significantly different from those of Sephardic communities, which derive their traditions from eastern or Babylonian Jewry. According to tradition, Sephardi are descended from the nobility of Jerusalem transferred in the sixth-fifth centuries B.C. to the communities of Babylon, Yemen, South Arabia, North Africa and the Iberian Peninsula, while Ashkenazi trace their ancestry to the Jews coming from Palestine to Italy in the first and second centuries A.D. and migrating further to Western Europe. Despite attempts through the centuries to reform "backward" Ashkenazi Jewry by the introduction of Sephardic culture, the majority of Hungarian Jews belong to the Ashkenazi tradition (Újvári, Frojimovics et al.).

ÁVÓ. (Hung. Államvédelmi Osztály translation: "State Security Department." After 1948 AVH "Államvédelmi Hivatal": "State Security Office.") The Hungarian secret police during the Communist regime.

Barkhes. (Yid.) Special bread used for the Sabbath; otherwise known as *challah.*

Bar mitzvah. (Heb.) A man's coming-of-age ceremony.

Bet ha-midrash. (Heb.; Yid. is besamedris) Literally "house of study," synagogue.

Beyt Yakov. (Heb.) Religious girls' upper school, a kind of teacher-training institution. Also called a *bes yankev.*

Bikur Kholim. (Heb.) Community association for visiting the sick.

Bimah. (Heb.) See *Almemor.*

Bnei Brak. An ultra-Orthodox town near Tel Aviv.

Bokher. (Heb.) See *Khazerbokher.*

Borukh Hashem. (Heb.) Literally, "may His name be praised," meaning "Thank God."

Brayt Parnose. (Heb.-Yid.) A good living.

Chulent. (Yid.) Sholet. A bean dish that is traditionally prepared the day before and cooked by warming overnight for serving on the Sabbath, in conformity with laws that prohibit cooking on that day.

Constanta. Romanian city on the Black Sea.

Danube bridges. The retreating Germans blew up Budapest's bridges across the Danube in 1944–45 to slow advancing Allied troops. Their loss was acutely painful to all Hungarians. Five main bridges were destroyed, three of which are shown on map 2: Margit Bridge (A1), the Széchenyi Chain Bridge (C1), and Erzsébet Bridge (D2). The others were the Szabadság (Liberty) Bridge (then called the Ferenc József Bridge) and the Petőfi Bridge (then the Horthy Miklós Bridge). Two railroad bridges were also blown up.

Daven. (Yid.) Pray.

Dayan. (Heb.) Someone who can judge in religious-halakhic matters.

Drayvokhn. (Yid.) Three weeks of mourning preceding Tisha b'Av (q.v.), marking the time when the Temple at Jerusalem was under siege.

Droshe. (Heb.) Sermon.

Erets* or *Erets Yisrael. (Heb.) The land of Israel.

Eruv. (Heb.) A ritual enclosure constructed by observant Jews to permit carrying objects on the Sabbath. The enclosure unifies private dwellings by linking them with wire and posts and allows the carrying of objects on the Sabbath within the resulting common space in accordance with Halakhic rules.

Feast of Tabernacles. See Sukkot.

Gabe. (Heb.-Yid.) From Heb. *gabbay*, shul attendant, sexton.

Gaon. (Heb.) Wise man.

Gemara. (Heb., Yid. *Gemure*) See Talmud.

Gemilat Khasadim. (Heb.) Community benevolent society.

Glass House on Vadász Street. During the war, there were buildings reserved for the protection of Jews, in the care of foreign embassies or the International Red Cross. These properties legally were not Hungarian territory, so local authorities who wanted to lay their hands on their Jewish inhabitants had no jurisdiction there. Perhaps the most famous of these properties was the architecturally distinctive building at 29 Vadász Street, which had glass walls and functioned as the office of the Building Glass Company (Frojimovics et al.).

Glatt kosher. (Heb.-Yid.) Following the strictest interpretation of the Law.

Goy. (Yid.) Gentile (pl. goyim).

Hajdúság. (Hung.) Historical and geographical region in the Great Hungarian Plain around Debrecen (map 1 B5), named in the seventeenth century for the Hajdús, Hungarian mercenary soldiers, mercantiles, and cattle drovers who settled there. Includes the towns of Hajdúböszörmény, Hajdúnánás, Hajdúhadház, and Hajdúszoboszló. Karady describes this area as an Orthodox stronghold with a high degree of Magyarization (q.v.) (171).

Hakhsharah. (Heb.) Training programs in which Zionist youth learned the technical skills needed for emigration to Israel and life on a kibbutz.

Halakah. (Heb.) Jewish Law.

Hanukkah. (Heb.) The Feast of Lights. Eight-day holiday beginning on the twenty-fifth of Kislev (November or December), commemorating the rededication of the Temple by the Maccabees in 167 BCE.

Hasidism. A branch of Judaism founded as a reform movement in Orthodoxy in the Ukraine in the middle of the eighteenth century, emphasizing mystical union with God as the path to true sanctity, in preference to Torah learning. The mentality of Hungarian Orthodoxy was influenced by the religious practices of the Ashkenazi Jews (q.v.) who immigrated from Germany and Moravia, and of the Hasidic Jews who came from Poland and Galícia. Today Hasidism is an "ultra-Orthodox" movement; some of the people described in this book became Hasids after they left Hungary and are shown returning to their Hungarian communities from America.

***Havdole* candle.** (Heb.) A braided candle used in a ritual marking the end of Shabbat.

Heder (Heb., translation: "room"). Traditional Orthodox elementary religious school. In heders, boys from age 3 were taught the Hebrew alphabet, the five books of Moses in Hebrew and the vernacular, with commentaries, the prayers, the Prophets, basic Jewish law, history, and customs, as well as Mishnah (see Talmud) (Danzger).

Hekhsher. (Heb.) The rabbi's seal of approval, indicating the kosher (q.v.) status of food products.

High Holy Days. Rosh Hashanah, Yom Kippur, Sukkot (q.v.).

House of Life. Translation of the Hebrew/Aramaic/Yiddish expression, *bet olamin/bet ha-khayim*, a euphemism for "cemetery."

Iyyar. (Heb.) The second Jewish month in the spring.

JDC. American Jewish Joint Distribution Committee or "Joint" was founded in 1914 to help Jews adversely affected by World War I. Starting at the end of World War II and continuing through the rise of Communist governments in Eastern Europe, the JDC played a large role in the care of those in displaced person camps and provided funds for economic rehabilitation of shattered communities as well as for those who wished to emigrate.

Jewish Agency (for Israel). The Israeli organization which handles immigration. Also known, because of its Israeli name, as the *Sokhnut*.

Jewish Laws. Passed in 1920, the *numerus clausus* law placed a ceiling on the percentage of Jewish students permitted in higher education institutes. The so-called "First Jewish Law" of 1938 limited the percentage of Jews who could participate in professional life, in administrative positions, and in commerce and industry. The Second Jewish Law of 1939 further restricted the percentage of Jews in economic positions. By early 1943, there was the initiation of a government program with the goal of eliminating Jews from public life and cultural activities; there were also further limitations on the participation of Jews in the economy, and Jewish land was effectively confiscated (Haraszti, "Hungary from 1918 to 1945").

Kaddish. (Heb.) Prayer for the dead which takes the form of a glorification of God and the affirmation of faith. The mourning son is required to recite the kaddish daily during the year after the funeral, following the thirty days of full mourning, and then once a year, first on the anniversary of the funeral, then on the anniversary of the death (Frojimovics et al.).

Kapedli. (Heb.-Yid.-Hung.) Traditional Jewish skull cap, usually velvet, worn at all times by observant Orthodox Jews. Also referred to by the Yiddish word Yarmulke.

Kashrut. (Heb.) Refers to the set of ritual laws concerning dietary restrictions and requirements of strictly observant Jews. Food that meets the requirements of the dietary laws is designated as kosher (q.v.).

Kever Avot. (Heb.) Visiting the grave of a parent is considered the source of great blessings, and is required on the *yortsayt* (q.v.) (Frojimovics et al.).

Khamets. (Heb.) Food made from grain-based flour allowed to rise through contact with water; yeast or leavening.

Khazerbokher. (Heb.-Yid.) Heb. *khazer* means "to repeat"; this word refers to repeating the studied text, the methodology employed in much Jewish study, which in English is designated as "to learn," as distinct from "to study." A *bokher* is a young man, not yet married, studying in a yeshivah.

Khazerfresser. (Yid.) From Heb. *khazir,* "pig," pork. Yid. *fressen* means to "gobble up."

Khevrah Kadishah. (Heb.) Community burial society.

Khumash. (Heb.) The Five Books of Moses, originally called the Torah. Gradually, the term *Torah* came to include the Hebrew Bible as a whole. See also Torah.

Khupah-Kidushin. (Heb., translation: "the wedding canopy," and "the blessings"). The two words together refer to the wedding ceremony itself.

Kiddush. (Heb.) Blessing over wine on the eve of the Sabbath or Festivals; reception after a service at which such a blessing is said.

Kile. (Yid.) Short for Hebrew *kehillah,* meaning "congregation."

Kipah. (Heb.) = *Kapedli,* but usually crocheted. See Yarmulke.

KISZ. See Pioneers.

Kőbánya. A remote part of Budapest located within the X district of the city (map 2 east of D4).

Korona. (1) Hungarian currency. The korona or crown was replaced on January 1, 1927, as part of the effort to fight inflation after World War I. (2) Slovakian currency, the *koruna.*

Kosher. Food items selected and prepared in accordance with the strict dietary regulations of Jewish law.

Kreizlerei. (Yid.) Little store with lots of goods.

Kugel. (Yid.) Very spicy pudding made of eggs and potatoes or flour.

Kvitel. (Yid.) Small label with wishes on it, to be left on a grave, or on the West Wall in Jerusalem.

Lag b'Omer. (Heb.) One-day semi-holiday, the thirty-third day of the counting of Omer, a period of mourning. On this day, the restrictions of the Omer are lifted: it is customary to light bonfires and be merry.

Leyn. (Yid.) Use chant to perform a ritual reading from the scroll of the Torah or another sacred text.

Lulav. (Heb.) Palm branches and other plants used for celebrating the Feast of Tabernacles.

Maftir. (Heb.) A selection from the Prophets which is read at a service after the main reading by a new reader, who is also called a *maftir.*

Magyarization. Hungarians call themselves, and the language they speak, Magyar. Thus, this refers to replacing one's previous language with Hungarian.

Karady describes the nobility's efforts in the late nineteenth and early twentieth centuries to persuade minority groups to communicate in Hungarian (169–71) and notes that "the linguistic Magyarization of Hungarian Jewry was an exceptionally successful but rather unique phenomenon" (170).

Mashgiakh. (Heb.) Religious supervisor who oversees the proper execution of Jewish laws relating to ritual practices.

Matzah. (Heb.) Unleavened bread.

Meah Shearim. Jerusalem neighborhood of ultra-Orthodox Jews.

Megillah. (Heb.) The Scroll of Esther. See Purim.

Menorah. (Heb.) Traditional Jewish eight-branched candle holder.

Mezuzah. (Heb., translation: "doorpost.") A parchment affixed to the right side of the doorpost of a Jewish home. This scroll contains verses from the Torah (Deuteronomy 6: 4–9, 11: 13–21). Pious Jews touch the mezuzah every time they enter or leave and then kiss their finger (Frojimovics et al.).

Mikveh. (Heb.-Yid.) Ritual bath.

Mindszenty, Joseph. Roman Catholic cardinal who opposed Communism and the Stalinist rule of Hungary. He was sentenced to life imprisonment in a show trial in 1949, but freed in the Hungarian revolution of 1956. However, he was compelled to take up asylum in the U.S. embassy and was not able to leave the country until 1971.

Minyan. (Heb.) The minimum number of ten worshippers needed for a worship service.

MIOK. Magyarország Izraeliták Országos Képviselete ("National Representation of Hungarian Israelites"). This organization was established in 1950 as the sole overseer of Hungarian Jewry. Its creation in effect meant the elimination of Orthodoxy in Hungary, as the newly formed body was primarily oriented toward Neolog Jewry. Before 1950, the independent body in charge of Orthodoxy in Hungary was MIOI, Magyarország Izraeliták Országos Irodája ("National Bureau of Hungarian Israelites"). See Orthodox Congregation.

Mizrakhi. (Heb.) Religious Zionist organization.

Moravia. A historical country now forming the eastern part of the Czech Republic.

Moshav. (Heb.) Smaller Israeli settlement similar to a kibbutz, but without the common ownership structure of the latter.

Moyhel. (Heb. Mohel.) A Jewish person trained to perform the ceremony of circumcision.

Nagy, Imre. Chairman of the Hungarian Council of Ministers from 1953 to 1955. He steered an independent course from Soviet policies, and this led to his removal. He served again by popular acclamation during the anti-Soviet revolution in 1956 and was executed when the Soviets took charge again.

Nagymihály. Michalovce, Slovakia (map 1 A5). Site of an important Orthodox conference in 1865 setting criteria for the building of houses of worship and for liturgy. See Trianon.

Neolog. Those Jews who followed the decisions of the 1868–69 National Jewish Congress, while those Jews who left the Congress were called Orthodox or autonomous Orthodox. The Congress established a national organization of Hungarian Jewry to meet the demands of the Austro-Hungarian government. Those who accepted this administrative reform were also open to other modest reforms which in their view were in keeping with tradition, like organizing a rabbinical seminary. In contrast, the Orthodox maintained that every innovation in ritual or administration represented a violation of tradition. See Orthodox Congregation. (Frojimovics et al.)

Netanya. Israeli area between Haifa and Tel Aviv.

Niggun. (Heb., translation: "tune" or "melody.") Refers to religious tunes without words.

Niszel, The. This restaurant at 14 Révay Street was the only kosher eatery in Budapest in the early '50s (map 2 B2). (Frojimovics et al.).

Numerus clausus. (Lat., translation: "closed number.") See Jewish Laws.

Ohel. (Heb.-Yid.) Literally "tent," plain white house in a cemetery, indicating the grave of a Hasidic *rebbe* (Frojimovics et al.).

Oleh. (Heb.) New immigrant to Israel, masculine form (pl. *olim*; fem. *olah*).

Orthodox Congregation. The full name of this organization was "Hungarian Autonomous Orthodox Israelite Congregation Central Bureau," but it was also called the Orthodox Central Bureau. In 1950, this body was essentially eliminated by subordinating it to MIOK (q.v.).

Pebble. In visiting a cemetery, Jewish custom calls for placing a pebble, not flowers, on the grave of the deceased (Frojimovics et al.).

Pengő. Hungarian currency which was replaced by the Forint on August 1, 1946, as part of the effort to fight inflation after World War II.

People's Tribune. Established by the government in 1945 to bring war criminals to justice.

Pesakh. (Heb.) Literally "passing over." Passover. Eight-day holiday beginning on the eve of the fifteenth of Nissan (March or April). The holiday commemorates the exodus from Egypt with a Seder, a ceremonial meal held in the home.

Pioneers. A Communist youth group like the Boy Scouts. The organization enrolled children to age 14, after which they became KISZ (Communist Youth Alliance) members.

Pirkhey Agudat Israel. (Heb.: Pirkhey, "blossom" or "flower.") The youth group associated with *Agudat Israel* (q.v.).

Pirkhey Tiferes Bahurim. (Heb.: Pirkhey = "blossom" or "flower") Group for boys younger than yeshivah age associated with a yeshivah.

Poyshe. (Heb.-Yid.) Sinner.

Purim. The Feast of Lots. Celebrated on the fourteenth day of Adar (February or March), a festival marking the saving of the Jews from Haman by Esther.

Rabbi. (Heb.) Teacher. Not interchangeable with Rebbe, the term for a rabbi used in Hasidism (q.v.), but it is used by some individuals as if it were.

Rajk, László. Communist Minister of the Interior in the government of 1946 who was known for his ruthlessness. He also served as General Secretary of the Communist-controlled Hungarian Workers' Party. In 1948, Rákosi, the Stalinist Hungarian ruler, in a show of loyalty to Moscow, turned upon former ally Rajk, charging him with collaboration with "excommunicated" Yugoslavs. Rajk was executed in what amounted to a scheme by Rákosi to rid himself of many rivals. Many others were accused, put to death or interned in a series of related party purges lasting until 1953 (Kontler).

Rashi. Rabbi Solomon ben Isaac (1040–1105), one of the leading commentators on the Bible and the Talmud. See also *Toysefes.*

Rebbe, ***Rav.*** See Rabbi. *Rav* may also be used for a teacher who is not certified, or a wonder-worker, also uncertified.

Rebetsen. (Yid.) Wife of a rebbe.

Red, white, and green rosette. This patriotic and national symbol originated in Hungary's 1848 Revolution against Austrian rule. Although Hungary's Jews were well integrated into society and felt very much a part of their country, some non-Jews viewed Jewishness as an insuperable barrier to being a "real Hungarian." The racist attitudes fostered in the Second World War contributed to the spreading and acceptability of this attitude. It may be for this reason that Groszberg is self-conscious about his Hungarian nationalist feelings. See Abelesz, "You're Hungarian? You're a stinking Jew!" (p. 25) and Rosenberg, "red, white, and green rosette" (p. 86).

Rosh Chodesh. (Translation: "beginning of the month," designates the first day of every month in the Hebrew calendar, marked by the birth of a new moon and is considered a minor holiday.) The name is borne by a monthly magazine published in Prague with support from the Lauder Foundation.

Rosh Hashanah. Jewish New Year. Celebrated on the first day of Tishri (September or October). The first of the series of ten penitential days completed on Yom Kippur (q.v.).

Rozgony. Rozhanovce, Slovakia (map 1 A5). See Trianon.

Sabbath-keeping company. After Stalin's death, it was possible for Jews to start a cooperative which was closed on the Shabbat.

Sabra. (Heb.) A Jew who is born in Israel, as opposed to an immigrant. See *Oleh.*

Sacred objects. The objects which a Jew uses to fulfill his daily obligation to prayer. They include the tefillin and tallit.

Seder. (Heb.) A ceremonial meal usually held at home on the first and second night of *Pesakh,* accompanied by the reading of the Haggadah, the story of the Exodus from Egypt. See *Pesakh.*

Shabbat. (Heb.) The day dedicated to the worship of God, "Sabbath" in English; however, Jews celebrate it from sundown Friday to sundown Saturday.

Shakter. (Yid.) See *Shokhet.*

Shames. (Heb.-Yid.) Sexton, beadle, or orderly of a synagogue.

Shas Khevrah. (Heb.) Community Talmud-study association.

Shavuot. (Heb.) The feast of the Giving of the Torah, "Pentecost," in May–June.

Sheftel. (Yid.) Do business.

Shekel. Israeli money.

Shema Israel. (Heb.) This prayer represents one of the best-known parts of the Hebrew liturgy, and its first sentence has often been used as a confession of faith (Újvári).

Shikseh. (Heb.-Yid.) Gentile woman.

Shivah. (Heb.) Thirty-day period of ritual mourning for a close relative. During this time, the bereaved does not participate in ordinary activities and does not cut his hair as an outward sign of grief.

Shnoder. (Yid.) Make financial contributions in a synagogue, after reading the Torah.

Shokhet. (Heb.: Yid. *Shakter*) Ritual slaughterer trained to follow the strict requirements of Jewish law.

Sholet. (Hung.) See Chulent.

Shtrayml. (Yid.) Round, big-brimmed fur hat worn by Haredi Jews, also sometimes called "ultra-Orthodox."

Shuk. (Heb.) A market.

Shul. (Yid.) synagogue. Hungarian Jews often call their place of worship a templom or "church," the word used by Christians as well of their places of worship.

Sider. (Heb.-Yid.) Prayerbook, also *Siddur.*

Sidra. (Heb., *parasha*) The portion of the Torah read during the weekly service.

Sokhnut. (Heb.) See Jewish Agency.

Soyfer. (Yid.) Scribe who writes Torah scrolls, *mezuzot* and tefillin (q.v.).

starred house. As part of the racist measures defined by the German occupation, Jews in Budapest (and elsewhere) were forced to move into houses designated for their occupation. These houses were marked by a yellow Star of David, and were subject to rules restricting the lives of the Jews. This program, started June 15, 1944, was said to aim at discouraging bombing of the capital city by dispersing targets the Allies would wish to avoid.

Status Quo. (Lat.) Or Status Quo Ante. Members of the five or six percent of Hungarian Jewish communities which would not affiliate with either the Neolog or the Orthodox organizations after the 1868–69 National Jewish Congress (Haraszti).

Sukkot or *Sukes* (Heb., translation: "booths" or "huts.") Feast of Tabernacles. Eight-day holiday beginning on the fifth day after the Day of Atonement. Booths (or tabernacles) are built to recall the forty years' wandering in the desert.

Szabad Nép. (Translation: "Free People.") Official newspaper of the Hungarian Communist Party, published in 1942, and from 1944 to 1956.

Szatmár. A region originally in eastern Hungary, now in the Ukraine and Romania (map 1 B6). See Trianon.

Szatmár Hasid. (Yid.) Member of a branch of so-called ultra-orthodox Judaism founded by Rabbi Moshe Teitelbaum (1759–1841), rabbi of Sátoraljaújhely (map 1 A5) in Hungary.

Tallit. (Heb.) Prayer shawl.

Talmid hokhem. (Yid.-Heb.) *Talmid,* literally "pupil," *hokhem,* literally "wise." An expert in Jewish learning.

Talmud. (Heb.) The "Oral Law," post-Biblical rabbinic teachings, consisting of the Mishnah, a collection of laws, and the Gemara, a running commentary on the Mishnah.

Talmud-Torah. (Heb.) Communally operated Orthodox Jewish schools developed in larger towns to educate orphans and the children of the poor who could not afford the *kheder* (q.v.). The name does not imply that the Talmud was taught there (Danzger).

Tefillin. (Heb.) Phylacteries. Leather cases containing passages from scripture, worn by religious men on the forehead and the left arm during weekday morning prayers.

Thilim. (Heb.) Psalms. T'hila or Tehila (pl. Tehilim) means "praise," and collectively the Psalms are considered songs of divine praise.

Tisha b'Av. (Heb.) Literally "the ninth of Av" (July or August), the date of the commemoration. A day of fasting and mourning commemorating the destruction of the temple in 70 CE.

Torah. (Heb.) The scripture, originally consisting of the Five Books of Moses. Gradually, the term Torah came to include the Hebrew Bible as a whole.

Toysfes. (Yid. for Heb. *Tosafot*) Commentary for the Talmud developed by the descendants of Rashi (q.v.).

Transcarpathia. At one time, this area was part of the Habsburg Kingdom of Hungary. It comprises parts of the once-Hungarian counties of Ung, Bereg, Ugocsa, and Máramaros (map 1 A6, A7–B7). Today it is part of the Ukraine. Also Subcarpathia, Carpathian Ruthenia, Carpatho-Ukraine.

Treyf. (Heb.-Yid.) Non-kosher (q.v.) food items.

Trianon. The treaty completed at Trianon after World War I (1920) represented the victorious Allies' dealing out justice to defeated Austria-Hungary by partitioning Hungary and distributing over two-thirds of her territory to other powers. The number of Hungary's Jews decreased by half as a result, as their homes were reassigned to Czechoslovakia and Romania (Katus 104).

Tsadik. (Heb.-Yid., translation: "righteous.") One who is very strict in religious observance, a saintly man, or a pious, true person. In a Hasidic context, a spiritual leader.

Tsores. (Heb.-Yid.) Troubles, misery.

Új Élet. (Hung., translation: "New Life") The official paper of the Hungarian Jewish organized community. The name of this periodical means "New Life." It was established in 1945 and publishes to this day.

Új Kelet. (Hung., translation: "New East.") A Hungarian-language Zionist Jewish newspaper which first appeared in Kolozsvár in Transylvania, now called Cluj-Napoca in Romania (map 1 C6). The paper was published in Transylvania from 1918 to 1940, when the area was annexed by Hungary and it was banned by Miklós Horthy, the Hungarian dictator. It was later revived in Tel Aviv, Israel.

Vidduy. (Heb.) Confession.

Wehrmacht. German army.

Wirthshaft. (Germ.-Yid., translation: "economy.") To do business, with the implication of doing so not completely legally.

Yad Vashem. Memorial museum set up to honor European Jews who suffered at the hands of the Nazis under Hitler as well as "the Righteous Among Nations" who rescued Jewish victims.

Yeshivah. (Heb.) Higher school for studying the Talmud, Talmudic academy.

Yeshivah Bokher. (Heb.-Yid.) A boy who studies in a yeshivah, from age 13 and up.

Yom Kippur. (Heb.) Day of Atonement. Celebrated on the tenth day of Tishri (September or October). The first prayer recited on this day is Kol Nidre.

Yortsayt. (Yid.-Germ.) Jewish ceremony at the cemetery commemorating the anniversary of someone's death. Also *yahrzeit* (Yid.). See Kaddish.

Bibliography

Bacskai, Sándor. *Az Első Nap: Emlékképek az Ortodox Zsidóságról*. New York, Budapest, Jerusalem: Múlt és Jövő Könyvek, 2004.

———. *Egy Lépés Jeruzsálem Felé*. New York, Budapest, Jerusalem: Múlt és Jövő Könyvek, 1997.

———. "The History of Hungarian Orthodox Jewry After 1945," unpublished paper.

Danzger, M. Herbert. *Returning to Tradition: The Contemporary Revival of Orthodox Judaism*. New Haven: Yale University Press, 1989.

Frojimovics, Kinga, et al. *Jewish Budapest: Monuments, Rites, History*. Budapest: CEU Press, 1999 (Hungarian edition 1995).

Hanák, Peter. "Discontinuous Society-Deformed Society." *Journal of Popular Culture* 29, no. 2 (Fall 1995): 57–66.

Haraszti, György. Tr. Veronika Szabó. "American Jewish Joint Distribution Committee." *The YIVO Encyclopedia of Jews in Eastern Europe*. 2010. http://www.yivoencyclopedia.org/article.aspx/Hungary/Hungary_from_1918_to_1945 Accessed September 3, 2012.

———. "Hungary from 1918 to 1945." *The YIVO Encyclopedia of Jews in Eastern Europe*. 2010. http://www.yivoencyclopedia.org/article.aspx/American_Jewish_Joint_Distribution_Committee Accessed September 4, 2012.

Karady, Viktor. "Religious Divisions, Socio-Economic Stratification and the Modernization of Hungarian Jewry after the Emancipation." In *Jews in the Hungarian Economy 1760–1945: Studies Dedicated to Moshe Carmilly-Weinberger on his Eightieth Birthday*, edited by Michael K. Silber. Jerusalem: Magnes Press, Hebrew University, 1992, 161–83.

Katus, László. "The Occupational Structure of Hungarian Jewry in the Eighteenth and Twentieth Centuries." In *Jews in the Hungarian Economy 1760–1945: Studies Dedicated to Moshe Carmilly-Weinberger on his Eightieth Birthday*, edited by Michael K. Silber. Jerusalem: Magnes Press, Hebrew University, 1992, 92–105.

Katzburg, Nathaniel. *Hungary and the Jews: Policy and Legislation 1920–1943*. Ramat-Gan, Israel: Bar-Ilan University Press, 1981.

Kniesmeyer, J., and D. Brecher. "Beyond the Pale: The History of the Jews in Russia." http://www.friends-partners.org/partners/beyond-the-pale/index.html. June 24, 2000.

Kovács, András. "Antisemitic Prejudices and Dynamics of Antisemitism in Post-Communist Hungary." Proceedings of the international conference "Anti-semitism in Europe Today: The Phenomena, the Conflicts." 8–9 November 2013, 1–23.

———. "Hungarian Jewish Politics from the End of the Second World War until the Collapse of Communism." In *Studies in Contemporary Jewry*, vol. 19: *Jews and the State: Dangerous Alliances and the Perils of Privilege*, edited by Ezra Mendelsohn. New York: Oxford University Press, 2004.

Kovács, András, and Aletta Forrás-Biró, eds. "Jewish Life in Hungary: Achievements, Challenges and Priorities since the Collapse of Communism." Budapest: Institute for Jewish Policy Research Report, 2011.

Manchin, Anna B. "Matzo Hussars and Creative (Anti)Semitism: Jewishness and Popular Culture in Post-Communist Hungary." *Shofar* 34, no. 3 (2016): 1–27.

Újvári, Péter. *Magyar Zsidó Lexicon*. Budapest: Makkabi Kiadó, 1929, reprinted 2000.

Vörös, Károly. "Mór Wahrmann: A Jewish Banker in Hungarian Politics." In *Jews in the Hungarian Economy 1760–1945: Studies Dedicated to Moshe Carmilly-Weinberger on his Eightieth Birthday*, edited by Michael K. Silber. Jerusalem: Magnes Press, Hebrew University, 1992, 187–95.

Index of Places

Italic pages numbers denote illustrations.

All cities, towns, villages, etc. are in Hungary unless otherwise noted. All streets are in Budapest unless otherwise noted.

† designates map 1 locations; †† designates map 2 locations

Abonyi St., east of B4††, 91
Akácfa St. (shul and girls' home), C3††, 50, 155, 170
Aknaszlatina, B6†, 174
Alföld, C4–B5†, 6
2 Alma St. (Orthodox nursing home), west of B1††, 139
Almásfüzitő, B3†, 48
America, 50, 75, 87, 94, 98, 99, 107, 115, 116, 121, 124, 130, 131, 143, 147, 148, 152, 153, 154, 164, 165, 167, 188, 193, 197, 200, 208
Amerikai Rd., northeast of the City Park (A4††), 174
Andrássy Rd., B3††, 47, 86
Andrássy St. (in Győr, B3†), 23
Arad, C5†, xxn10, 69, 70
Aradi St., B3††, 49
Aranyosmarót, A3†, 90
Aréna Rd. (today, Dózsa György Rd.), 90
Austria, xvin6, xviii, 30, 31, 41, 94, 145, 197n12, 217

Bajcsy-Zsilinszky Rd., B2–C2††, 32, 35, 40, 85
Bakony, B3†, 20
Balassagyarmat, B4†, 178
Balaton, Lake, C3–B3†, 19, 20
Balatonfüred, B3†, 155, 167
Balatonszemes, C3†, 52
Balmazújváros, B5†, 53
Bánffyhunyad, C6†, 51, 194
Bars county, A3–A4†, B3†, 90
Békéscsaba, C5†, 10n††, 49, 54
Beled, B3†, 15, 41
Berettyóújfalu, B5†, 12n*, 53, 148
Berhida, B3†, 19
Bet ha-midrash, 116, 194, 206
Bethlen Gábor Sq. (shul), B4†† (02), 80
Beyt Yakov school, 73
Biecz (Poland), 162
Big Jew St. *See* Eötvös St.
Biharkeresztes, B5†, 50
Bnei Brak (Israel), 43, 112, 119, 138, 162, 206
Bodrogkeresztúr, B5†, 89
Bor (Serbia), 66, 68, 69
Böszörmény, 120. *See also* Hajdúböszörmény
Brassó, C8†, xxi
Buda (Budapest), 6, 8, 75, 92
Buda castle, C1††, 168

Budapest††, B4†, xiii, xivn3, xxn10, xxii, xxiii, xxvi, xxvii, 1, 7, 8, 9, 10nn*†, 21, 34n13, 39n19, 44, 46nn2–3, 47, 49, 52, 53, 55, 56, 57, 58, 59n27, 60, 64, 91n2, 96, 98, 99, 100, 104, 109, 110, 112, *113*, 115, 139, 140n38, 144, 147, 148, 151, 152, 156, 163, 166, 170, 171, 173, 174, 179, 180, 187, 188, 192, 202, 205, 206, 210, 212, 215

Budapest Varieté (6 Kálvária Sq.; south of D4†† where Karácsonyi and Bross Sts. meet), 109

Building Glass Company (29 Vadász St.), B2††, 32, 35, 207

Carpatho-Ukraine. *See* Transcarpathia

City Park, A4††, 134

Constanta (Romania), 180, 206

Continental Hotel, C3†† (01), 87

Corvin restaurant (4 Kisfaludy Ln.), D4††, 109

Csanády St., A2††, 93

Csenger, B6†, 178

Csepel, south of D4††, 34, 37

Csillebérc, west of A1††, 135

Csorna, B3†, 27, 53, 68, 166, 192, 194

Czechoslovakia, xivn2, xxi, 55, 56, 131, 143, 159, 163, 164, 217

Danube bridges, 18, 25, 206; Erzsébet Bridge, D2††, 206; Margit Bridge, A1††, 40, 86, 206; Széchenyi Chain Bridge, C1††, 206

Danube River, A1–D2††, xxn10, 34n13, 48, 67

Deák Ferenc St. (Little Jew St., in Makó), 173

Debrecen, B5†, xxn10, 7, 12, 52, 53, 99, 100, 105, 106, 117, 119, 120, 122, 139, 142, 148, 151, 153, 179, 207

Defense Ministry, 40

Déli R. R. station, just west of C1††, 28

Dés, B7†, 71, 72

23 Dessewffy St. (shul), B2†† (03), 39, 40, 153, 166, 167, 169

Dob St., C2–C3††, 51, 92, 135, 139

35 Dob St. (shul), C3†† (04), 6, 12, 49, 50n11, 57, 98, 102, 112, 122, 133, 135n36, 137, 143, 170, 174

Dobozi St., 170

Dombrád, B5†, 99

Dózsa György Rd., A4–B4††, 102

Dűltfáspuszta (today, Isztimér), B3†, 22

Eger, B4†, 10n*, 54, 147

Elektromos field (in Pest), north of A2††, 17

Eötvös St. (Big Jew St., in Makó), 58, 173, 175, 181, 187

Eperjes, A5†, 90, 164

Erets (*Erets Yisrael*), 30, 54, 68, 86, 87, 98, 207

Erló (Heb., Eger), 82

Erzsébet Kattler Prayer House (shul; 4 Jósika St.), B3†† (20), 169, 170, 171, 172

Erzsébet Királyné Rd., northeast of City Park (A4††), 32

Erzsébetváros, B3–B4††, C3–C4††, 169

Fehérgyarmat, B6†, 107

Ferihegy (airport), southeast of D4††, 174

Fertőrákos, B2†, 27

Fertőszentmiklós, B2†, 33

Fő Sq. (in Pápa), 193

70–78 Fő St. (prison), A1†† (05), 60, 61

Fonyód, C3†, 97
Frigyes barracks (in Győr), 26

Galánta, B3†, 47, *48*, 49, 90, 127
Galícia, A6–A7†, xv, 72, 208
Garay St., B4–C4††, 90, 128
48 Garay St. (shul), B4†† (10), 91, 102, 127, 143, 155, 170
Glass House (29 Vadász St.), B2†† (11), 35, 48, 207
Göd, B4†, 85
Görömbölytapolca (today, Miskolctapolca), 52
Gyöngyös, B4†, 2
Gyöngyvirág Rd., west of B1††, 137
Győr, B3†, 23, 24, 25, 26, 41, 94, 202
Győr-Sopron county, B2–B3†, xxn10, 32

Hajdú-Bihar county, C5–C6†, 11
Hajdúböszörmény, B5†, 7n12, 12n*, 53, 207
Hajdúhadház, B5†, 7n12, 54, 207
Hajdúnánás, B5†, 12n*, 53, 56, 207
Hajdúság, 7, 52, 207
Hajdúszoboszló, B5†, 7n12, 12n*, 148, 207
Hanna kitchen (32 Nagyatádi Szabó St. [today, Kertész St.]), C3††, 96, 113, 116, 126, 130, 138
Hatvan, B4†, 18
Hédervár, B3†, 25
Hernád St., B4††, 102, 122, 139, 170
Holló St., C2††, 92
1 Holló St., C2†† (09), 51, 57
Horthy Miklós Hospital (in Kőbánya), 48
Hunfalu (today, Huncovce, Slovakia), A4†, xiv, 157
Hunfalva, xiv, 46, 157, 158. *See also* Hunfalu

Huszt, B6†, 189, 194
Hűvösvölgy, northwest of A1††, 51, 53, 135
Hűvösvölgyi Rd., west of A1††, 51, 54
Hűvösvölgyi St. (mistake for Hűvösvölgyi Rd.), 137

Israel, xiii, xviii, 7, 29, 40, 41, 42, 43n21–22, 54, 56, 58, 65, 71n5, 73, 94, 107, 120, 130, 133, 140, 142, 145, 146, 147, 148, 149, 151, 159, 163, 164, 165, 167, 176, 178, *181*, 185, 197, 205, 207, 208, 212, 214, 217. *See also Erets*
Israeli embassy (37 Vilma Királynő Rd. [today, Városligeti fasor]), B4†† (19), 39, 40, 41, 58, 61, 62, 63, 147

Jászberény, B4†, 17, 18
Jazur (near Tel Aviv), 57
Jewish secondary school (in Pest, corner of Szent Domonkos and Abonyi Sts.), just east of B4††, 10
4 Jósika St. (shul). *See* Erzsébet Kattler Prayer House
József St. (shul), 80
Juhász Gyula School of Education (University of Szeged, Szeged), 150

Kaba, B5†, 120
Kácsfürdő (part of Kács, B5†), 52
Kálmán Imre St., B2††, 84
Kamara Varieté (46 Teréz Körút), B2††, 109
Kapás St., A1††, 92
Kapuvár, B2†, 15, 16, 17, 26, 27, 29, 31, 32, 38, 41
Kassa (today Košice, Slovakia), A5†, xiv, xv, xxn10, 156, 160, 161, 162n14, 163, 164

Kattler (shul). *See* Erzsébet Kattler Prayer House
Kazincbarcika, B5†, 105
Kazinczy St., C2–C3††, 82, 135
Kazinczy St. (shul) (today Puškinova St. in Kassa), xiv, 156, 164
7 Kazinczy St. (in Miskolc), 99
16 Kazinczy St., C3†† (08), 144
27–29 Kazinczy St. (shul), C3†† (07), 6, 80, 92, 93, 125, 133, 154, 170
Kecskemét, B4†, 60
Kedem (winery, Marlboro, NY), 153
Kelenföld, south of D1††, 63
Kerepesi St., C4††, 39
Kertész St., B3–C3††, 188
32 Kertész St., C3†† (12), 60, 110, 126
Killián Barracks (intersection of Ferenc Körút and Üllő Rd.), directly south of D3††, 40
Király St., C2–C3††, 6, 17, 39, 155
26 Király St. (shul and Agudah's offices), C2†† (13), 49n7, 50, 51n13, 57
41 Király St. (daytime center for girls), C3†† (14), 57
Kiskörút (ringroad), C2–D3††, 39, 40
Kisvárda, B5†, 12, 50, 51, 99, 104, 120, 139, 148, 179
Klauzál Sq., C3††, 92, 155
Kőbánya, east of D4††, 8, 48, 83, 210
Kölcse, B6†, 101
Kolozs county, B6–B7†, C6–C7†, 194
Kolozsvár (Cluj-Napoca, Romania), C6†, 138, 146, 217
Komárom, B3†, 24
Kópháza, B2†, 27, 91
Korona (hotel in Makó), 174, 176, 182
Körút (ringroad with unique names in different sectors: Szent István [A2††], Teréz [B2††], Erzsébet [B3–C3††], József, [C3–D3††]), 59
Kossuth (Lajos) Sq., B2†† (15), 40
Kótaj, B5†, 97
Kővár, northwest of A1††, 149, 152, 167
Kővari meat processing plant, 149
Kozma St. (location of a large Jewish cemetery), east of D4††, 167, 168
Kunmadaras, B5†, 6

Laskod, B5†, 104
Laudon St. (today, Káldy Gyula St. [C2††]), 49
Lazarovits and Friedmann (kosher butcher), 104, 114, 139
Lipótváros, A1–A2††, B1–B2††, C1–C2††, D2††, 39
Little Jew St. *See* Deák Ferenc St.
Lóránt Rd., west of C1††, 137

Magyarkanizsa, C4†, 197
Majakovszkij St. (today, Király St.), 99, 151, 170
Makó, C5†, 10n*, 50, 52, 53, 56, 111, 112, 125, 173, 173n1, 174, 175, 176, *177*, 178, 179, 180, *181*, 185, 190, 197
Makó Jewish School, 126, 173
Máramaros county, A6–A7†, B6–B7†, 172, 217
Máramarossziget (southeast of Aknaszlatina), B7†, *xix*
Margit Bridge. *See* Danube bridges
Markó (prison), B2†† (06), 61, 64, 75
Mátészalka, B6†, xxii, 12n*, 100, 104, 108, 114, 119, 120, 148
Mezőkovácsháza, C5†, 50, 52, 53, 119
Mezőnyárád, B5†, 52
Miskolc, B5†, xxn10, 2, 3, 6, 7, 10, 36, 49, 52, 73, 97, 99, 100, 107, 119, 120, 123, 139, 148, 179

Miskolctapolca, B5†, 52
Moravia, xv, 90, 208, 211
Mór Weisz Bread Factory, 51
Mosonmagyaróvár, B3†, 21, 26
Müllers' prayer house (shul) (in Újpest), 103
Munkács, A6†, 50, 51, 158, 165
13 Murányi St., east of B4††, 90

4 Nagyfuvaros St. (shul), C4†† (16), 39
Nagymező St., B2–B3††, 40, 158
Nagymihály (today, Michalovce, Slovakia), A5†, 161, 164, 212
Nagyrét (meadow in Hűvösvölgy), 53
Nagyvárad (Oradea, Romania), B5†, xxn10, 50
Neolog Congregation (shul) (12 Síp St.), C3†† (17), 1, 57, 92, 118, 149
Neolog Old People's Home (on Erzsébet Királyné Rd.), 32
Netanya (Israel), 101, 119, 138n37, 139, 212
Nikolsburg (today, Mikulov, Czech Republic), 90
Nyár St., C3††, 138
Nyírbátor, B6†, 12n*, 148
Nyírbéltek, B6†, 112, 114
Nyíregyháza, B5†, 10n*, 12, 100, 112, 114, 148
Nyugati railroad station, A2††, 40, 85

Óbuda (Budapest, far north of Víziváros [B1††]), 8, 28, 161
One Stop Kosher restaurant (98 Rutledge St., Brooklyn, NY), 188
Óra Rd., west of C1††, 137
Óra St. (mistake for Óra Rd.), 136
Oroszvár, B3†, 55

Paks, C4†, 8, 10n*, 54, 94, 95, 98
Pápa, B3†, 16, 28, 41, 53, 100, 188, 189, 190, 191, 192, 193, 194, 195, 195n10, *196*, 201, 202
Parliament, B1†† (18), 86
Pásti St. (in Debrecen), 117
Pest (Budapest, on east side of Danube), 6, 8, 10, 12, 17, 18, 19, 25, 26, 28, 32, 34, 38, 41, 43, 44, 48, 50, 53, 66, 71, 73, 74, 75, 76, 77, 79, 80, 83, 85, 86, 90, 91, 96, 98, 101, 104, 105, 106, 107, 108, *113*, 114, 119, 120, 122, 139, 157
Pétfürdő, B3†, 18
Petlendpuszta, B3†, 16
Petőfi St. (shul) (in Pápa), 193
Piliscsaba, B4†, 18, 93
Platán Hotel (2 Fő Sq., Pápa), 188, 192, 195, 200
Poland, xv, 8, 17, 56, 172, 208
Pozsony, B3†, xx, xxi, 5, 9, 46, 55, 82, 119, 164, 200, 201
Pozsonyligetfalu (once, independent village; today, part of Pozsony), 55
Práter St. (two blocks south of Baross St., just beyond D4††), 38
"Puper" yeshivah (institution for Jews who originated in Pápa; Williamsburg, NY), 195
Püspökladány, B5†, 12

Radomyshl (in Ukraine), 162
Rajka, B3†, 55
Rákóczi Rd., C2–C3††, 109
Rákospalota, 103
Rákosrendező railroad station (19–21 Teleki Blanka St.), northeast of A4††, 18, 85, 180
Romania, *xix*, xxi, 8, 39, 53, 56, 67, 67n3, 71n5, 131, 138n37, 143, 145, 146, 173n2, 206, 216, 217

Royal restaurant (19 Márvány St.), west of C1††, 109
Rozgony (today, Rozhanovce, Slovakia), A5†, 161, 214
Rózsafa restaurant (26 Kacsa St.), A1††, 109
Russia, 20, 22, 70, 131
Ruthenia, Carpathian. *See* Transcarpathia

Salgótarján, B4†, 67, 68, 78, 89, 119
Sárvár, B2†, 28, 166
Sátoraljaújhely, A5†, 68, 216
Síp St., C3††, 12
12 Síp St. (shul). *See* Neolog Congregation
Small Vehicle Cooperative (corner of Csanády and Visegrádi Sts.), A2††(21), 93, 95
Soltvadkert, C4†, 8, 39, 179, 194, 199
Sopron, B2†, 29, 41, 54, 91
Sopron county, B2–B3†, xxn10, 27
Sopronkeresztúr, B2†, 194, 197n12
St. István Hospital (on Nagyvárad Sq.) east of D4††, 17
9 Stalin Road (in Soltvadkert), 179
Subcarpathia. *See* Transcarpathia
Svábhegy (mountain), west of B1††, 137
Szabadság, Mt. (Mt. Szécheny), west of D1††, 96, 106, 134, 136, 170
Szabolcs-Szatmár county, B5–B6†, 11
Szatmár (Szatmárnémeti; today, Satu Mare, Romania, east of Csenger [B6†]), 99, 148, 189, 194, 216
Szatmárcseke, B6†, xxii, 107
Szeged, C4†, xxn10, 173, 175, 176, 184
Székesfehérvár, B3†, 119, 120
Szeretet Hospital (Izraelita Szeretet Kórház, 53–55 Amerikai Rd., beyond A4†† on other side of City Park), 139
Szőgyén, B3†, 24
Szombathely, B2†, 16, 30, 31, 73, 90, 194
Sztropkó, A5†, 162

Tátra St., A2††, 81
Temesvár, C5†, xxn10, 67, 69, 70
Tét, B3†, 73
Thököly Rd., C4††, 102
Tibolddaróc, B5†, 52
Tiszafüred, B5†, 148
Tiszántúl (part of Alföld), 6, 11
Tőketerebes (today, Trebišov, Slovakia), A5†, 168
Tököl, B4†, 34
Transcarpathia, A6–A7, B6–B7†, xviii, *xix*, xxn10, 8, 47, 217
Transdanubia, C2–B3†, xxn10, 188, 194
Transylvania, C6–C8†, D7–D8†, xxn10, 8, 17, 46, 47, 217
Tselem (Yid. for Deutschkreutz, Austria), 197
Tselem yeshivah, 197
Turnu Severin, D6†, 67
Tüzér St. (other side of Dózsa György Rd., northeast of Csanády St.), 81n9
Tyukod, B6†, 99

Újpest, B4†, 85, 103, 149
Üllői Rd., D3††, 86
Ungvár, A6†, 164

Vác, B4†, xix, 47, 68, 71, 73, 74, 75, 80, 81, 83, 84, 85, 86, 103
Vadász St., B2††, 35
Vajdahunyad castle (in City Park), 135
Városlődi Rd. (in Pápa), 195
Városmajor Rd., west of C1††, 169
Várpalota, B3†, 18, 19, 35

5 Vasvári Pál St. (shul), B3†† (22), 80
Verpelét, B4†, 68, 144
Veszprém, B3†, 195
Vilma Királynő Rd. (renamed Városligeti Esplanade in 1991), B4††, 39
Vilmos Császár Rd. (1914–19; today, Bajcsy-Zsilinszky Rd.), 85
Visegrádi St., A2††, 93, 139, 152
Visegrádi St. (shul), A2†† (23), 80
Vörösmarty St. (shul), A3–B3††, 170

Wesselényi St., C3–B3††, 56

Yad Vashem museum, 21, 44, 158, 218

Ždiar (in Slovakia), 163
Zemplén county, A5–A6†, B5†, 168
Zugló (official name of District XIV), northeast of A4††, 169

Index of Subjects

Names in bold refer to people quoted in the narrative of this book.

Abelesz, Benjamin, 30, 36, 37
Adasz Jiszraél, 194
Adler, Rachel, 50
Agricultural Cooperative group, 101
Agudah, 47, 49, 49n7, 50, 51n13, 53, 54, 55, 56, 57, 58, 64, 87, 205
Akhdut, 55
Aliyah, 39, 54, 94, 205
Államvédelmi Osztály (ÁVÓ), 30, 31, 34, 34n15, 54, 55, 58, 59n28, 63, 78, 84, 206
Allgemeine Judische Zeitung, 46
anti-Semitism, xxiii, xxiv, 6, 7, 56, 58, 83, 86, 92, 136, 163, 179, 183
anti-Zionism, xxiii, 11, 56, 58, 163
Apponyi, Albert, 5
Arrow Cross, 20, 25, 28, 48, 49, 91, 205
Ashkenazi, xv, 5, 16, 46, 197, 205, 208
autobiography (Communist), 36, 163
ÁVÓ. *See* Államvédelmi Osztály

Barta, Dr. Lajos, 131
Béke Cooperative, 181
Benedikt, Mark, 90
Benedikt, Mordekhai, 90
Benedikt, Sándor, 92, 96, 100, 102, 103, 106, 108, 109, 110, 112, 116, 117, 118, 119, 122, 126, 127, 128, 137, 141, 142, 143, 145, 154
Benedikt, Vera, 122, 127, 137, 143
Berger, Jakab, 99
bet din, 79n7, 82, 99
Blasz, Jenő, 52
Bnei Akivah, 57
Brach, Shaul, 162
Braun, Miklós, 96, 98n, 99, 103, 112, 114, 130, 133, 134, 136, 140
Braun, Simon, 52
Brüll, Ignác, 53
Brüll, Zalmen, 119, 123
Budai, György, xxii, 112, 115, 118, 123, 125, 126, 128, 129, 130, 132, 134, 136, 137, 151, 174
Budapesti Izraelita Hitközség (BIH). *See* Orthodox denomination

Ceaușescu, Nicolae, 145
Central Intelligence Agency (CIA), 95
Chaskel, Zwi, 61, 62
Christian Democratic People's party, 54
Christians (Christianity), xvi, xviii, xxi, 4, 5, 18, 28, 30, 52, 54, 162, 173, 175, 215
Christmas, 10, 21
Claims Conference, 100, 102

Communists (Communism), xxi, xxiii, xxiv, 7n13, 18, 20n4, 23, 24, 26–27, 28–29, 34, 36n17, 49, 49n9, 54, 54n18, 59n25, 65, 78, 82, 92, 110n15, 131, 133nn30–31, 135, 143, 148, 163n17, 206, 208, 211, 213, 216
community. *See* Orthodox denomination
congregation. *See* Neolog; Orthodox congregation; Status Quo
Congressional congregations. *See* Neolog
Csatáry, László, 163
Czikk, Dr. Juraj, 164
Czitrom, József (Jehosua), 10n*

Dak, Moshe, 61, 62
Deutsch, Dr. Adolf, 47
Deutsch, Éva. *See* Dickmann, Mrs. Zoltán
Deutsch, Mendel, 105, 114, 116, 120, 123, 124, 131, 132, 133, 148, 154
Dickmann, Ervin, 106, 117, 120, 129
Dickmann, László, 141
Dickmann, Mrs. Zoltán (née Deutsch), 106, 107, 118, 127, 141, 142, 148

Easter, 125, 191
Ehrenfeld, Rachel, 50, 197
1868–69 National Jewish Congress, xvi, xvii, xx, xxn11, xxii, 1n2, 3, 4, 212, 216
Elbaum, Nachman, 200, 201
emigration (Jewish), 7, 8, 61, 64, 65, 95, 122, 142, 145, 207
Engel, Shmuel, 162n14
Ernst, Fülöp, 49
eruv, 72, 72n6, 207

Farkas, Ensign László, 18, 19, 20, 21
Feast of Tabernacles, 92, 191, 207, 210, 216
Feld, Lajos, 162, 163
Ferencvárosi Tornaklub (Fradi), xiv, 156, 157
Fixler, Herman, 102, 107
Fodor, László, 175
Foltyn, Pál, 163
forced labor, 6, 16, 17, 19, 20, 23, 24, 33, 35, 49, 52, 53, 91, 92, 105
Fradi. *See* Ferencvárosi Tornaklub
Frank, Ábrahám, 49, 55
Frankfurt, Andor, 107
Friedmann, Ervin, 50, 55, 57
Frisch, Efraim, 56
Fuchs, Lipót, 50

Gáti, Ödön, 52
Gemara, 116, 117, 118, 131, 207, 216
Gentiles, xviii, 20n4, 44, 136, 139, 207, 215
German Reform movement, xvi
Gerő, Ernő, 110
Gestapo, 23, 25
Glancz, Áron Duved, 72, 74
Gombó, Gábor, 179, 180, 184, 185, 198
Gorbachev, Mikhail, 142
goy, xix, 71, 83, 86, 207
Gromyko, Andrei, 56
Grósz, Béla, 167, 168, 169, 172
Grósz, Károly, 50
Groszberg, Ervin, xviii, 61, 93, 135n36, 214
Groszberg, Jenő, 99
Groszberg, Lipót, 46
Groszmann, Sámuel, 164
Grünfeld, Márton (Mordche), 10n*
Grünwald, Jákov Jehaszke, 16, 194, *196*, 202
Grünwald, Jákov Jehaszke (the younger, grandson of Jákov Jehaszke Grünwald), 191, 194, 195, 198, 202

Grünwald, Jószef (Joszéf) (son of Jákov Jehaszke Grünwald), 194, 195
Günzler, Vilmos (Zev Wolf), 68
Guttmann, József, 158

Halberstam, Avraham Shalom, 162n15
Halberstam, Yekutiel Yehuda, 138n
Hannukah, 125, 208
Hasid, xv, xxin12, 5, 16, 43, 111, 121, 151, 169n1, 175, 176, *181*, 182, 184, 189, 192, 194, 195, 197, 199, 201, 208, 212, 213, 215, 217. *See also Szatmár Hasid*
Herczog, László, 103, 114, 115, 119, 123, 124, 128, 132, 133, 135, 137, 149, 151
High Holy Days, 72, 91, 93, 142, 208
Hirsch, Márkus, 161
Holocaust, xv, xxi, xxii, xxiii, xxiv, xxv, 53, 54, 56, 100n9
Horovitz, Ahron, 162n15
Horváth, György, 163
Hungarian constitution, xvin6, 59
Hungarian Independence party, 54, 54n18
Hungarian Orthodoxy, xiii, xv, xvi, xxiii, 4, 5, 8, 43, 47, 58, 205, 208
Hungarian revolution of 1956, xxn11, xxiii, 211

Jahrzeit. *See yortsayt*
Jewish Agency (*Sokhnut*), 42, 43, 87, 88, 94, 146, 147, 208, 215
Jewish Congress. *See* 1868–69 National Jewish Congress
Jewish Easter. *See Pesakh*
Jewish Laws, 6, 16, 160n, 209, 212
Jewish schools. *See* Talmud-Torah
Joint Distribution Committee (JDC), 6, 27, 39, 42, 50, 51, 58, 69, 71, 94, 95, 102, 130, 159, 208
Jónás, Béla, 35

Jungreisz, Ignác (Yitzchok Tzvi HaLevi), 162n12
Jungreisz, Moses (Moshe HaLevi), 158, 162n12
Jungreisz, Sándor (Amram), 2, 10n*, 57, 82

kaddish, 104, 108, 209
Kahán-Frankl, Samu, 2, 3, 9, 57, 58
kashrut, 129, 209
Kattler, Erzsébet, 170
Katz, Éliás, 119
Katz, Éva, 63
khamets, 81, 209
khazerfresser, 109, 209
kheder, 73, 117, 118, 179, 181, 182, 216
Khevrah Kadishah, 74, 161, 209
Khrushchev, Nikita, 58
Khumash, 116, 209
kibbutz, 141, 147, 207, 212
kiddush, 93, 129, 164, 210
kile, 99, 107, 210
KISZ. *See* Pioneers
Kohanites, 195
Kohn, Márton, 161
Kolman, Mendel, 200
Kornitzer, Géza, 64
Kornitzer, Mózes, 102
kosher, 20, 21, 30, 31, 38, 49, 52, 70, 96, 99, 104, 139, 144, 148, 151, 153, 155, 159, 164, 167, 169, 174, 176, 188, 207, 208, 209, 210, 212, 217. *See also khazerfresser*; *treyf*
Krausz, Majer, 114, 115, 116, 117
kulak, 34

Lag b'Omer, 53, 210
Lebovits, Jakab, 10n*
Lemberger, Asher, 178
Lemberger, Avram, 178

Lemberger, Efraim, 178
Lemberger, Mendel, 178
Lemberger, Nándor (Moses Nátán), 10n*, 179
Lemberger, Rachel, 179
Lemberger, Shlomó, 178
Lemberger, Simon, 178
Levin, Pál, 55
leyn, 155, 210
Link, Gyula, 49

Magyarization, xvii, xviii, 207, 210, 211
Magyar Tornaklub (MTK), xiv, 133, 156, 157
mashgiakh (ritual supervisor), 81, 82, 99, 130, 139, 145, 147, 152, 211
matzah, 32, 81, 82, 92, 99, 153, 159, 174, 175, 211
Mayer, Dr. Móric, 11
Mengele, Josef, 18, 162
mikveh (ritual bath), 11, 27, 159, 181, 191, 197, 211
military police, 17, 22, 29
Mindszenty, József, 40, 64, 211
Ministry of the Interior, 76, 84n11, 95, 147, 213
minyan, 72, 80, 88, 103, 150, 156, 167, 211
MIOI (National Bureau of Hungarian Israelites), 11, 211
MIOK (National Representation of Hungarian Israelites), 3, 10n*, 11n18, 97, 100, 118, 211, 213
Mizrakhi, 53, 87, 211
MKP. *See* Communists
moshav, 42, 212
Moskovits, Bernát (Báruch Cví Hakohén), 10n*, 95, 98
Moskovits, R. Mordkhe Arye, 53
Mother Theresa (Anjezë Gonxhe Bojaxhiu), 189
Mózes, Imre, 115, 116, 117, 118
MTK. *See* Magyar Tornaklub

Nagy, Imre, 38, 64, 212
National Assembly of 1840 (Hungarian), 160
National Israelite Assembly of 1950, xvii, xxii, xxv, 1, 2n*, 11, 57
nationalization, 10, 72, 80, 101
National Jewish Congress. *See* 1868–69 National Jewish Congress
National Neolog Bureau, 58
National Office of Religion, 118
National Peasant Party, 29
National Pioneer Council. *See* Pioneers
Neolog (Congressional), xvi, xvii, xxn10, xxi, xxiii, 1n2, 2, 3, 4, 5, 6, 7, 8, 9, 9n16, 11, 12, 32, 50, 57, 58, 71–72, 81n9, 82, 97n6, 161n10, 162, 175, 178, 211, 212, 216
Neolog rabbinical schools, 5
New Year's. *See* Rosh Hashanah
niggun, 117, 212
numerus clausus. *See* Jewish Laws

Office of Religious Affairs, 100
ohel, 162, 202, 212
Olti, Vilmos, 64
Orthodox Central Bureau, 1, 2, 9, 11, 46n3, 47, 213
Orthodox community, xv, xviii, xx–xxiii, 1n1, 2n4, 5, 6, 8, 11n18, 12, 46n3, 53n16, 55, 63n30, 137, 150, 158n5, 161n10, 169nn1–2, 178, 206, 207, 208, 209, 215, 217
Orthodox congregation(s), xvin6, *xix*, xxn10, xxi, xxiii, 2, 3, 4, 6–12, 15, 30, 31, 32, 42, 47, 49n7, 50, 50n11, 52, 57, 64, 67, 72, 74, 90, 91, 92, 95, 98–105, *113*, 119,

128, 130, 132, 139, 140, 140n39, 141, 145, 146, 149, 152, 159, 160, 161, 163, 164, 168, 170, 173, 178, 179, 184, 188, 189, 191, 193, 194, 195
Orthodox denomination, 4, 7, 10, 100
Orthodox Division, 9, 12, 63n30, 96, 98, 100, 149
Orthodox rabbinate, 5, 9, 100
Orthodox Rabbinical Council, 9, 10n*, 12
Orthodox youth movement, 47, 197
Orthodox Zsidó Élet, 98
Ortutay, Gyula, 1, 2, 7, 10, 56, 57

Parliament, 31n8, 110n14, 185
partisans, 17, 23, 66, 68, 69
Paskusz, Mór, 96, 98, 100, 102
People's Tribune, 20, 35, 213
Pesakh, 10, 23, 25, 49, 62, 81, 159, 213, 214
Péter, Gábor, 78
Peter and Paul (feast), 29
Pfeiffer party. *See* Hungarian Independence party
philo-Semitism, 175
Pioneers (KISZ), 133, 150, 174, 213
Pirkhey Agudat Israel, 47, 51, 53, 213
Pirkhey Tiferes Bahurim, 47, 213
pogrom, 6
Pohl, Sándor, 163
Posen, Simon, 54
"*Puper*" yeshivah (Williamsburg, NY), 195
Purim, 59, 71, 213

Raj, Feri, 96, 140
Raj, Tamás (Tomi), 96, 110
Rajk, László, 64, 84, 213
Rákosi, Mátyás, 56, 64, 65, 110n15, 175, 213
Rashi, 116, 214, 217
red, white, and green rosette, xix, 54, 86, 214
Reich, Jakab Koppel, 49
Reiner, Dr. Imre, 57, 58
Reisman, Miksha, 157, 158, 165
Rézmovits, Jóska, 142
Roóz, Ella, 51
Rosenberg, Frigyes (Fritzi), xix, xxii, 70, 78, 82
Rosenberg, György (Gyuri), 108, 115, 117, 118, 122, 124, 126, 129, 130, 134, 136, 142, 153
Rosenberg, Sámuel, xiv, 157
Rosh Chodesh, 164, 214
Rosh Hashanah, 20, 208, 214
Roth, Sándor, 50
Rubinstein, Leibish, 174, 178, 188, 189, 195
Rubinstein, Miklós, 97, 98
Rubinstein, Moyshe, 188, 199, 201, 202
Rubinstein, Simon, 174, 175, 184
Russian army, 7, 20, 21, 24, 26, 34, 39, 40, 66, 86, 92

Sabbath (Shabbat; Saturday), 3, 10, 15, 31, 32, 33, 36, 37, 38, 40, 42, 47, 55, 59, 68, 71, 72, 73, 79, 81, 83, 88, 89, 92, 93, 103, 107, 110, 118, 120, 124, 127, 129, 131, 134, 138, 145, 150, 151, 155, 156, 168, 169, 171, 172, 179, 180, 181, 183–85, 189, 197, 198, 199, 200, 206, 207, 208, 209, 214
Sabbath-keeping cooperatives (companies), 11, 83, 93, 142, 171, 179, 214
Saturday. *See* Sabbath
Scheiber, Sándor, 127
Schnitzler, Zsigmond (Sraga Slomó), 10n*
Schreiber, Ede (Jochanan), 10n*
Schutzstaffel (SS), 25, 163
Schwartz, Anna, 51
Schwartz, Isidor, 51

Sebestyén, Dr. Antal, 99, 102, 140
Sephardi, 182, 205
shakter (ritual slaughterer), xxii, 9, 72, 73, 74, 104, 107, 112, 113, *113*, 114, 139, 147, 148, 153, 170, 215. *See also shokhet*
shames, 89, 160, 192, 215
Shas Khevrah, 125, 161, 215
Shavuot, 77, 157, 215
Shema Israel, 168, 215
shokhet, xxii, 27, 73, 99, 117, 140, 145, 215. *See also shakter*
shul, 39, 59, 67, 69, 70, 72, 80, 81, 82, 85, 87, 91, 99, 102, 103, 126, 127, 135, 143, 150, 152, 153, 154, 155, 156, 166, 167, 169, 170, 171, 175, 176, 179, 184, 187, 191, 192, 193, 207, 215. *In Index of Places, see also* Akácfa St.; Bethlen Gábor Sq.; 23 Dessewffy St.; 35 Dob St.; Erzsébet Kattler Prayer House; 48 Garay St.; József St.; Kazinczy St. (in Kassa); 27–29 Kazinczy St.; 26 Király St.; Majakovszkij St.; Müllers' prayer house (in Újpest); 4 Nagyfuvaros St.; Neolog Congregation; Petőfi St. (in Pápa); 5 Vasvári Pál St.; Visegrádi St.; Vörösmarty St.
Singer, Jenő, 52
Slánsky case, 59
Slánsky, Rudolf, 59n25
Smallholders party, 1
Small Vehicle Cooperative, 93, 95
Social Democrats, 28, 29
socialism, 7, 59, 101
Sofer, Akivah, 46
Sokhnut. *See* Jewish Agency
Sós, Endre, 3, 100
soyfer, 102, 119, 215
SS. *See* Schutzstaffel
Stalin, Joseph, 29, 34n11, 36, 37, 59n26, 60, 64, 214
Star of David, *48*, 185, 216
Status Quo, xvii, xxn10, xxi, 1n3, 5, 106, 216
Stein, Benő, 49, 50, 55, 57
Steinberger, Jenő (Stea), 57, 65, 115, 135
Steiner, Marcell, 100
Steiner, Yeshaya, 89n14
Stöckler, Lajos, 2, 3, 8, 11, 38
Stoltz, Eta (Mrs. Károly Stoltz), 22, 34, 44
Stoltz, Károly, 22, 44
Sussman, Simon, 49
Sussman, Viktor, 49
swastika. *See* anti-Semitism
Szabad Nép, 56, 59, 216
Szaberszky, Jóska, 78
Szabolcsi, Miska, 78
Szálasi, Ferenc, 19, 26n5, 175
Szatmár Hasid, 89, 99, 120, 216
Szegfű, György, 97, 123
Székely, László, 60
Szemere, Sámuel, 140
Szenes, László (Laci), 109
Szenes, Mrs. László, 108, 109, 110, 115, 121, 128, 129, 131, 132, 138, 154, 155
Szenes, Tamás (Tomi), 108, 109, 110, 116, 120, 121, 122, 124, 126, 127, 128, 132, 137, 138, 142, 144, 145, 147, 154, 155
Szigeti, Attila, 31
Szófer, Jochanan, 9
Szófer, Mózes, 4, 9

tallit, 168, *177*, 183, 214, 216
Talmud, 97, 112, 116n19, 116n21, 121, 125, 126, 135, 140, 155, 162n14, 170, 214, 215, 216, 217, 218
Talmud-Torah, 7, 8, 47, 52, 57, 63, 64, 65, 93, 98, 100, 102, 103, 104, 115, 119, 135, 151, 161, 164, 171, 173, 179, 216
tefillin, 21, 60, 85, 166, 168, 214, 215, 216
Teitelbaum, Márton (Patyi), 111, 174

Teitelbaum, Rózsika (Rózsi), 98, 173, 174, 177
Tisha b'Av, 17, 63, 77, 206, 217
Torah, 5, 20, 40, 51, 129, 152, 157, 161, 170, 175, 176, 184, 205, 208, 209, 210, 211, 215, 217
treyf, 21, 105, 174, 180, 217
Trianon (treaty), xiv, xxi, 5n8, 46, 46n1, 217
tsadik, 168, 178, 202, 217
201st Home Defense Chemical Warfare Company, 18

Új Élet, 2, 2n*, 8, 53, 96, 97, 98, 101, 158, 165, 167, 169, 217
Új Kelet, 39, 217
Ungar, Ábrahám, 15, 27, 28
Ungar, Yitzchok Shlomó, 43

Veres, Peter, 29
Vorhand, Moyshe (Moses), 173, 180, *181*
Vorhand, Zeev, 178

Warsaw ghetto, 172
Weber, Béla, 183
Weber, Joseph, 190
Weber, Zsuzsanna (née Gombó), 179
Weinberger, Kálmán, 104, 117, 121, 123, 124, 152
Weinberger, Tibor, 104, 114, 116, 117, 120, 121, 123, 125, 126, 127, 129, 134, 136, 137, 145, 153
Weiser, Eliezer, 73, 103n
Weisz, Gyula, 171, 172
Weisz, Ignác (Yitskhak), 104, 112, 113, *113*, 114, 115, 117, 119, 130, 132, 134, 138, 151, 174
Weisz, Izrael (Srulcsi), 99, 107, 111, 114, 119, 124, 126, 127, 129, 137, 146, 147, 151
Weisz, Khaim, 111, 117
Weisz, Leibish, 114, 120, 121, 123, 124
Weisz, Mór, 51
Weisz, Moyshe, 98, 99, 107, 128, 140, 142, 149, 155
Weisz, Yidesz, 130
Weiszberger, Gizella (née Horovitz), 102, 139
Weiszberger, Pinkhasz, 119
Weizmann, Chaim, 58
Wollák, László, 195
World Jewish Congress (WJC). *See* Neolog
World War I, xxi, xxin12, 46n4, 72, 162n14, 208, 210, 217
World War II, xxn11, xxiv, xxv, *48*, 208, 213

yortsayt, xiv, 33, 157, 180, *196*, 202, 218

Zionism, 5, 58, 59
Zsidó Híradó, 46
Zsidó Újság, 47
Zsigmond, László, 21, 22, 24, 25, 26
Züszmann, Alfréd, 2, 3, 10, 11

SÁNDOR BACSKAI is a Hungarian writer, editor, and photographer.

EVA MARIA THURY is associate professor in the Department of English and Philosophy at Drexel University.

Sándor Bacskai describes taking the cover photograph: "This photograph was taken in 1994 during the World Conference commemorating the fiftieth anniversary of the death of Orthodox Chief Rabbi Mózes Vorhand. The conference is described in the chapter 'One Step toward Jerusalem.' Some of the visitors who visited Makó then had worked in the local Peace cooperative in the fifties. This Sabbath-keeping union was set up to allow Jews who adhered to their religion to refrain from going to work on Saturdays and religious holidays, and instead to work on Sundays. Of the Jews returning in 1994, some were Hasid and some not: those who had been involved in the Peace organization took the opportunity to visit the cooperative building, and naturally, they brought along their children who had been born in America or Israel. This photograph was taken when some of the Hasid children and young people were heading from the hotel to the Peace building.

"I was following behind and took some other pictures, including one of a tractor coming along the other side of the road (this was not as successful a photograph), and there were also some in which some locals were staring at the visiting Jews. The aircraft appeared unexpectedly in the sky: it was probably an old crop-dusting machine. When I noticed it, I only had enough time to grab my camera; I was not sure that the photograph would be successful. But when I developed the film at home, I saw that I had not only captured the plane, but that its position in the picture was fortuitous. It added an ominous if somewhat anachronistic note to the composition, evoking a time of menace for the young Jews of Makó."